100 YEARS OF
BASEBALL

"What People Are Saying"

"For an intimate, dramatic story of baseball read "100 Years of Baseball." by Lee Allen. Allen has written a thorough history of the great game: from the beginning to the present day. The result is a book that provides drama, excitement, humour and intrigue."
-- Suburbanite Economist

"In 100 Years of Baseball, Harry Wright is called the "forgotten father of baseball." Above all others, he is the one who foretold of the gigantic future of organized baseball. That was way back in 1857. Down through the years as baseball grew, Lee Allen traces the development . . . the New York Knickerbockers of yesteryear; Jackie Robinson; the dark days of 1919, and the New York Yankee world series monopoly."
-- Long Beach Press Telegram

"No one who wants to know baseball history should be without this book"
-- Portland Press Herald

"A full-fledged history of professional baseball with its crises, climaxes and heroes from the Knickerbockers of 1858 to the shenanigans of Durocher and MacPhall."
-- Oakland Tribune

100 YEARS OF BASEBALL

THE INTIMATE AND DRAMATIC STORY OF
MODERN BASEBALL FROM THE GAME'S
BEGINNINGS UP TO THE PRESENT DAY

LEE ALLEN & ANDY GONDLE

100 Years Of Baseball: The Intimate And Dramatic Story Of
Modern Baseball

Bibliographical Note: This edition is an abridged republication of the first edition published in 1950. For this edition, selective editing and editorial additions have been made.

Publisher: Bibliopoesy, a division of SEO Amigo Pty Ltd.
ISBN 13:   978-1495309175
ISBN 10:   1495309177

Disclaimer and Terms of Use: The Author and Publisher has strived to be as accurate and complete as possible in the creation of this book, notwithstanding the fact that he does not warrant or represent at any time that the contents within are accurate due to the rapidly changing nature of the Internet. While all attempts have been made to verify information provided in this publication, the Author and Publisher assumes no responsibility for errors, omissions, or contrary interpretation of the subject matter herein. Any perceived slights of specific persons, peoples, or organizations are unintentional. In practical advice books, like anything else in life, there are no guarantees of income made. This book is not intended for use as a source of legal, business, accounting or financial advice. All readers are advised to seek services of competent professionals in legal, business, medical, accounting, and finance field.

1. Baseball 2. History 3. Sport 4. USA

Ordering Information: Books may be purchased in quantity and/or special sales by contacting the publisher by email at sales@bibliopoesy.com

TO THE $\mathcal{F}$*AN*

a breed of which I am one and
a group which apparently can
endure anything.

Foreword

BASEBALL IS an integral part of American culture. It is ingrained in our history and in the hearts of many. It is no surprise that a book such as this is greatly in demand. A book that focuses not simply on a single ball club or an individual player, but that brings together a wide range of histories and personalities that forged a national pastime.

There was a time when sports stories did not count as news. The stories of games played, won and lost were hidden inside newspapers among advertisements for patent medicines. The history of sports did not have a popular beginning, but as the popularity of games such as baseball continued to grow, so did the desire to know more about them.

Newspapers were the main resource for learning about the sport of baseball. It was not an easy game to learn and understand. The logistics of play, how to score, the mistakes that are made- all come together to turn a simple game of stickball into something much more complex and, yet, readily embraced by the American public.

As a child that grew up in the shining age of the Yankees, I have come by my love of the game honestly. During the time when baseball greats like Mickey Mantle and Roger Maris were ruling the plate, it is no surprise that the sport became a part of my soul.

Since I could not realize my own dream of becoming a professional player, I took great pleasure in being someone who could tell the story of the games. In the book 100 Years of Baseball, Lee Allen takes a deeper look at the beginning of our nation's pastime and the stories that took it out of the hidden parts of the newspapers into a full-blown section for all to enjoy on the weekends.

-Andy Gondle

CONTENTS

"April will come back again,"

Thomas Wolfe.

"The wonderful and inspiring thing about baseball is the universality of its appeal. The big leagues are only the pinnacle of a structure that reaches down through a host of minor organizations to the nationwide foundation which manifests itself in games in every hamlet and village East or West, North or South. Manly sports are both the cause and evidence of a nation's virility. Baseball, in the hot period, is the safety valve of barriers; it is the country's summer tonic. Because it is honest and fair and square, and the gamblers in it have been discouraged, it holds its place in the affections of the people. What do thirty thousand howling fans care about Montenegro or wool if three are on and Baker's at the bat?"

Philadelphia *Ledger*, 1914.

"This is a funny business," said Bug Holliday yesterday. "We get paid to knock the cover off the ball, and pitchers get paid to keep us from hitting it."

Cincinnati *Enquirer*,
June 27, 1892.

Harry Wright, Forgotten Father 1

HIGH ABOVE the southern shore of Lake Otsego, the Glimmer-glass of the novels of James Fenimore Cooper, a two-story brick building known as the National Baseball Museum brings grandeur to the sylvan resort of Cooperstown, New York. There, in a series of bronze plaques that honor retired heroes of the diamond, is baseball's Hall of Fame.

But there are numerous omissions from this galaxy of horsehide greats, and the most flagrant is that of Harry Wright, the man who first conceived of baseball as the business that it has become. Although Harry Wright was to baseball what George Washington was to the presidency, his name has not been included among those officially tapped for fame, probably for the very good reason that those charged with making such selections are not familiar with his story. Yet Harry Wright is truly the father of professional baseball, and his paternity has been established beyond all doubt.

William Henry (Harry) Wright was born at Sheffield, England, January 10, 1835 and was only a small boy when he emigrated to America with his father, a noted cricketer. Shortly afterwards his younger brothers, George and Sam, were born. All the Wrights were expert at cricket, and when Harry reached young manhood, he obtained a job as a professional of the British sport with the St. George Club at Hoboken, New Jersey. On his days off he used to go to the Elysian Fields at Hoboken where men and boys were playing a game that was new to him, a game known as baseball. And all through the summer of 1857 he watched the progress of these contests, fascinated by the discovery of a game more exciting than cricket.

These early players were the members of a club known as the Knickerbockers. This team had been formed in 1845 and the guiding spirit behind it was Alexander Joy Cartwright. It was he who drew up the game's first rules, limited the contestants to nine on each side, established ninety feet as the proper distance between bases, and provided for the game's first uniforms. Cartwright's efforts gave baseball much needed uniformity and ended the haphazard practice of using different rules in each community which played the game.

Learning the new sport, first as a spectator and then as a participant, Harry Wright became a member of the Knickerbockers in 1858. He played his first game with them in July of that year as an outfielder, making three catches without an error but going hitless against Matt O'Brien of the Atlantics, an early Knickerbocker rival from Brooklyn.

It was at precisely this time that the Knickerbockers were losing control over the game they had so successfully pioneered. Other teams had sprung up throughout the East, and many of them clamored for modernization of the rules. But the Knickerbockers, baseball's first reactionaries, refused to discuss changes in the code. And it came about that other teams banded together to form an organization of ball clubs, the first such organization in history.

Alarmed by the possibility of losing control, the Knickerbockers attended the association's inaugural meeting on March 10, 1858 in large numbers, hoping to stampede the convention. But with each club limited to three delegates by the chair and with twenty-five clubs in attendance, the Knickerbockers were unable to stem the tide. The result was baseball's first governing body, the National Association of Baseball Players (not to be confused with the National Association of Professional Baseball Players formed in 1871).

Harry Wright continued to play for the Knickerbockers, but since baseball was still an amateur endeavor, he relied on his occupation as a cricket professional to provide him with a living.

In 1865 he journeyed west to Cincinnati to organize a cricket club among the bluebloods of that teeming Ohio River community, but when he got there he discovered that baseball was crowding out cricket as a popular pastime. Men and boys were playing the new game on every vacant lot, and interest in the sport was at fever pitch. Wright soon learned that although cricket appealed to the effete upper classes which still emulated the leisurely pursuits of England and New England, the masses were solidly for baseball.

The two best teams in Cincinnati during the baseball season of 1868 were the Buckeyes and the Red Stockings. Harry Wright by this time had been induced to take over the management of the latter, and under his direction the club fought furiously for patronage with its rival. And when Wright imported four paid players from the East, the Red Stockings not only defeated the Buckeyes but caused them to disband.

Although baseball had begun as an amateur game that was civic in nature, the desire to win soon made it necessary to import players and pay them for their services. Probably the first professional player was James P. Creighton, a pitcher for the Excelsiors of Brooklyn, who died at the height of his fame after rupturing his bladder while pitching against the Unions of Morrisania, New York, a small Westchester community. At least it is known that Creighton was paid sub rosa for his skill as early as 1860. Alfred James Reach, later the founder of a sporting goods firm, was another early professional though certainly not the first, as was generally claimed.

Two years after Creighton received money for his services admission was charged at games for the first time on the Union Grounds in Brooklyn, and when each spectator became required to lay down ten cents for the privilege of watching the sport, the players, after expenses had been deducted, split the gate. It was this admission charge that made the professional aspect of the sport inevitable.

Professionalism was strictly forbidden by the National Association, which ruled the game from 1857 to 1871. But the rule was largely ignored, and the Association, operating behind a crude constitution through loosely organized delegates of state associations, had very little power. The situation was much like that which exists today in collegiate football, with colleges giving lip service and lip service only to the theory that the pastime is an amateur one, with the emphasis on the building of character.

Harry Wright and his Red Stockings were tired of this hypocrisy and disgusted with the weakness of the National Association of Baseball Players, which issued laws which could not be enforced. During the winter of 1868-69 the players of the old Red Stockings and the followers of the team held many discussions in which the situation was thoroughly mulled over; and Harry Wright decided that the answer was to form a team consisting entirely of professionals, a team which proudly and defiantly proclaimed itself as professional.

As a consequence of this decision, the Cincinnati Red Stockings of 1869, the game's first professional club, came into being. And that is why unhallowed Harry Wright is the true parent of professional ball.

The decision to turn pro was not popular in all circles, and it was especially loathsome to two classes: the idle dilettantes and the gamblers. The idlers hated the idea of professionalism because they thought the game should be played only by "gentlemen" in their leisure and only incidentally for the pleasure of the public. Conditioned by the British concept of amateurism, they feared that if skill were the only qualification for membership in baseball clubs, "undesirable" people would soon be playing the game; and they felt that the determining factor should not be skill but "race, color and previous condition of servitude." Thus it can be seen that baseball, in order to achieve competence, had to be freed from the undemocratic influences of then aristocratic New York, influences which were originally British. But it is a curious fact that Harry Wright, who was responsible for the liberation because he made democracy work in Cincinnati, was himself born a British subject. And certainly the dilettantes considered him no gentleman.

The gamblers were opposed to professional baseball for a different and much more practical reason. Astutely knowing that gate receipts and salaries would give clubs a financial stake in the game that had previously been the monopoly of the betting gentry and alert to the fact that professionals would be much more difficult to manipulate for their sordid purposes than amateurs, they screamed to high heaven.

But ignoring both the social register set and the gamblers, Wright held steadfast to his purpose and combed the country for the game's outstanding players. His aim was to form the strongest possible club, a team that would be unbeatable. And his accomplishment became exactly that.

Charlie Gould, first baseman of the Red Stockings, was the only native Cincinnatian on the club. Catcher

Doug Allison and Left Fielder Andy Leonard were from New Jersey, although Leonard had been born in Ireland. Second Baseman Charlie Sweasy was from New Hampshire. Right Fielder Cal McVey was from Montrose, Lee County, Iowa. Harry Wright himself played center field, and he brought on his brother George to play shortstop. Pitcher Asa Brainard and Third Baseman Fred Waterman were also from New York.

But not even in Cincinnati was it recognized to what degree Harry had succeeded in his aim when the 1869 season began. After the Red Stockings had defeated a picked nine in their first local appearance on April 17, the Cincinnati Enquirer gave this chilly welcome to Wright's team:

"The baseball season for 1869 was opened yesterday by a game between the first nine of the Cincinnati Club and the field. The playing on both sides was very poor. There was quite a large number of spectators present, but the enthusiasm of last summer was lacking."

From that lack-luster start the Red Stockings went on to become the talk of the sporting world. They engaged in 65 games without once losing, and their perfect record was marred only by a five-inning tie with the Haymakers of Troy, New York. Actually, Cincinnati, under present rules, would have been awarded that contest by forfeit, as the Haymakers, who were in collusion with gamblers, left the field when they had tied the score rather than risk defeat. John Morrissey, a notorious politician and owner of the Haymakers, had wagered $60,000 that the Red Stockings would not win, and he never had to pay off.

The Red Stockings traveled from Massachusetts to California, willingly taking on all comers. Statistics of the season show that they traveled almost 12,000 miles by rail and boat, playing before more than

200,000 people, and scoring 2,395 runs to 575 for their opponents. George Wright batted .518 in 52 games, scoring 339 runs and smashing out 59 home runs. The team as a whole produced 169 homers, an average of almost three per game.

The only club that was considered likely to beat the Red Stockings that year was the celebrated nine from New York known as the Mutuals. Every time the Reds would win that season, indignant fans would shout, "Wait until you play the Mutuals; they'll show you a thing or two!" And when the Red Stockings did finally cross bats with the New Yorkers, it proved to be quite a struggle, but Harry Wright's boys won, 4 to 2. That was an unheard of score in those days of double figures, and the contest was considered the finest ever played up to that time.

But the importance of the Red Stockings to baseball history does not lie in their extraordinary achievement on the field. Their contribution consisted of establishing the fact that baseball could succeed as a professional venture. They drew so much attention to the game that clubs began to spring up throughout the land as indiscriminately as dandelions. These clubs grew so strong that by 1871 they were able to form baseball's first major league, the National Association of Professional Baseball Players.

The Red Stockings, however, were not the first team to go on tour. That honor had been won in 1860 when the Excelsiors of Brooklyn visited several cities in western and central New York. Seven years after that the Nationals of Washington, a team composed mostly of young men who worked in federal bureaus, became the first eastern club to cross the Alleghenies. Making an extended junket through primitive country, the Nationals lost only one game, a defeat suffered at

Rockford, Illinois when they were bested, 29 to 23, by a 17-year-old pitcher named Al Spalding.

Baseball had received a great impetus during the Civil War when it provided a stimulating diversion from the monotony of camp life among soldiers of the Union army. A game played on Christmas Day, 1862 between clubs selected from the 165th New York Volunteer Infantry, Duryea's Zouaves, was witnessed by over 40,000 soldiers. That game, played at Hilton Head, South Carolina, was the talk of the military world for weeks thereafter, and when the war was over, men who had observed baseball for the first time, Confederate prisoners of war among them, introduced the sport in their home localities.

When the Red Stockings visited all these places where baseball was beginning to thrive, teams were formed in their wake for the sole purpose of defeating them. However, Harry Wright's nine managed to win its first 27 games in 1870 before bowing to the Atlantics of Brooklyn, 8 to 7, in 11 innings, on the afternoon of June 14. This famous game has been described in numerous baseball writings. But before the season was over the Red Stockings lost five other games, two of them to a new team from Chicago known as the White Stockings.

By this time interest in the Reds on the part of the home fans began to wane, the game's first demonstration that rooters are a fickle breed. And when other clubs began to make lucrative financial offers to the Cincinnati players, the dissolution of the club became certain. So complete was the disintegration of the Reds that when it came time to pay the club's outstanding bills the lumber from the park was sold to stall off creditors.

But Harry Wright moved on with the game. Taking with him his brother George in addition to Charlie

Gould, he assumed control of the Boston club as playing manager. He remained in the Hub for eleven years, first lending a rare dignity to the chaotic National Association, then serving as one of the pillars of the much more solid National League. For two seasons, 1882-83, he managed Providence of the National, and then launched a new chapter of his life as pilot of the Philadelphia team, a term of service that lasted ten seasons more. An early day Connie Mack even though he didn't live to attain the latter's age, he was one of the first baseball figures to be venerated.

Wright lived in a turbulent era, when mud-slinging was indulged in by newspapers towards almost every player and official. But a single printed criticism of Harry Wright cannot be found. He managed professional teams for twenty-six years in all. Here is his complete record as a pilot:

YEAR	TEAM	LEAGUE	WON	LOST	PCT.	FINISH
1868	Cincinnati	None	41	7	.854	—
1869	Cincinnati	None	64	0	1.000	—
1870	Cincinnati	None	62	6	.912	—
1871	Boston	N.A.	22	10	.688	2nd
1872	Boston	N.A.	39	8	.830	1st
1873	Boston	N.A.	43	16	.729	1st
1874	Boston	N.A.	52	18	.743	1st
1875	Boston	NA.	71	8	.899	1st
1876	Boston	N.L.	39	31	.557	4th
1877	Boston	N.L.	42	18	.700	1st
1878	Boston	N.L.	41	19	.683	1st
1879	Boston	N.L.	54	30	.643	2nd
1880	Boston	N.L.	40	44	.476	6th
1881	Boston	N.L.	38	45	.458	6th
1882	Providence	N.L.	52	32	.619	2nd

1883	Providence	N.L.	58	40	.592	3rd
1884	Philadelphia	N.L.	39	73	.348	6th
1885	Philadelphia	N.L.	56	54	.509	3rd
1886	Philadelphia	N.L.	71	43	.622	4th
1887	Philadelphia	N.L.	75	48	.610	2nd
1888	Philadelphia	N.L.	69	61	.531	3rd
1889	Philadelphia	N.L.	63	64	.496	4th
1890	Philadelphia	N.L.	78	53	.595	3rd
1891	Philadelphia	N.L.	68	69	.496	4th
1892	Philadelphia	N.L.	87	66	.569	4th
1893	Philadelphia	N.L.	72	57	.558	4th
	Grand Total		1436	920	.610	—

During the Union Association disturbance of 1884 and the Brotherhood War which followed a little later, Wright remained loyal to the National League, not necessarily because he approved of the league's position but because he did not approve of playing on Sunday, which was common practice in the outlaw circuits.In his latter days he built the Philadelphia team starting from scratch and might have won a pennant had not his health declined. During his Cincinnati period he had been married in the presence of his team, his adoring players presenting their manager and his bride with a gold watch wrapped in a $100 government bond. Shortly after the death of his wife in 1892, Harry himself began to fail. After the 1893 season he gave up management of the Phils, and Nicholas E. Young, the league president, created the post of supervisor of umpires especially for him. That job was in the nature of an honorarium, and after his death it was abandoned and not restored for years.

An attack of pneumonia complicated by a rupture of the pleura caused Wright's family to remove him to a sanatorium at Atlantic City in September, 1895, and there, on October 3, at the age of 60, he expired.

And although his memory is neglected today, he was mourned throughout the country when word of his passing spread. A day was set apart by all professional baseball clubs, designated as Harry Wright Day, to establish a fund for a monument to him.

But the celebration was not successful. April 13, 1896, the day upon which Harry Wright was honored, was a rainy and dismal one in most places around the land. Total receipts of the occasion reached the paltry figure of $3,349.79. New York City's contribution was a mere $322. At its annual meeting the following winter the National League pledged itself to supply more money and authorized the monument committee to proceed with the memorial shaft.

That was official baseball's last gesture toward Harry Wright. Harry is not in the Hall of Fame or even on the Honor Roll, a list of sub-immortals and second-string deities created in 1946 to include writers, managers, umpires and executives.

One gentleman who is in the Hall of Fame is Morgan Gardner Bulkeley, a totally inconspicuous sporting personage who served as president of the National League in the circuit's maiden year of 1876 and who then successfully avoided any connection whatever with the game in the remaining forty-six years of his life. Bulkeley took up the science of politics and the insurance business and ended up as a United States Senator from Connecticut. He made no contribution whatever to baseball, and his presence among the elite at Cooperstown is as ill-advised, as ridiculous and as mysterious as Harry Wright's absence.

Bill Hulbert's
Shotgun Wedding 2

SOME IDEA of the character of the National Association, baseball's first major league and a wheel which revolved for five years starting in 1871, can be inferred from the fact that the Mutual franchise of the circuit was owned and operated by William Marcy (Boss) Tweed, political worthy, forger and larcenist who found baseball of the era a fertile field for his skulduggery. Thus it is noteworthy that the game's first recorded crook was not a player but a magnate. A product of New York City, Tweed had a hand in virtually all the financial possibilities of life in that metropolis, and that baseball became included within the orbit of his manipulations is not surprising.

The gamblers that Harry Wright had so stoutly opposed were discouraged when baseball succeeded on a professional basis, but not so discouraged that they did not finally manage to seduce club officials, players and umpires.

In fact, when Wright journeyed from Cincinnati to Boston to launch professional baseball in the Hub, he considered the abandonment of the professional principle, fearing that the high moral tone of Massachusetts would not permit professional sport. However, he was dissuaded from this belief by Albert Goodwill Spalding, the young pitcher from Rockford, Illinois who had been recommended to Wright by Henry Chadwick, the veteran writer of the game. Wright had gone to Rockford to sign Spalding and two other players, Ross Barnes and J. Fred Cone, and this trio formed the nucleus of the Boston Red Stockings.

The National Association was formed at a meeting in New York, March 4, 1871, and although it struggled through five seasons, it has long been terra incognita for historians. All that seems generally known is that corruption was rife, and the chief ingredients of life in the league were bribery, contract breaking, and the desertion of players.

But the National Association was definitely a major league. More than half of the players who appeared in 1871 box scores were still on the job when the National League was formed five years later, and still others were prevented from continuing their careers in the National because of advancing age. But more than a hundred National League performers, many of whom reached stardom, got their starts in the old N.A.

The first season of the National Association saw ten different clubs participating, although one team didn't finish the season, and the games of another didn't count in the official standings. The Kekiongas of Fort Wayne, Indiana, disbanded in July, and a month later the Eckfords of Brooklyn replaced them. However, games played by the Eckfords were thrown out. The clubs which did remain, in the order of their finish, were: the Athletics of Philadelphia, the Red Stockings of Boston, the Mutuals of New York, the Olympics of Washington, the Haymakers of Troy, the Forest Cities of Cleveland, and the Forest Cities of Rockford. J. W. Kerns, who succeeded the notorious Morrissey as president of the Haymakers of Troy, also served as president of the league.

The schedule that first year was a brief one, with no club playing more than 35 championship games, and the Athletics, who won the pennant, battled through only 29, winning 22 and losing seven. Boston was in second place, with 22 victories and ten defeats, and Chicago third with a record of 20 and ten. Actually, Chicago had been in first place for most of the season, but was deprived of a chance for the flag because of the Chicago fire that ravaged the city in October. That celebrated fire began on October 8, and on that day the White Stockings were scheduled to meet Rockford on the Lake Street grounds. The Rockford players were actually entering the city when they saw the blaze that put Chicago out of the race. Since that time numerous clubs have been figuratively burned up over losing a pennant, but thanks to Mrs. O'Leary's bovine, the White Stockings of 1871 were the only nine literally burned out of one.

The Athletics of 1871, then, were the first team to win a major league pennant. Managed by Elias Hicks Hay hurst, the roster of those primitive champions is best pieced together today as follows:

PLAYER	POS.	BIRTHPLACE AND DATE		DIED
Bechtel, George A.	Sub	Phila., Pa.	'49	
Berkenstock, Nathan	Sub	Pennsylvania	'31	2-23 '00
Cuthbert, Edgar E.	OF	Phila., Pa. 6-20	'45	2-6 '05
Fisler, Weston	1B	Camden, N.J. 7-5	'41	12-25 '22
Heuble, George A.	OF	New Jersey	'50	
McBride, James	P	Pennsylvania	'46	10-10 '16
Malone, Ferguson G.	C	Ireland	'42	7-18 '05
Meyerle, Levi S.	3B	Phila., Pa.	'49	
Pratt, Thomas J.	Sub	Pennsylvania	'50	9-28 '08
Radcliff, John J.	SS	New Jersey	'46	7-26 '11
Reach, Alfred J.	2B	London, Eng. 5-25	'40	1-14 '28
Sensenderfer, John P.	Sub	Phila., Pa. 12-28	'47	5-3 '03

By way of preparing for its second season, the National Association decided that a player and not a club executiv. should serve as president of the league, and so at the circuit's first annual convention at Cleveland, President Kerns was deposed and the job given to Bob Ferguson, a player of the Brooklyn Atlantics and the game's first switch hitter.

Chicago had not sufficiently recovered from the fire to field a team, and Rockford decided to abandon professional ball, but the other seven teams of 1871, including the Atlantics, were ready to go on, and the number of clubs was increased to 11 when franchises were granted the Lord Baltimores of Baltimore, the Mansfields of Middletown, Connecticut, the Eckfords of Brooklyn and the Nationals of Washington.

Although Rockford disappeared from the baseball map after only one professional season, that small Illinois community made a valuable contribution to the game's history. It has already been told how Harry Wright found three famous early players at Rockford, and in addition to those, Rockford also produced Bob Addy, an outfielder who is credited with being the first player to steal a base by sliding; William (Cherokee) Fisher, a pitcher who drifted to Rockford from Philadelphia; and, most famous of all, Adrian Constantine Anson, who was to play professional baseball for twenty-seven years, a longer period of major league service than any other player ever achieved. Anson, whose names of Adrian and Constantine were derived not from Roman emperors but from two towns in Michigan his father found pleasant, was the first white child ever born in Marshalltown, Iowa. Anson received a salary of $66 a month at Rockford, but when the Athletics offered him $1,250 to come to Philadelphia the following year, Hiram Waldo, the Rockford manager, told him to go ahead. Waldo then surrendered the franchise.

The eleven-club National Association had rough going in 1872. Ferguson was absolutely without experience as a league official, although he was one of the most popular of players, and many of the teams were poorly managed and not supported by the fans. Only six clubs finished the season; in the following order: Boston, Baltimore, Mutuals, Athletics, Atlantics and Eckfords. The first four clubs paid regular salaries to their players, and the last two were operated unsuccessfully as cooperatives. The Eckfords won only three championship games all year while losing twenty-six. Although the league schedule was modest in proportions, it was padded with various exhibition games on days when nothing was at stake, and the players were kept busy from April through October.

For three years more the league struggled on with various changes of franchise, and as time passed it became apparent that dishonesty was a general practice. Though a man of integrity, Bob Ferguson found himself helpless in the face of all the chaos. A player by choice and an executive only by election, he had little tact, could not handle men, and lacked the qualities of a reformer. His experience made it quite clear that at that early date players could not manage their own affairs. Management and playing called for different qualities, and a firm hand was needed if the game were to survive.

The Association's fifth and last season was its worst. Thirteen clubs entered the field, and only seven completed the schedule. Drunkenness among the players in 1875 became so prevalent that it presented a problem almost as serious as the throwing of games. The only club which avoided the practices which almost destroyed the game in its infancy was Harry Wright's Boston Red Stockings. And the character assumed by Wright's team paid handsome dividends, as Boston won the pennant for the fourth consecutive year.

But elsewhere all was confused. The situation was especially bad in Brooklyn where the Atlantic club fostered so much open betting that one section of the grounds was known as the Gold Board, with activity that rivaled that of the stock exchange.

Discovering that their salaries represented only a fraction of what they could make by dealing with the gamblers, the players traveled from city to city like princes, sporting diamonds, drinking champagne at dinner every night, and ostentatiously paying the tab by peeling off folding money from wads of the stuff that mysteriously reproduced themselves. Of course, this was the era of the Robber Barons, and compared to the really big business transactions that went on while Ulysses S. Grant sat benignly in the White House, the activity of baseball players was indeed of the small fry variety. But it served to furnish a sordid miniature of the nation's social and economic health.

One early baseball magnate to whom all this was revolting was William A. Hulbert, a new official of the Chicago White Stockings. Hulbert had been born at Burlington Flats, Otsego County, New York, but was removed by his parents to Chicago at the delicate age of two. He attended Beloit College, and then returned to Chicago where he eventually became a member of the Board of Trade. Becoming interested in baseball as a sport, he was persuaded in 1875 to take on executive duties with the White Stockings, but while attending a league convention at Philadelphia he was horrified by what he saw and he vowed to inaugurate reforms. Shocked by the charges of crooked play and disgusted with the drunkenness, Hulbert soon learned that the game's loosely enforced contractual arrangements with players supplied still another source of trouble.

One day in Baltimore a player on Hulbert's team, William H. Craver, was arrested and put in jail. Investigation revealed that he had previously signed with Baltimore and had received an advance of $1,200. Although Hulbert had no prior knowledge that Craver had jumped his contract with Baltimore, he settled with the Maryland club for $600, and the player was released from the hoosegow and permitted to perform for Chicago.

Hulbert knew that the city of Chicago wanted good baseball but could not get it because teams from the East continually stole players. And so he decided that the only way to fight back was by the use of the same methods.

One day Hulbert approached Al Spalding, the ambitious hurler, and said, "Look here, Spalding. You're a western man. Your home is in Rockford. Why not sign with Chicago in 1876?"

Spalding, always alert to the possibility of adding to his income, agreed when he found that he and Hulbert could come to terms. Spalding also made it possible for Hulbert to sign three other Boston stars, Cal McVey, Ross Barnes and Deacon Jim White. The signing of these four great players—baseball's original Big Four—caused a furor when word of their capitulation to Chicago leaked out. In addition Spalding helped Hulbert obtain Cap Anson from the Philadelphia club. Those five players, along with Paul Hines, John Glenn and John Peters from the old Chicago team of the National Association, were to form the nucleus of Hulbert's first National League club.

The news that Hulbert had retaliated in kind by robbing the East of its greatest stars might not have become public knowledge had not the newspapers in Chicago found it impossible to keep from bragging. The National Association had a rule on its books prohibiting any player from signing a contract before the season ended with any club other than the one to which the player belonged. But the Chicago papers began to gloat over Hulbert's coup, and in Boston the shocked fans began to ask, "What goes on here?"

Barnes, White and McVey all denied signing with Chicago, but Spalding, possessed of a moral code which permitted him to jump his contract but not to lie about it, freely admitted his part in the proceedings.

From that time on the Boston fans bitterly assailed the Big Four, heaping abuse upon them throughout the remainder of the 1875 season. But those Boston players, the best in the game, outdid themselves in an effort to counteract the ridicule, and the Red Stockings finished the year with 71 victories and only eight defeats, the most phenomenal record ever made by a major league club in an organized league. Completely oblivious to the taunts of the home fans, Boston did not lose a single contest on its own grounds all season long.

But Hulbert was worried. Fearing that the National Association would expel the players he had signed, he decided to anticipate action by his fellow magnates. He wrote letters to Colonel John A. Joyce of Cincinnati, Charles A. Fowle of St. Louis, and Charles E. Chase of Louisville, all gentlemen who were presumably interested in decent baseball, inviting them to a meeting at Louisville to discuss conditions. Although there is a legend rampant to the effect that this meeting took place at a chop house, the actual site was the Galt House, one of the city's leading hotels. Hulbert's group, which also included Spalding and Louis Meacham, a Chicago baseball writer, met for four or five days in January, 1876. These four clubs, which were representative of Chicago, Cincinnati, St. Louis and Louisville, voted to form a new organization to be called the Western League. A committee consisting of Hulbert and Fowle was appointed to write to eastern clubs interested in reform, and a letter was sent to the Bostons, Hartfords, Athletics and Mutuals, inviting them to still another meeting, this one to take place at the Grand Central Hotel in New York at noon on Wednesday, February 2, 1876.

This New York meeting was attended by all those who had gathered at Louisville, in addition to Morgan Bulkeley of Hartford, William H. Cammeyer of New York, G. W. Thompson of Philadelphia and Nathaniel T. Apollonio and Harry Wright of Boston. Bulkeley acted as chairman of the affair with Harry Wright as secretary, but the confab was stricdy Bill Hulbert's show.

All clubs except Cincinnati and Louisville, which were not members, resigned from the National Association, thus sounding the death knell of that circuit; and with the eastern teams ready to come into the new loop, the name, Western League, was abandoned, and the new organization was called the National League, the same National League which, despite various vagaries of fortune, has operated continuously for three quarters of a century.

Although the outcome of that meeting was a notable achievement, all did not go smoothly. The eastern owners were loathe to abandon their liaison with gamblers. But Hulbert, before the general meeting, had made separate appointments with each of the promoters, carefully spaced a half hour apart. As each magnate entered the room, Hulbert locked the door and began to lecture sternly concerning the reforms he insisted upon. So the birth of the National League was in reality the aftermath of a series of shotgun weddings, with Bill Hulbert playing the role of the bride's indignant father. The eastern teams, soaked in corruption, played the bridegroom with the utmost reluctance.

Here are the reforms that Hulbert introduced as part of baseball's new code for the infant National League:

1. The circuit was to consist of a league of clubs and not an association of players.

2. Each club was to post an entry fee of $100, ten times greater than the amount which had been required to enter the National Association, in addition to annual dues of $100.

3. To be eligible for membership, a city was required to have a population of 75,000, and was not to be within less than five miles of another league club. (This established the principle of a club's rights over the city it represented. One of the faults inherent in the National Association was the fact that there were three teams in Philadelphia.)

4. Player contracts were to be written and not verbal, with the provision that any player made ineligible by one club would remain ineligible to all others.

5. All players found guilty of dishonest playing were to be barred from the game for life.

Hulbert, of course, could have had the league presidency for the asking. But he felt that some concession should be made to the eastern teams to compensate them for their cooperation in living up to the radical western idea of honest baseball. And so he urged that Morgan Bulkeley of Hartford, who could be used by the game as a front because of his acceptance in political and industrial circles, take office as the league's first leader. Bulkeley agreed, but he remained in office for only one year and contributed nothing.

During that year Bill Hulbert stood over his shoulder, with a solicitous eye on his offspring.

What were Hulbert's motives in founding the National League? Was it pure altruism, a conviction that the game needed stern measures to save it from ruin? Partly. But the original idea was created in an attempt to make legal the theft of the Big Four from Boston.

The Debutante
National League   3

In THE inaugural season of Bill Hulbert's National League the eight clubs battled through a schedule of seventy games, with each team meeting its opponents ten times, five each at home and on the road. Teams clashed three times a week, usually on Tuesday, Thursday and Saturday afternoons. In most cities play did not get under way until 4 o'clock, enabling business men to complete their daily toil before adjourning to the ballyard. Admission to the grounds was pegged at fifty cents, a figure that was considered high.

The first championship National League game took place at Philadelphia, Saturday, April 22, 1876, with the visiting Boston team nosing out the Athletics, 6 to 5. This historic contest was witnessed by 3,000 fanatics, not a bad outpouring. Early in the following week the other six clubs swung into action, and Hulbert's dream of an organized circuit was a reality.

The National League's first winning pitcher, victor in that 6 to 5 struggle between Boston and Philadelphia, was Joseph E. Borden, one of the game's most shadowy figures. Sometimes appearing in box scores as Borden, but usually as Josephs, this hurler was destined to be the game's first and greatest flash in the pan. Borden had pitched a no-hit game for Philadelphia of the National Association, July 27, 1875, the first recorded no-hitter in professional baseball, and he also was to author the first flawless effort in Hulbert's new loop.

The season was just a month old when Borden blanked Cincinnati without a blow in a contest at the Hub on May 23, the Beantowners winning, 8 to 0. According to the record books the National League's first no-hitter was tossed by George Washington Bradley of St. Louis against Hartford on July 15, 1876, nearly two months after Borden performed the stunt, but a thorough investigation of the records indicates that the Boston pitcher and not Bradley deserves the accolade as the league's first hitless flinger.

The reason why Borden's feat never attracted the attention of the keepers of the annals is because all box scores indicate that in the game in question Borden yielded two safeties. Although the game was played at Boston, the score was sent to the league office by Oliver Perry Caylor, a writer for the Cincinnati Enquirer, and during the season Caylor, at variance with contemporary scorers, counted bases on balls as hits. Later, in 1887, bases on balls were to count as hits, but in the league's first campaign only Caylor scored them as such. Borden granted passes to two Cincinnati batters, passes which appeared as hits in the box score. Since this was his second no-hit outing, Borden became the first of 14 major league pitchers who have twice blanked the enemy without a blow.

Any fan looking at that box score today would have difficulty in finding how it differed from the score of a game played in 1950 except for the unusually high total of errors. But note that nine of the 20 errors were made by the teams' catchers. This is because passed balls in 1876 were credited as errors. Wild pitches were also considered miscues, and Borden had two of those. So in reality more than half of the errors in that score were battery errors and would so be counted today. Here is the corrected box score of Borden's previously unknown accomplishment:

BOSTON	AB	R	H	PO	A	E	CINCINNATI	AB	R	H	PO	A	E
Wright, ss	5	1	1	1	2	0	Gould, 1b	4	0	0	8	0	0
Leonard, 2b	5	1	2	2	1	1	Booth, ss	4	0	0	3	6	1
O'Rourke, cf	5	0	0	1	0	0	Jones, cf	4	0	0	0	0	0
Murnane, 1b	4	1	0	8	0	0	Pearson, c	4	0	0	6	1	6
Schaefer, 3b	4	1	0	4	3	0	Snyder, lf	3	0	0	4	0	0
Manning, rf	4	1	2	4	0	0	Sweasy, 2b	3	0	0	0	1	2
Morrill, c	4	1	0	5	2	3	Foley, 3b	3	0	0	1	0	3
Whitney, lf	4	2	1	2	0	0	Clack, rf	2	0	0	5	0	2
Borden, p	4	0	0	0	1	2	Fisher, p	2	0	0	0	1	0
	39	8	6	27	9	6		29	0	0	27	9	14

Earned runs — None. Bases on errors — Boston, 7. Bases on balls-Cincinnati, 2. Two-base hit — Manning. Left on bases — Boston, 4; Cincinnati, 2. Struck out — O'Rourke, 2; Jones, 2; Booth, Schaefer. Time of game — 1:50. Umpire — Mr. Hodges of the Howard Club.

Fielding wasn't the highly developed skill in 1876 that it is now. Gloves were not used then, and catchers played directly behind the bat only when runners were on the bases. Cincinnati, tailenders in the National's opening year, made 623 errors in 65 games, an average of not quite ten per contest, but how many of the bobbles would be charged today is questionable. Scorers were probably more exacting, and the fielding game had not yet evolved into the almost perfect mechanism that it is today.

Otherwise the score might well be yesterday's, save for one additional detail of the summary, the line which lists the umpire as "Mr. Hodges of the Howard Club."

If umpires are an abused lot today, in 1876 their task was doubly hazardous. There was no such thing as a league staff of umpires, and was not to be for three more years. Most of the fans who attended the game were roughnecks, and many of them arrived at the park inebriated. Heckling the umpire afforded them more pleasure than watching the game itself. Hulbert had anticipated this, and tried to find a suitable way of selecting the officials. The practice most generally followed provided for the visiting team to supply the home club with a list of five suitable umpires in that locality. The home team would then select two of these and then ask the visitors to choose between the two. It was an awkward arrangement but the best that Hulbert could think of at the time.

Borden won few games after his no-hitter against the Reds, but he did achieve 13 victories as against 11 defeats before a sore arm ended his usefulness. Humbly he filled out the season as grounds-keeper of the Boston club, and a few years later he bobbed up at Philadelphia, ironically stitching the baseballs he once propelled so well, in a factory. He died as unusual a death as any player who ever trod the diamond, a victim of the legendary flood at Johnstown, Pennsylvania, May 31, 1889.

Early professional players customarily met death under fantastic circumstances. Often, if they worked in factories, they were crushed by falling weights. Some others were murdered, and an extremely high percentage of them, out of all proportion to their number, committed suicide in strange ways. If Borden's fate seems bizarre, consider the fate of his battery mate, Boston's first National League catcher, Lewis J. Brown.

After his retirement because of a sore throwing arm, Brown obtained employment as a bouncer in a dive on Boston's La Grange Street. The bistro operated on the sly after the proprietress, Mrs. Joe Goss, the widow of a famed pugilist, who once fought John L. Sullivan, lost her license because of irregularities. One of the sports who visited the establishment was Chris O'Brien, a big fellow, and one day Brown and O'Brien engaged in a friendly wrestling match. The Widow Goss, fearful that the noise would attract the police, asked them to cease, and when they didn't, she hit Brown over the knee with a piece of gas pipe. He was removed to City Hospital, where he informed officials that he had fallen against a stone cuspidor. A week or so later pneumonia set in and he died, meeting his maker just four months before Borden became engulfed at Johnstown. And then the Widow Goss, as a sentimental gesture, had him buried in the same grave with her departed husband.

Hulbert's coup in signing the Big Four paid handsome dividends, and the Chicago team roared through the debutante National League like a prairie fire. Hulbert's organizational skill was matched by the field management of Al Spalding. The highest paid player of the year with a salary of $3,000 and a $500 bonus, Spalding won 47 games and lost 13, to become the league's first leading pitcher. His slab work assured Chicago of the pennant, the White Stockings finishing six full games ahead of second place Hartford with 52 triumphs and only 14 setbacks. Cal McVey, one of the old Cincinnati Red Stockings, was at first base for Chicago; Ross Barnes, the league's leading hitter, played second; John Peters was at short; and Cap Anson, later famous as a first baseman, performed at third. John Glenn, Paul Hines and Bob Addy roamed that first championship outfield; and Spalding's catcher was Deacon Jim White. A utility man on the team, Oscar Bielaski, was possibly the first professional player of Polish descent and the only one of that nationality to enter the league for years to come.

Barnes managed to win that first batting crown with a mark of .403, but did so by the use of a most unorthodox baseball device known as the "fair-foul" hit. Years before, Barnes had marveled at the skill of Dicky Pearce, a shortstop who was supposed to have invented the bunt. Barnes then practiced bunting faithfully, and developed a technique for laying down bunts which rolled foul. In those days there was no rule providing for fouls on balls which originally struck fair and then rolled outside the lines. Instead, they were termed fair-foul hits and enabled the batsman to reach base. Barnes became the batting champ by the frequent application of fair-foul hits, but in the winter that followed the fledgling season the rule was changed, and the decline of Ross Barnes as a player coincided with the shift in legislation.

Hartford and St. Louis finished in a virtual tie for second place, the Connecticut team winning 47 and losing 21 for a percentage of .691, and the Missouri nine copping 45 and dropping 19 for a .703 figure. However, Hartford was awarded second place. Known as the Dark Blues, Hartford achieved eminence largely because of the stout pitching of Tommy Bond and the slugging of Dick Higham, an outfielder who had formerly been a catcher and who soon was to attain ignominy as baseball's first crooked umpire. The leading slugger of the St. Louis team was Lipman E. Pike, a lefthanded hitting outfielder and the game's first professional player of Jewish ancestry, but the Missouri team's strong finish was mostly traced to the magnificent pitching of George Washington Bradley.

Bradley won 44 games, three fewer than Spalding, and lost 19. Sixteen of his triumphs were shutouts, a record for whitewashings that held up for forty years, or until Grover Cleveland Alexander duplicated the figure for the Phillies in 1916. It has already been noted that Bradley, like Borden, etched a no-hit game into the annals, and he also had three one-hitters.

Boston, mediocre without the Big Four, ended up in fourth place. When Borden's arm went lame, pitching duties at the Hub were shared by John Manning and George H. (no kin to George Washington) Bradley. But by far the best Boston player was James Henry (Orator Jim) O'Rourke, outfielder who could also go behind the bat. A man of amazing stamina, O'Rourke caught a major league game in 1904, and was active as a player at Bridgeport in his fifties.

The second division clubs, then as now, had their difficulties. The Louisville Grays, boasting a whale of a pitcher in Jim Devlin, were the best of the lot, finishing fifth, and were followed by the Mutuals, the Athletics and the Cincinnati Reds. The Reds were hopeless tenants of the cellar, winning only nine games while losing 56. The team had one streak of 18 consecutive defeats, and one of the club's pitchers, Charles Wilson (Dora) Dean, had a personal losing string of 16 in a row. Though not as successful on the field as his rivals, Dean achieved a much greater success in life than did most of his contemporaries, founding a prosperous electrotype business at Nashville which he conducted until he died at the age of 83 in 1935. At 80 Dean still played tennis and went swimming, and presumably he had long forgotten his failures on the diamond.

The Athletics and Mutuals failed to make their last trip through the West, and for this Bill Hulbert, proving that he meant business, had them expelled from the league. The National operated as a six-club circuit for the next two years, not expanding again until 1879.

But despite the delinquency of the Athletics and Mutuals, the league played 257 of the 280 scheduled games that first year, in addition to three ties. Bill Hulbert ran his show with an iron hand while the nominal league president, Morgan Bulkeley, sat in idleness at Hartford.

Baseball had made immense strides in one season under Hulbert. There was satisfaction everywhere but in Cincinnati, where a losing team riled the local populace. Just how little the sentiments and even the phraseology of the fan have changed throughout the years is best demonstrated by the following letter, an antiquated squawk by a Red rooter which appeared in the Cincinnati Gazette on May 12, 1876, when the season was little more than two weeks old:

"It seems that the present Red Stocking Baseball Club was gotten up more for the purpose of making money for individuals than as a pride for Cincinnati. Any person knowing anything about baseball knows that no good man can be had for little or nothing. Why wasn't Nichols retained? Guess he wanted a little more money. Why wasn't Mack, of last year's Stars, engaged? And how about engaging Malone? Does he, too, want more money? It is sad that the present Red Stocking nine should be the acknowledged successors of the once famous Red Stocking club."

Long-suffering fandom had begun a vigil that has lasted for three quarters of a century, and the operators of the Cincinnati franchise learned early that cellar air breeds discontent. And in the following year the miseries of the Cincinnati team almost wrecked the league.

Cincinnati's club was owned by an industrialist named Josiah L. Keck, a man who also operated a rendering business, melting down horses into soap; and there were those fans unkind enough to suggest that he might just as well melt down some of his players. At any rate, after Keek's Reds had lost 14 of their first 17 games in 1877, the owner refused to pay the expenses of the club on its first eastern swing, explaining, "I lost money on the trip last season, and I don't intend to take such a risk again this year."

So the Reds didn't go East, and the team's players tried to negotiate with other clubs. Hulbert, though president of the league by now, couldn't forget that he was also president of the White Stockings, and he took advantage of the chaotic Cincinnati situation to sign two of the team's players, Infielder Jimmy Hallinan and Outfielder Charlie Jones, the game's first formidable hitter of home runs. Hulbert sent Louis Meacham, the Chicago sports writer who had helped organize the National League, to Cincinnati to corral the pair, and Meacham was able to accomplish his purpose easily when he found that Hallinan was in jail on a drunk charge and ready to sign anything that would mean freedom.

But meanwhile a responsible group of Cincinnati citizens, rallying to the team's cause, bought up Keck's stock and assumed his indebtedness, then asked that the Reds be reinstated.

Hulbert, however, found a loophole in the fact that the Reds had not paid their dues to the league, a matter of $100, and he insisted that the franchise be forfeited. But at a special meeting he was overruled and a compromise effected. Jones returned to Cincinnati after playing only three games for Chicago. Hallinan remained with the White Stockings, but a broken finger caused his retirement within a week, and in two years he was dead of gastritis.

The Reds resumed their schedule under new ownership and finished the season, ending up last again, although the games indulged in by the club were eventually declared null and void.

Hartford was another trouble spot. The immortal Bulkeley lost money on his Dark Blues in 1876 despite his second place finish, and then he worked out a deal whereby the Hartfords played their 1877 home games at the Union Grounds in Brooklyn. This slight to the

Hartford fans was of no consequence to Bulkeley, who yielded the league presidency to Hulbert after one year and then permanently removed the city of Hartford from the major league scene after one year more.

Hulbert's piracy of the Cincinnati players in 1877 was not successful, and his White Stockings did not repeat as champions. This was largely because Al Spalding practically retired, appearing in only two games. Spalding's removal left Tommy Bond of Boston as the best pitcher in the circuit and, bolstered by Bond, the Beaneaters breezed to the flag, seven full contests ahead of the Louisville Grays. Just how much help Boston received from Louisville that summer was a moot matter, for what went on in the Falls City toward the end of the campaign was strange indeed and furnished Hulbert with a headache much more splitting than the comparatively trivial events at Cincinnati and Hartford.

The Louisville
Crooks   4

"Gentlemen, what can I do to prove to you I regret my crooked work with the Louisville nine? I have suffered poverty; been obliged to beg; seen my wife and child want for something to eat; been living on charity. And I thought I would come to Utica to this convention as my last hope. I am sorry that I did wrong. I want just one more chance. I think I have repented of my crooked work and don't, for God's sake, refuse to give a man a chance to redeem himself."

THE ABOVE speech, which sounds as if it were culled from the script of one of the melodramas performed on showboats of the era, was supposedly part of an address made by James Alexander Devlin, the most prominent of four Louisville players expelled from baseball, at the Boggs Hotel, Utica, New York, February 19, 1879, before an august gathering of National League officials. Devlin, a pitcher, along with Outfielder George Hall, captain and home-run hitter of the Grays; Shortstop Bill Craver; and Third Baseman Al Nichols had been permanently exiled for throwing games, December 5, 1877, at the league's second annual meeting at the Kennard House in Cleveland. Until his death in 1883 it was Devlin's annual custom to make such a plea for reinstatement, a supplication which invariably fell upon deaf ears.

Little has been published concerning the Louisville scandal, although the chronologies of baseball

41

frequently included in the dusty records books often give the meager information that Devlin, Craver, Nichols and Hall (always listed in that order, for some reason) were found guilty of throwing National League games in 1877. What was it all about?

Bill Hulbert's new league, founded in an effort to put an end to the sordid liaison between baseball and gambling, survived its first campaign without a breath of scandal, but in the circuit's sophomore season the ugly monster reared its hideous head again.

Devlin was one of the best pitchers of his time. Frequently likened to Job by the biblically inclined sports writers of his day because he continually suffered from a chronic case of boils, and also described by the press as a sleep-walker, Jim overcame the twin hazards of skin eruption and somnambulism to become a hurler rated only slightly less efficient than Al Spalding and Tommy Bond, and he was believed to be worth every cent of his 1877 salary of $2,000. Hall, the small, handsome outfielder who had hit five home runs for the Athletics in 1876, a total which made him the loop's first king in the four-master department, earned even more, $2,800. Craver was the team's regular shortstop and a player of more than ordinary attainments. Of the four only Nichols was a lesser light. He didn't even appear in a game with the Grays until August, as Bill Hague was the regular third baseman. Then Hague, like Devlin, became visited with boils, and Nichols was added to the roster at the behest of several of the players.

It had been a rugged season for the Grays. Traveling to Cincinnati on the river steamer, General Lytle, to open the campaign, the Louisville team sat through three postponements because of rain, an annoyance because league rules specified that each player must pay his club fifty cents per day while on the road.

Manager Jack Chapman had a tough time keeping his players out of the saloons, and even on the ball field they were a source of trouble. A game at Cincinnati on May 15 was declared "no contest" because of unruly conduct by the Louisvilles. The trouble started in the seventh inning when the Grays, leading 8 to 5, were batting. Outfielder Bill Crowley, an extraordinarily uncouth character who frequently carried his bat into the hotel dining room by way of demonstrating that the ball-player's veneer of culture was still thin in 1877, was mistakenly given a base on balls when the umpire, one Brady, got mixed up in regard to the count. Brady appealed to the scorer and then ordered Crowley to bat again, but the player refused. Hall, the next hitter, went to the plate, but Brady wouldn't recognize him. Meanwhile, Crowley sat down on first base, hugging his knees. In desperation Brady declared Crowley out, and when that happened, the Louisville team picked up its bats and departed from the field, and the game was forfeited to the Reds. And although the rules specified that the winning team gain possession of the ball, Devlin stole it. Ten minutes later the field became drenched with rain, and a crowd of thoroughly disgusted fans went home wet.

Hall had a brother-in-law named Frank Powell who lived in Brooklyn and who had been telling George for almost a year that he was a fool not to throw games and thereby increase his income. Pondering this advice over a period of months, Hall finally addressed a letter to Devlin, proposing that they throw games, and left the billet doux in Devlin's room at the Burnet House in Cincinnati.

Meanwhile, Devlin had drummed up an acquaintance with one Richard Tobin, a cigar clerk at Earle's Hotel in New York. Tobin introduced Devlin to a gambler named McLeod at the latter's home, 141

Broome Street. McLeod told Devlin that if he ever wanted to make any money to let him know, and that if he should ever desire to throw a game, he should send McLeod a telegram containing the word, SASH.

Upon receiving the little note from Hall, Devlin wired McLeod that an exhibition game at Lowell, Massachusetts was to be thrown. McLeod then sent Devlin one hundred dollars, and Jim gave twenty-five of it to Hall. When the subsequent investigation revealed these financial details, newspapers engaged in a field day of punning, saying such things as, "You can hire a Hall fairly cheaply these days; for only twenty-five dollars."

The next games thrown were three exhibitions at Indianapolis for which Devlin received three hundred dollars. By this time, however, Devlin decided to hold out on Hall, and from that time on George never received his rightful share of the spoils.

Nichols was next taken into the ring, and because he was a rather obscure player, it was decided that he should act as go-between, and it was arranged that McLeod's wires should be sent to him. That was where the Louisville boys made one of their first mistakes.

Vice President Charles E. Chase of the Grays thought it was most peculiar that a player so slightly regarded as Al Nichols should be the recipient of so many telegrams in every city the team visited and thought that the little in-fielder might be involved with gamblers. And so, when the club left for an August series in St. Louis, Chase ordered Manager Jack Chapman to leave Nichols at home and seize any telegrams that might come for him at the Mound City, sending them to the team's directors. The next day Chase told Nichols that all the team's players were under suspicion of selling games and asked him to sign a paper giving Chase the authority to open and read any wires that might come for him.

"I don't know anything about games being thrown," Nichols insisted, "although I've heard that Craver is throwing them. But I won't permit you to open my wires."

"Your refusal is an admission of guilt," Chase pointed out.

"All right, then, open them," Nichols replied.

Chase then read two wires addressed to Nichols which had been forwarded by Chapman. They were both from P. A. Williams, a pool-seller from Brooklyn. One wanted to know why Nichols had not been heard from, and the other inquired as to whether arrangements (presumably for throwing a game or games) had been completed.

Nichols said that he had no idea what the wires were all about, but when the team returned, Hall went to Chase and confessed his part in the venture, blaming Nichols for the whole scheme.

Dan Devinney, an umpire, then got into the act, claiming that George McManus, manager of the St. Louis Browns, had offered him two hundred and fifty dollars to throw the Louisville game of August 1 to St. Louis. However, since Louisville had won the game in question, 3 to 1, Chase never bothered to pursue that allegation or locate McManus.

Chase then suspended Craver, Hall, Nichols and Devlin for all time, and the league confirmed the banishment. There was not a shred of evidence against Craver, whose suspension was actually the result of mere insubordination, as he refused to permit the directors to open his telegrams.

Thereafter, Devlin made a pathetic appearance at every league gathering, pleading for the reinstatement that was never granted. Finally giving up, he returned to Philadelphia and joined the police force, but he soon contracted tuberculosis. A benefit game played for him in 1883 yielded a thousand dollars but came too late, and the errant pitcher died at his home there, October 10, 1883.

Craver also became a policeman at Troy, New York and served honorably on the force until his death, June 17, 1901. He was highly esteemed by all who knew him at Troy, and his obituary did not identify him as having been involved with the Louisville crooks. Hall went home to Brooklyn, became an engraver, and prospered, but like Devlin he went to an early grave. Only Nichols continued to play baseball for a living. He was with the Franklin club of Brooklyn in 1884, and is believed to have performed for Jersey City of the Eastern League in 1886 under the name of Williams.

There is no question but that the action of the four Louisville players cost the Grays the pennant. The team was in first place as late as August 13, but then lost seven successive games in the East and slid out of contention. The work of the Grays in a late-season series against Hartford cost Louisville its last chance for the flag and was also suspect.

One of the games that Devlin admitted throwing was a contest at Cincinnati on September 6, but how he conspired to throw that one is uncertain, inasmuch as the Reds didn't win the verdict until the tenth inning when Lipman E. Pike slashed a home run to right field for the only score of the contest. Hall and Nichols insisted to the last that the only games they threw were exhibitions and that their conduct in championship frays was consistently decorous.

Be that as it may, it was Chase's stern action and Hulbert's equally firm confirmation of it that saved baseball in 1877. Crooked playing had never before been punished, and the players were incredulous in face of the demonstration that the new league meant business. The treatment of the Louisville crooks set the precedent for equally drastic action more than forty years later when the Chicago Black Sox were found guilty of conspiring to throw the 1919 World Series to the Reds.

Newspapers throughout the country treated the Louisville scandal with mixed amusement and cynicism, but in the main they applauded Chase and Hulbert for their stand. And in St. Louis, where Devlin and Hall had signed to play in 1878, it was certainly no joking matter.

"The days of professional baseball are numbered," moaned the Globe-Democrat, "and the hundreds of young men who have depended on the pastime as their means of earning a livelihood will be obliged to change their plans of operation."

But thanks to Hulbert that lugubrious prophecy was not fulfilled, and the professional game survived its darkest hour.

It has often been alleged that these early professional players were of the worst possible type, and although there were several notable exceptions, the charge is generally true.

One early player was shot to death during a lynching attempt at Glens Falls, New York after being accused of murdering a little girl under particularly atrocious circumstances. Another served a term in the penitentiary for arson after setting fire to a hotel at Franklin, Pennsylvania. Still another was arrested for highway robbery after slugging a minister of the gospel and lifting his wallet and watch. And the list of such picturesque but nevertheless damning episodes could be continued indefinitely.

But it must be remembered always that many of these early players were alcoholics who would have found the gutter by late adolescence had they not discovered that their baseball talent could be converted into an affluence that was entirely unexpected and certainly not understood. Baseball was and is a perishable business. Conditioned to high living and the worship of the mob, those primitive players were not psychologically equipped to cope with the business of making a living in less exciting ways once their careers had terminated. Baffled by the turn of events, many of them sought solace in the bottle, which in many instances led to the passing of bad checks and other, more sinister offenses.

But certainly the players were no more culpable than the magnates who exploited them, as will be seen.

Melancholy Monopoly   5

THE INVENTOR of the turnstile, that remarkable mechanical device which records admissions to ball parks and other places of commercial amusement, has not yet been honored with a hallowed niche at the Cooperstown shrine, an enormous oversight on the part of the type of baseball magnate that confines his interest in the pastime to the turnstile's merry click. However, although the game's tycoons have neglected the inventor, they early became enamored of his invention, which was made standard equipment at National League parks in 1878.

This mechanical means of counting the gate was provided for at the circuit's second annual meeting in Cleveland, the same meeting at which the banishment of the Louisville players was confirmed. And so, by a strange coincidence, simultaneous means were found to lock players out and spectators in. And it was exactly at this time that club owners learned of still another way of increasing their take, by despoiling the outfield fences with advertising matter.

Hulbert's firm policy with the Louisville crooks was a sound one, and had the league's strong hand restrained itself all would have been well. But the magnates, intoxicated with their newly found power, began to use their right to suspend with utter disregard.

Edward (The Only) Nolan, a highly regarded pitcher from Paterson, New Jersey, was banned by Indianapolis after the 1878 campaign because he lied to a club official, asking for a day off to visit his brother William. When investigation revealed that Brother

William was as fictional a character as Lewis Carroll's Father William, Nolan was declared ineligible and was not able to regain employment until 1883, after he had been deprived of his livelihood for four seasons.

Then there was the treatment of players by the Boston club. Boston's affairs were run by the Triumvirs, an interesting trio of magnates named Arthur H. Soden, William H. Conant and James B. Billings. Soden was the president and the strongest Triumvir, and his reign, which began in 1877, was to last for three full decades. Revered by his fellow magnates and hated by the players, he had all the controversial characteristics such as frugality and austerity that are interpreted as virtues or vices according to one's point of view.

Soden blacklisted one player, Sadie Houck, for refusing to tip his hat to the magnate. Another, John O'Rourke, brother of the more famous Orator Jim, was released because his salary was too large. But the athlete who suffered most at Soden's hands was Charles Wesley Jones, an outfielder and one of the game's most celebrated sluggers.

Jones was one of the most colorful players of his era, but he has been entirely neglected by historians of the game. His name appears in the record book only once, for his feat of becoming the first player to hit two home runs in a single inning. Born in Alamance County, North Carolina, April 3, 1850 as Charles Wesley Rippay, he adopted the name of Jones to prevent his mother from learning he had become a professional player. He played for Cincinnati the first three years the National League operated, then moved to Boston. It will be recalled that he was one of two players Hulbert tried to steal from the Reds in 1877.

When the Beaneaters refused to pay Charlie any salary, he committed the terrible crime of asking Soden how much the club owed him. For this he was made ineligible and had to sit on the sidelines for over two years. The amount of money Soden owed Jones was $378. The magnate fined him $100 of this, left him stranded in Cleveland, and then announced to the press that Charlie was an ingrate and blackguard.

Jones played outlaw ball at Portsmouth, Ohio during the period of his exile, and finally won his way back into the American Association in 1883, at the same time that "The Only" Nolan attained his reinstatement. Had it not been for the birth of the Association as a major league rival of the National, Nolan and Jones probably would have remained on the blacklist for life.

Charlie Jones was something of a Beau Brummel, and a Cincinnati clothing firm gave him all the new suits he needed merely to wear them on the streets as an advertisement for the concern.

Several years after his reinstatement, Jones began running around with a woman from Newport, Kentucky named Ollie Smith. One day Charlie and Ollie were sitting in a Cincinnati saloon when they spied Jones' wife walking up and down on the sidewalk in front of the place. The pair boldly walked outside and tried to board a Vine Street car, but Mrs. Jones, screaming "Catch him! Hold that man and woman!" caught up with them and threw the contents of a mysterious package into their faces. The weapon was cayenne pepper and it scored a bulls-eye, striking Charlie in the eyes and temporarily blinding him.

That strange, off-the-field injury practically ended his career. He remained with the Reds for a season and a half, drifting to the Metropolitans in 1887, and then to Kansas City, where he closed his career in 1888. No longer did the galleries shout demandingly, "Home run, Jones!" for Charlie could no longer respond.

Not able to maintain his sartorial standards, Jones filled out his baseball life in the shabby garb of an umpire, and there his trail ends.

That Jones and others like him were unfairly made ineligible there can be but little doubt. Magnates were learning that the gate was more interesting than the sport, a point of view that the players and public did not share.

As early as 1877 a player named Ritterson, who had been with the Athletics during the previous year, signed to play for a professional team called the Ludlows of Ludlow, Kentucky, for the handsome salary of $50 a month. Ben Schott, the owner of the Ludlows, imported Ritterson from Philadelphia. Although he had not practiced all winter, Ritterson caught five innings until his battered and bruised fingers forced him to yield to another player. Schott then fired him on the spot, told him to get back to Philadelphia the best way he could, and refused to pay him anything. Thanks to the generosity of George Hall, one of the Louisville crooks, a fund of $30 was collected from players on the field and Ritterson was able to leave the city.

These abused players, finding themselves victimized at every turn throughout the season, then had to face the annual nightmare of winter. Frequently alcoholic and usually unfit for other work, baseball's first professional players, when unable to collect advance money from their clubs, survived the off-seasons the best way they could.

An entire team at Oswego, New York placed the following advertisement in a local paper following the 1877 season:

"We the undersigned members of the Oswego baseball club, seeing the season is over and wishing to remain in town the coming winter, would beg to inform the citizens of Oswego that we are willing to work at anything. Pay no object."

National League players, better known than the obscure members of the Oswego nine, were often able to find winter jobs as bartenders or policemen. But even to players with employment the off-season loomed lugubriously. One St. Louis newspaper of the era summed up the situation in verse:

"The melancholy days have come,
The saddest of the year,
When those who tread the diamond field
No longer toss the sphere.

"No meals at big hotels; no flowers;
No picnics to remember;
No compliments; no sly, sweet looks—
No baseball—just November."

Not only the players but the National League itself had hard going in the late seventies. The expulsion of the four Louisville players was followed by the eviction of the entire Louisville franchise prior to the 1878 season. Hartford and St. Louis also departed, but the league continued as a six-club circuit by taking in Providence, Milwaukee and Indianapolis.

Providence lasted as a National League member for eight years and added a brilliant page to the game's annals. Managed by the famed Wright brothers, first George and then Harry, the Rhode Island club was the first to gain publicity by attempting something new. Providence erected the first wire screen in front of the grandstand behind home plate in 1879, a precaution designed to prevent the public from mayhem. When it was shown that such a protective screen also prevented numerous lawsuits which might have been filed by spectators struck with baseballs, other clubs followed suit. Previously the field seats for spectators behind the catcher were referred to as "slaughter pens" because of the high incidence of injury to spectators. Providence was also the first club to equip its players with individually styled bats, with the name of each player burned into the wood.

Indianapolis and Milwaukee, however, made no contribution to the game equal to that of Providence, and both quit after one season. But in 1879 the league expanded to eight clubs again by admitting Buffalo, Cleveland, Troy and Syracuse. Then, in 1880, Worcester replaced Syracuse.

Cincinnati, St. Louis and Louisville, all river towns, were considered wicked by the effete cities of the Atlantic coast, and in those places the news that Louisville and St. Louis had been forced out of the baseball picture was hailed with delight. But Cincinnati remained as a trouble spot, and the sharpshooters of eastern baseball determined to disenfranchise the rowdy metropolis on the Ohio.

The National League called a special meeting at the Cataract House, Niagara Falls, New York on May 25, 1880 and passed a resolution which forbade the sale of malt or spiritous liquors on league grounds. This resolution was aimed directly at Cincinnati. The Reds voted against the legislation and continued to violate the rule, and the beer flowed freely at the Cincinnati park all during the 1880 season.

A Worcester newspaper, The Spy, then started sniping at the practice and insisted that the Reds be expelled from the league. Worcester was also incensed because the Cincinnati team leased its grounds to clubs which played baseball on Sunday. The National League, of course, played no Sunday baseball, for its pious executives would not dream in desecrating the Sabbath in so abhorrent a fashion. In fact the National League, steadfast in moral purpose, did not begin playing on Sunday until the Sabbath successes of the American Association proved that it was profitable. Sunday baseball was constantly under fire from church pulpits throughout the nation, and one earnest advocate of the measure to prohibit Sunday play was a Kentucky Senator whose Negro mistress disapproved of the practice.

The eastern magnates finally got their way. When the Reds, at the winter meeting following the 1880 campaign, signified their intention of selling beer and leasing their grounds for Sunday games again in 1881, they were immediately expelled from the league, and their place in the sacrosanct entente was given to the city of Detroit.

Players were not the only abused figures in the game at this stage of the sport's history. Umpires were treated even more wretchedly, if such a thing seems possible. Originally a National League arbiter received five dollars a game for his services and was paid by the home club. It was soon found out that an umpire tended to favor the home team to escape the wrath of the crowd, and another system had to be devised. By 1879 a regular staff was chosen. Umpires were culled mostly from the ranks of old players, but many of them were ignorant and dissolute, and all were continually badgered by fans and players alike. By 1886 there was a sign in the park at Kansas City which read, "Please Do Not Shoot the Umpire; he is Doing the Best he Can."

But one umpire who didn't do his best was Richard Higham, a member of the National League staff in 1882 and a former catcher and outfielder who had hit .314 for Hartford in 1876. Now, very often, baseball executives in attendance at some winter banquet honoring an official will state flatly that there has never been a case of a dishonest umpire. Apparently they do not know about Richard Higham, whose work became so shockingly bad in 1882 that an investigation made by the Detroit club proved he was in collusion with gamblers. Higham devised a novel plan of advising gamblers how to bet on games at which he officiated, and he was trapped when confronted with concrete evidence at a special league meeting at the Russell House, Detroit, June 24, 1882. Handwriting experts were introduced and they proved that a letter to which Higham admitted authorship was identical to another missive which instructed the recipient how to bet. Confronted with the identical handwriting in the two letters, Higham confessed, was expelled on the spot, and then went to Chicago and began making a precarious living as a racetrack tout, which he continued until his death in 1905. Only once before his death was Higham again in the public prints, and that happened at Kansas City in 1889 when he was horsewhipped for circulating damaging reports concerning the character of Mrs. Fred Allen, the wife of a bartender.

Another umpire with a background that was not exactly impeccable was Herman Doscher, an arbiter so highly favored by Al Spalding that the latter chose Doscher to officiate in the "spring world series" between the White Stockings and Browns in 1887. Doscher managed Cleveland in 1882, and he had secretly signed a contract to pilot Detroit the following year. Sent by the Cleveland team to scout two players at Troy, New York, Pete Hotaling and Jake Evans, Doscher signed them, not for Cleveland but for Detroit. He also tried to induce three of his Cleveland players to move to Detroit with him. Doscher denied all this, but a check with the National League office revealed that his signed Detroit contract was already in the safe of the league secretary, Nicholas E. Young. Doscher was then suspended, but through the influence of friendly club executives, he was reinstated and permitted to umpire.

But despite the squabbles between magnates and players, despite the sad plight of umpires, despite the general practice of drunkenness in the ranks, baseball carried on as a profitable National League monopoly. Every season on the playing field events occurred which captured the fancy of the populace.

Paul Hines, an outfielder in Providence and the first gardener to appear at his position wearing sun glasses, performed what is regarded by some record books as the first unassisted triple play. Other historians have cast doubt upon the feat, in the belief that Hines had assistance, but George Wright, who was on the field that day, always insisted that Hines made the tri-killing without aid.

"Boston had men on second and third," said Wright, "and Hines was in center field. The batter hit what would now be called a Texas Leaguer behind shortstop, and the runners raced for the plate. Hines came in fast, made a shoestring catch, and then ran on to tag third before either runner could return."

Not much attention was paid to slugging feats, and home runs were few and far between. Pitchers were kings in the seventies. Two of the most remarkable pitching feats of all time were registered within a week of each other in 1880. John Lee Richmond, a graduate of Brown University, pitching for Worcester on June 12, retired 27 Cleveland players in order, without a runner reaching base. Five days later John Montgomery Ward, another collegian from Penn State and one of the smartest men who ever played baseball, duplicated the stunt for Providence against Buffalo. In three quarters of a century those were the only two perfect games pitched in the National League, although the American has witnessed four such performances.

Another remarkable game in which Providence figured saw the Grays defeat Detroit, 1 to 0, in eighteen innings, August 17, 1882. Ward pitched that one for Providence too, and his club won when Charles (Old Hoss) Radbourne, normally a pitcher but, on this occasion, stationed in right field, connected for the circuit in the final frame. No 1 to 0 game in history was ever longer than that one, although the Giants and Cardinals reeled through a joust of equal length in 1933, and twice in the American has a game of identical longevity been decided by the same score.

Bill Hulbert, whose organizational genius made the National League possible and whose administration as the loop's second president was largely beneficial, died at Chicago of heart disease, April 10, 1882. Although at times he took advantage of his position as league president to aid his Chicago team and although he sometimes appeared almost as heartless as his fellows in dealings with the players, Hulbert was scrupulously honest and he created order out of chaos.

The club owners met shortly after Hulbert's death and chose Arthur H. Soden to fill out the term of office.

Beer and Whiskey Circuit 6

THE FACT that the National League had deprived the cities of Cincinnati, Louisville and St. Louis of their franchises by no means meant the end of baseball in those places. On the contrary, freedom from the National afforded each of those towns an opportunity to play baseball in an atmosphere that was leisurely and unrestrained.

Alfred H. Spink, who, with his older brother, William, was one of the game's great writers and builders in St. Louis, formed a team during the spring of 1881 which he called the Browns, relying on the magic of that old name to lure the customers. Spink wrote to O. P. Caylor, the Cincinnati baseball scribe, suggesting that the latter pick up as many professional players as he could at the Queen City and call them the Reds. Caylor did so, and took the revivified Reds to St. Louis for a tilt with the resurrected Browns. This game was played on May 22, 1881, and a huge crowd flooded the park and cheered every move the players made. So hungry were the fans for baseball that they leniently overlooked the fact that the game was a sloppy one, the Brownies winning, 15 to 8.

Spink had found a backer for the Browns in Christ Von Der Ahe, an incredible character who was something out of Rabelais. An immigrant who came to America from the German province of Westphalia in 1864 when he was 17, Von Der Ahe stayed in New York for several years and then drifted to St. Louis, where he clerked in a grocery and then became the proprietor of a modest delicatessen at Sullivan and Spring avenues in the city's west end. Christ at this time was a lavish, pleasure-loving young man who knew nothing about baseball and who spoke with a Teutonic accent as thick and generous as the cheeses he luxuriously sliced at his place of business.

"Vot a fine, pig crowd," he said to Spink after the exhibition with the Reds. "But the game, Al. How vas the game? Vas it a goot game? You know, I know nawthing."

The game might not have been good, but it more than satisfied the starved sports of St. Louis, and it was arranged that there would be more contests. In Brooklyn a former National Association catcher, Bill Barnie, organized a club to which he gave the old name, Atlantics, and took the team to St. Louis for a brawl with the Browns. In Philadelphia an aggregation was formed by Horace B. Phillips to provide Spink with still another competitive ally. These teams all visited St. Louis on a percentage basis, with the players retaining sixty per cent of the gate and the remaining forty going for such necessary items as advertising, park expenses and profits. And the news of this rich new Missouri vein of baseball prosperity spread throughout the land.

At this time there was a young man named Ted Sullivan, a product of Chicago who had gone to Dubuque, Iowa to run the news agency that supplied all the railroads in that area. He hired as a news butcher at Dubuque another young chap with whom he had attended college at St. Mary's, Kansas, a fellow named Charlie Comiskey. Sullivan, always interested in sports, organized a team known as the Dubuque Rabbits, and young Comiskey became the club's first baseman. The Rabbits were still another team that hopped down to St. Louis that eventful summer for a game with the Browns, and Sullivan induced so many promising players to come to the city that he was asked to remain and join in the development of the Browns. Comiskey was also invited to become a permanent fixture of the club.

Most of the games at St. Louis were played on Sundays, and so tremendous was the response that it was decided to form a permanent league in 1882. In the autumn of 1881 a conference was held at Cincinnati's Hotel Gibson, and franchises were granted to six clubs: St. Louis, Cincinnati and Louisville of the west, Baltimore, Philadelphia and Pittsburgh in the east. Organizers of the new league, which was called the American Association, included Spink and Von Der Ahe of St. Louis; Caylor and Louis Kramer of Cincinnati; J. W. Reccius and John Botts of Louisville; H. D. (Denny) McKnight and Horace B. Phillips of Pittsburgh; Bill Barnie of Baltimore; and Charlie Mason, Lew Simmons and Billy Sharsig of Philadelphia. McKnight was elected as the circuit's first president. Although Barnie had organized his team at Brooklyn, it was feared that the patronage there would be slight, which necessitated the shift to Baltimore.

The organization of the American Association as a fullfledged rival of the National ended the monopoly that the latter wheel had enjoyed for six seasons, and the austere magnates of the haughty National of course greeted the newcomer with mingled disdain and contempt.

There were three principal differences between the two leagues when they first took the field as rivals in 1882. The Association permitted games on Sunday, allowed beer to be sold on the grounds, and charged twenty-five cents admission instead of the fifty-cent ante extracted by the National.

"We have brought baseball to the people" was the Association cry, and how the public loved it! But the National League moguls replied that the new league was a disgrace. Truthfully charging that the capital for the Association was largely provided by brewery and distillery interests, a campaign of calumny was launched in which the new loop was referred to constantly as a beer and whiskey circuit, as if the people cared.

Christ Von Der Ahe, the Association's guiding spirit and sort of a poor man's Hulbert, was utterly unlike any of the League magnates. Naïve, generous and honorable in his dealings, he spent his newly found wealth with a lavish hand. Nothing was too good for his players or his fans. And the other Association magnates seemed cut from the same cloth.

Barnie, a bill-poster who didn't have $50 to his name when he visited St. Louis in 1881, made $65,000 with his first Baltimore club. Simmons, Sharsig and Mason, the gay triumvirate in charge of the Athletics, cleared $300,000 in two seasons, the greatest profit ever made in the game up to that time. Sharsig went about wearing a diamond horseshoe the size of a walnut on his shirtfront, a three-inch diamond ring on his hand, and a gold watchcharm as large as a hen's egg on his vest.

These gaudy and carefree club owners, a new type, brought to the Association a color that made a flamboyant contrast to the cadaverous, pinch-penny and putty-faced aspects of National League life. Nowhere was the difference in the leagues so clearly shown as in the choice of uniforms. Association teams were dressed fit to kill, the players dashing about the field in silks so literally gorgeous as to make the rainbow envious. There were no team uniforms for a while, but players were individually arrayed in all shades of scarlet, orange, blue and tan, white and vivid purple. Each player wore his own combination of colors, as a jockey sports the silks of his stable.

This started a craze for resplendent uniforms that reached the sandlots, and town teams the country over tried to outdo themselves in glamorous garb. One Cincinnati newspaper expressed its reaction to the gaudy state of affairs in verse:

> Darling Mabel's zebra stockings
> Gently hang across the tub,
> Brother Tom will find them useful
> When he starts his baseball club.

Meanwhile, the National League officials looked on with dyspeptic envy. Had Bill Hulbert lived, the National might have settled any differences with its rival and enjoyed the competition for public favor, but his death and the emergence of Arthur H. Soden as his successor meant war. Responding to the popular success of the new league in the only way they knew how, National League barons began to induce Association players to jump their contracts. Three players, Billy Holbert, Dasher Troy and Sam Wise jumped to the National before the Association season began, and as a consequence baseball found itself in the courts for the first time. Injunctions and orders of restraint were issued to prevent the absconders from appearing in National uniforms, but the courts upheld the jumpers and the Association, baffled by such dignified legal proceedings, humbly submitted, but warned its member clubs not to have anything to do with National League teams.

This edict became embarrassing to the Cincinnati Reds, winners of the Association's first pennant. Paced by Will White, a tireless pitcher who had the distinction of being the first professional player to wear glasses on the field, the Reds were all set to meet the Chicago White Stockings, 1882 National League champions, in what might have turned out to be the first world series. Resorting to a subterfuge which sounds more like something the National League would have thought of, the Reds released all their players on the day the Association closed, and then the same men formed a new club to meet Cap Anson's strong nine.

Two games were contested by the clubs at Cincinnati, on the chill afternoons of October 6 and 7, each crowd numbering about 2,700. White blanked the Chicagoans, 4 to 0, in the opener, but on the next day Larry Corcoran, an ambidextrous pitcher, wielded a whitewash brush of his own, Chicago taking the 2 to 0 verdict. At that point Denny McKnight, the Association president, warned the Reds that continuance of the series would mean their expulsion from the new league, and the Reds, earlier deprived of major league baseball for an entire year because of expulsion from the National, hurriedly abandoned play. The Association then fined the Reds one hundred dollars for their audacity in fraternizing with the enemy.

Only a handful of the 108 men who appeared in championship games during the Association's first season had been in the National League the previous year. Tapping vast new sources of playing material, the Association in that first campaign introduced such illustrious performers as Charlie Comiskey, Lewis (Pete) Browning, Billy Gleason, Guy Hecker, Leach Maskrey, George McGinnis, John (Bid) McPhee, John (Cub) Stricker and William (Chicken) Wolf.

In meeting the challenge of the new circuit, the National dropped Worcester and Troy from the ranks, replacing those cities with teams from New York and Philadelphia. That is how the teams now known as the Giants and Phillies got into the National League. As a further means of obtaining talent, all suspended players, with the exception of the four Louisville crooks, were reinstated, and the magnates adopted a conciliatory attitude toward the Association for the first time.

When the Association held its own winter meeting, a club known as the Metropolitans was admitted to offset New York's National League team, and Columbus, Ohio was also granted a franchise, expanding the loop to eight clubs. The Association also voted to sign any National League players it could obtain to make up for those athletes who jumped to the older alliance of teams. Then the National threatened its players with fines of one hundred dollars each and the loss of two months' salary to prevent any further jumping of contracts.

Before Bill Hulbert died, he had been perplexed by a problem created by National League clubs that were accustomed to play exhibition games in small towns and then steal the best of the local players. There was no rule against such a practice, but Hulbert thought that it reflected discredit upon the game. Simultaneously, a man named Abraham G. Mills published an article decrying the practice of piracy and outlining a plan to eliminate it. Hulbert was so impressed with the article that he invited Mills to call upon him, and at the meeting he recognized the author as a man who had been president of the Olympics of Washington of the old National Association.

Between them Hulbert and Mills worked out what was known as the League Alliance, the first agreement between leagues. It was devised to establish harmony between the National League and two satellites, the International Association and League Alliance, which sprang up in 1877.

Mills replaced Soden as president of the National in 1883, and his first task was to establish peace with the Association, an honorable peace that he hoped would be an outgrowth of the League Alliance plan he had initiated to govern the relationship of leagues. So it came about that a meeting was held by committees of three from each major, Soden, Mills and John B. Day of the National League, Caylor, Simmons and Barnie of the Association. The Northwestern League, a minor organization, was also represented at this conference by one of its officials, Elias Mather.

There emerged from that meeting what was known as the National Agreement, a cornerstone of what has come to be called baseball law. This agreement, to which the Association made docile obeisance, bound the clubs to respect each other's contracts, and provided for a reserve list of 11 players.

This reserve clause, which has become the most controversial law in baseball's structure, was first thought of by Arthur H. Soden as a means of binding a player to his club. The National League first attempted the scheme in 1879, with each club granted the privilege of reserving five of its men. Soden and Mills were both for the extension of the reserve rule, and when the Tripartite Agreement was drawn up, it provided that each club could reserve 11 men. Later the number was increased to 14, practically an entire roster, and the principle of holding men under reserve was firmly established.

Proponents of the reserve clause claim that it is the only method known to assure honest baseball, that if a player were free to go to the highest bidder, it would be impossible to build a team. Opponents of the device claim that the contract is inequitable because although the club retains all rights over the athlete, he retains no rights whatever and that baseball under the reserve rule is a form of peonage. In three quarters of a century the validity of the reserve clause has sometimes been affirmed in court, but usually it has been denied. The issue is not yet settled, and it is likely that many additional lawsuits will be filed before it is.

The player of today may have numerous complaints about the way that baseball is conducted, but not one player in a thousand cares whether or not the reserve clause is legal. He knows that it is part of the game and accepts it as he accepts night baseball, hot double-headers in St. Louis and various other unpleasant aspects of major league life. If the reserve clause made it necessary for Walter Johnson, generally acclaimed as the greatest pitcher of all time, to do all his pitching for Washington, a team usually in the second division, well, that was Johnson's hard luck. So thinks the player.

And certainly the ball-player of the eighteen-eighties, interested mainly in obtaining enough advance money from his club to get through the winter, was not bothered by legal phraseology or the fine print of his contract. Players, then as now, went where the money was, and cash on the line to them meant more to them than their contracts.

Denny McKnight and his American Association might have fought the point with the National League and settled baseball's most perplexing problem for all time. But the Association, founded in a carnival spirit, was not especially interested. A convention to Christ Von Der Ahe, who was the real power behind the Association, was not the solemn conclave that it was to Spalding or Soden. It was, instead, an opportunity to stage a Roman holiday among congenial spirits with fermented spirits, and such legislation as was necessary was only a boring prelude to the pleasures of the night.

Spalding and Soden died rich men, and they lived for a long time. Von Der Ahe would have died penniless had it not been for the generosity of his old friend, Al Spink, who never forgot Christ and who staged a benefit game for him that raised $5,000, enough to make his last days at least as comfortable as they could be. For Christ was to go the way of most revelers, and his trail included a ball park that burned to the ground, a fistful of legal papers that spelled d-e-b-t and the ingratitude of those he had lavishly assisted all his life.

But Von Der Ahe's American Association, which lasted for a full decade as a rival of the National League, provided the fans with more colorful drama than the National could ever dream of, and besides, it forced concessions on the Spaldings and the Sodens that otherwise would never have been made.

St. Lucas
and the Onions   7

Henry V. Lucas, a rather portly young man with a full, good-natured face and scion of a family reputed to own half the real estate in St. Louis, first became interested in baseball at the age of nineteen when his uncle, John R. Lucas, operated the original National League club at the Mound City during the summer of 1876. Inheriting more than a million dollars in his own name upon the death of his father, young Lucas later became a daily attendant at games played by the Browns during the first two years the American Association operated. He became a steadfast friend of the players, marveling at their talent and overlooking their weaknesses, and nightly, over foaming mugs of beer, he listened by the hour to their grievances.

Believing that the players were held in bondage by a system of illegal contracts and viewing the agreements reached by Abraham G. Mills as a peril to freedom, Lucas vowed to go to the rescue of the athletes; and when he found that Al Spink and Ted Sullivan, those two great builders of the game, were in complete sympathy with his views, he determined to form a major league of his own.

During the summer of 1883 a minor circuit known as the Union Association was founded at Pittsburgh by a man named H. B. Bennett of Washington. Lucas believed that he could take over the franchises of this obscure league and form a loop so strong it could compete with the National and Association for patronage. Both majors were prospering in 1883, and it was the mistaken opinion of Lucas that there was room for a third.

Ted Sullivan was dispatched to various cities in the land, organizing franchises, securing players, and enlisting the aid of the newspapers, beating the drums for the new freedom. The new league received a tremendous bit of prestige when George Wright, the veteran shortstop and manager, was induced to join the ranks and place a club at Boston. Wright's interest in this venture was strictly economic. He had founded a sporting goods house and saw the possibility of using the Union Association as a market for the baseballs he manufactured. The National League used the Spalding ball, and the Association depended on a pellet supplied by Al Reach. There was no chance for Wright to market his product on a grand scale unless there were a third major.

In addition to Boston and St. Louis, teams were formed at Cincinnati, Chicago, Baltimore, Philadelphia, Washington and Altoona, Pennsylvania, the most obscure city ever granted a major league franchise. Except for Altoona the league appeared to be on solid footing.

National League magnates openly scoffed at the venture and predicted that Lucas, giving his players carte blanche in regard to salary and winking at their nocturnal delinquencies, would find his offspring drowned in a river of whiskey. They openly sneered at the Unions, calling them the Onions, and sarcastically dismissed the altruism of the new magnate by calling him St. Lucas.

Lucas retorted in kind by saying that the reserve rule "reserved all that was good for the owners, leaving the remainder for the players," and promised a fight to the finish.

In a statement of policy William Warren White, an old National Association player who had become secretary of the Unions, expressed his views by saying, "We have come to stay, peacefully, quietly, decently, determinedly; and while recognizing the honest rights of others, propose to maintain our own rights."

First player to break the reserve rule and sign with the Unions was Tony Mullane, a young pitcher who jumped from Christ Von Der Ahe's Browns to the St. Louis Union club, which was called the Maroons. But Mullane later repented and returned the advance money Lucas had given him, signing then with Toledo of the Association, a transaction that took place with Von Der Ahe's blessing.

But though Mullane skipped out on them, numerous players joined forces with the Unions, such established stars as Tommy Bond, George Washington Bradley, Hugh (One-Armed) Daily, Jack Glasscock, John (Father) Kelly, Jim McCormick, Edward (The Only) Nolan, Dave Rowe and Orator George Shaffer.

The American Association met the increased competition by expanding to twelve clubs, admitting Toledo and Indianapolis in the west and Brooklyn and Washington in the east, and thus hoped to corral all the available high class players. But chiefly through the efforts of Ted Sullivan the Unions introduced a host of previously unknown players, recruits who were to leave their mark upon the game. Among the famous performers who started their major league careers with the Onions were Clarence (Kid) Baldwin, Bob Caruthers, Ed (Cannonball) Crane, John T. Clements, Frank Foreman, Charlie Ganzel, Al Maul, James (Chippy) McGarr, Joe Quinn, George (Germany) Smith, William (Peek-a-boo) Veach and Perry Werden.

It was originally planned that the eight Union Association clubs would each play 112 games, meeting each of their seven opponents 16 times. But it soon became apparent that there were weak sisters in the league which could not support clubs. Altoona gave up the ghost by the end of May, and the franchise was shifted to Kansas City. And before the Unions struggled through the season they had representatives in Pittsburgh, Milwaukee and even such unlikely major league centers as St. Paul, Minnesota and Wilmington, Delaware. St. Paul had the briefest major league experience of any city in history, the Apostles winning only two and losing six before calling it quits, and yet the Saints produced one of baseball's great catchers in Charlie Ganzel.

Because of the entrance of the Onions into the field, more major league teams operated in 1884 than at any time before or since, 34 of them in all. In addition to the eight from the National League, the Union and American associations each produced thirteen, the American reaching that figure when the Washington franchise was moved to Richmond, Virginia.

Clubs in the National and American fought the Unions by jointly contributing to a pool, providing bonuses to restrain players from jumping their contracts. Tony Mullane, already mentioned because he was the first to leap, was benefited by this system, for when the Toledo club could not raise the $600 advance money for him, the pool came to the rescue.

It was impossible to make money in major league baseball in 1884 with 34 clubs operating, especially when, in so many localities, there were such furious fights for patronage. Philadelphia tried to support clubs in all three leagues, and eight other cities were represented in two. Players could be supplied to keep all three circuits going, but spectators simply were not available in large enough quantity.

The intentions of Henry V. Lucas were as noble as those of any personality whose life has ever touched the game, but his method of allowing players to discipline themselves was doomed to failure. Players were no more ready to manage their own affairs by 1884 than they had been in the old National Association under Bob Ferguson, and baseball's first 'third major' was an unfortunate and costly experiment.

Although the Onions lasted for only that one brief season, they produced one of baseball's really great teams, the St. Louis Maroons. Managed by Ted Sullivan, who recruited the best of the contract-jumpers for his own club, the St. Louis team won 91 games and lost only 16, a phenomenal percentage of .850. Billy Taylor was the chief pitcher for the Lucas nine, and his catcher was George Baker. Joe Quinn was at first, Fred Dunlap at second, Milton Whitehead at short and John Gleason at third, with George Shaffer, Dave Rowe and Louis (Buttercup) Dickerson making up the outfield.

The Maroons rode roughshod over all opposition from the season's start, being forced to the limit only by Cincinnati. In mid-season Cincinnati put together a team almost as strong as the Maroons by inducing three famed players, Pitcher Jim McCormick, Shortstop Jack Glasscock and Catcher Charles (Fatty) Briody to desert Cleveland's National League team. But it was far too late for the Outlaw Reds to win, and although McCormick's magic pitching inspired the team to win 30 out of its last 32 outings, St. Louis finished more than twenty full games ahead of them.

Only twice in major league history has a pitcher struck out 19 batters in a nine-inning game, and both feats were recorded when the Onions were in season. The first to do it was Charles Sweeney, who accomplished the trick for Providence in a National League game at Boston on June 7. Sweeney's catcher that day was Vincent (Sandy) Nava, the first Cuban to appear in the majors. But despite his strikeout pace, the Providence hurler had to work hard to win the decision, 2 to 1. Exactly one month afterward Hugh (One-Armed) Daily, pitching for the Chicago Unions, whiffed 19 Boston players while holding the Beaneaters to a single hit and winning, 5 to 0.

Daily's left hand and forearm had been amputated after he had been maimed in an explosion that took place in the Front Street Theatre at Baltimore, where he had a job mixing chemicals for a fireworks display. Since he pitched in an era in which gloves were not required, the injury did not in the least impair his effectiveness, and for a few brief seasons Hugh Daily was one of the pastime's most celebrated hurlers.

But the greatest pitching of the season was not accomplished by either Sweeney or Daily, although the former made the performance possible. Sweeney received so much credit and acclaim after his whiffing bee that he was induced to jump to the Maroons. That left Providence with only one other pitcher, Charles (Old Hoss) Radbourne. Suspended earlier in the season for insubordination, Old Hoss was reinstated immediately when the dereliction of Sweeney was discovered, and from that day on he accumulated the most amazing string of pitching triumphs ever known. Pitching day after day, the Old Hoss, who was then 30, ended up with 60 victories against 12 defeats, including a streak of 18 successes in a row. It goes without saying that Radbourne's hurling enabled Providence to win the flag. But the Old Hoss was not yet finished. That autumn the Providence club engaged in a primitive version of the world series with the Metropolitans of New York, champions of the Association. Jointly bound by Mills' National Agreement and united in their stand against the outlaw Onions, the League and

Association were finally able to agree upon a legal post-season meeting of their respective champs. That first series was conducted on a "best three out; of five" basis, but Radbourne saw to it that only three contests were required, as he defeated the Mets on successive days, 6 to 0, 3 to 1, and 11 to 2.

That ended the greatest season for pitching the game has ever known, and although on numerous occasions that summer the Old Hoss could hardly lift his arm to comb his hair, apparently the arduous schedule he followed did not blight his career for he was still on the major league scene seven years later.

However, formidable batting averages survived that season's dazzling performances on the mound. Fred Dunlap, second baseman of the Maroons, pulverized Onion hurlers with a .420 mark, and Tom Esterbrook of the Metropolitans paced Association batsmen with a figure of .408. The National League hitting crown was worn by Orator Jim O'Rourke, by this time a member of the Buffalo club. It was the third straight year that the city near the Niagara had provided the batting king, as big, friendly Dan Brouthers, first baseman of the Buffalo team, had become the league's first repeater as champion in 1882 and 1883.

The Onions might have carried on for another season had Lucas retained his enthusiasm for the project, but he had lost heavily in that one campaign and didn't see why he should continue to underwrite the deficit. The Onions lost perhaps $250,000 in one year of existence, but how much Lucas lost personally cannot be determined. National League magnates maintained that the venture had wiped out his entire fortune, but that was a gross exaggeration.

Cleveland had to abandon its National League franchise because of the war with the Unions. Crippled by the early desertion of Fred Dunlap and Orator

George Shaffer to the Maroons, the team was dealt a death blow when McCormick, Glasscock and Briody leaped to the Union Reds, and after finishing seventh, the promoters surrendered the franchise, but first disposed of all players by selling them to Brooklyn. Lucas then obtained permission to place his Maroon team in the National League, filling the slot Cleveland had occupied, and he succeeded in doing this despite the heated and understandable ire of Christ Von Der Ahe, the St. Louis Association competitor. Christ became placated only when it was pointed out that the National League prohibited baseball on Sunday, which meant that the Maroons would be unable to battle Christ for patronage on the Sabbath, the biggest baseball day of the week.

Deserted by its founder, the Union Association met for the last time at Milwaukee on January 15, 1885. Kansas City and Milwaukee were the only teams which voted to carry on, and when Lucas didn't even send a wire to the gathering, the Onions dolefully disbanded.

When 27 men who had broken their contracts by vaulting to the Unions were welcomed back into the fold, Abraham G. Mills indignantly resigned as president of the National League. This was sheer hypocrisy, for Mills had once made a trip with Cap Anson to Newark to induce Larry Corcoran, the ambidextrous pitcher, to break his contract with the Chicago Unions. But Mills quit, and he was replaced by Nicholas E. Young, who became the National's fifth president in the first decade of its existence.

As a matter of fact, Al Spalding had also been involved in a humorous bit of hypocrisy caused by Mills. When the jumping of contracts was such a problem, Mills wrote a letter over Spalding's signature to players all over the country, telling them about the sacred aspects of such a pact and asking the players to respect whatever agreements they had signed. But when the White Stockings were in need of players and Spalding tried to induce them to jump their contracts, he invariably had thrust under his nose one of the letters he had signed decrying the very practice he was now urging.

All three leagues lost money in 1884 because of the Union experiment, and once the outlaw circuit was dissolved, baseball resumed its normal growth and prosperity. Had the magnates only learned the lesson inherent in the Union struggle, the lesson that unfair practices directed against the player would breed discontent that might lead to revolt and subsequent financial ruin for all, everything would have been well. But when the competition from St. Lucas and his Onions was removed in 1885, a move which also enabled the American Association to reduce its ranks to a normal, eight-team wheel, the powers that ruled the game became even more imperious than they had been before, a colossal blunder that almost wrecked the game.

Strawberry Shortcake and Grass 8

IT WAS the fictional Sir Roger De Coverley, speaking in one of the celebrated *Spectator* essays of Joseph Addison, who pointed out that there are two sides to every story. This axiom of philosophy is certainly as true in labor relations as in any other human endeavor, and was particularly true of the baseball relations of capitalists and players in the eighteen-eighties.

That the magnates were particularly and unnecessarily cruel toward their hired hands has been pointed out, but many of them sincerely believed that they were following the only sensible course they could take, that the players were so profligate and dissolute they could respond only to iron discipline. And certainly it must be admitted that certain early professional performers in baseball were eccentric enough to tax the patience of the most tolerant club owner.

There was, for instance, Dave Foutz, a successful pitcher for the St. Louis Browns. Foutz was a faro fiend. At the conclusion of the 1884 season he left the Mound City with a poke of $2,300. Within two months he wired Christ Von Der Ahe that he was broke. Von Der Ahe dispatched $100 toward his relief, which lasted a week. Another hundred lasted another week. And when a third century disappeared in the same fashion, Christ paid the hurler's railroad fare back to St. Louis and then took care of his board for the rest of the winter.

Foutz was fortunate that he was employed by Von Der Ahe, the most lavish of the owners.

Various other players continued to be plagued by that least understood of maladies, alcoholism. Though by the end of the eighties many of the pastime's most prominent lushes had been weeded out, there were still numerous occasions on which performers missed playing because of what newspapers of the era enjoyed calling the "blind staggers." Baseball was growing up and becoming more efficient. When a player's proclivity for the bottle interfered with his ability to take the field, his mates suffered financially. Club owners were justifiably annoyed when an otherwise capable performer would disrupt the unity of his team by going on a bender. And yet, very often, the worst offenders in this respect were among the most popular idols of the fans.

Magnates also had reason to consider themselves superior to their help in the light of the strange superstitions that permeated the workers of the baseball vineyard. Ball-players were as credulous as Bulgarian peasants, and anyone who has studied the newspapers of the period can only conclude that the athletes spent all their off-hours looking for hairpins, avoiding cross-eyed folk and black cats, and establishing a pattern of compulsion neuroses. Every player seemed to believe that a certain person, place or situation was his Jonah; it might be a team-mate or even his wife, which led to the breaking up of teams and even marriages because of the superstitious whim.

The Chicago team of the National League, traveling by train to Providence in 1883, became convinced that the presence of three cross-eyed men on the train meant that the White Stockings would lose all three games of their series in the Rhode Island city. And when the

Grays did defeat their visitors three straight, every Chicago player was convinced he knew the reason.

James (Chief) Roseman, an outfielder with the Metropolitans, called time during a game at New York in 1885, taking advantage of the interlude to kiss the forehead of a Negro lad who was sitting in the bleachers, a strategy which, however, failed to enable the Metropolitans to win.

Even the most otherwise intelligent performers entered into the spirit of the superstition craze. John K. Tener, a pitcher who later was to become a bank president, Congressman from Pennsylvania and governor of that state, was convinced that he was knocked from the box one day by last-place Indianapolis only because that morning he had seen three cross-eyed girls, witnessed a passing funeral, and had had his luncheon tea spilled upon him by the waiter.

Perhaps the most superstitious player of the lot was Fred Pfeffer, second baseman of the White Stockings, and his mania was so complex that it is almost impossible to describe. Pfeffer saw to it that his right stocking, though of the traditional Chicago white, contained a few stitches of black thread in the heel. This was done to distinguish it from the left one. If he made no error on a given day, then Fred would put the stocking with the black thread on his right leg again. But if he had made an error, when he got back to the hotel (players did not yet dress at the park), he would pull out the thread and sew it into the heel of the other stocking, making that one the right. Thereupon, convinced that his stockings were adjusted, Pfeffer would assume his second base position with increased confidence. More interesting, but unavailable, would be information in regard to the number of times Pfeffer changed his stockings during a season.

These three delinquencies, prodigality, a love for booze and a devotion to superstition were more common among players of the picturesque American Association than they were among the austere athletes of the National League, and yet all three traits were abundant in the personality of Mike (King) Kelly, perhaps the greatest National League player of his time. And somehow a player of that type, no matter how great, seemed out of place on the roster of the high-minded White Stockings of Al Spalding, even more out of place than Fred Pfeffer and his penchant for sewing. Manager Cap Anson, though aware of Kelly's talent on the field, had to agree with Spalding that the King might be better off in a different realm. And so, despite the fact that Kelly led the National League in 1886 with a batting average of .388, he was peddled that winter to the Boston club.

The transaction was made at Poughkeepsie, New York on noon of St. Valentine's Day, 1887, with Boston paying $10,000 for Mike's services. This was the greatest sum ever expended for a player's contract up to that time, and the deal created a furor. In a way it made up for Bill Hulbert's theft of the original Big Four eleven years earlier, although whereas Hulbert stole the contracts of Spalding, White, Barnes and McVey, the Beaneaters paid out hard cash for the King. Boston fans were jubilant over the acquisition, but in Chicago a fog of gloom settled over Lake Michigan.

Boston's original offer for the King was $5,000, and Spalding told the Massachusetts promoters to double that figure. The lofty idea of obtaining Kelly did not originate with Soden, still leader of the Triumvirs, but with his treasurer, Jim Billings, who had an idea he might swing the deal as the King had announced that he would quit the diamond rather than play another year for Spalding. Billings then raised the ante to $9,000, but when he saw that Spalding remained adamant, he agreed to the original figure asked.

Cap Anson, manager of the White Stockings, was playing at billiards with his friend, George Slosson, an early master of the indoor sport, when news of Kelly's sale reached the public.

"I tell you," Cap said, "the Chicago club without Kelly is stronger than it ever was before."

But Slosson, taking aim of his cue, replied, "Anson, you may shout as long and loud as you like; the Chicago club has lost its best playing card."

Previous to making the deal Spalding, who had accused Kelly of drinking, a charge that Mike never bothered to deny, had said that the King would eat grass before playing with any team other than Chicago.

But several weeks after the sale, in his role of publisher of the Spalding Baseball Guide, the Chicago president found it embarrassingly necessary to write to the King for his picture to illustrate the book in accordance with the custom that batting kings were so displayed. And the King really wrote a regal message in reply, saying, "It gives me pleasure to send along my picture. However, I shall not be eating grass this summer. My address will be in care of the Boston club, and I shall be eating strawberry shortcake."

Then Kelly told a New York reporter, "I will forgive Spalding for everything he has ever done to me. His work in releasing me to the Bostons was the action of his life."

At this time the White Stockings and Browns were the best clubs in their respective leagues. Both winning flags in 1885, the clubs met in an inconclusive world series, each team winning three tilts, with one being declared a tie. When it became evident that the same teams would triumph again in 1886, Von Der Ahe challenged Spalding to another set of championship games and was overwhelmed when Anson, speaking for Spalding, made the daring suggestion that the winner keep all the receipts. Sportsman that he was, Christ thought the proposal was wonderful.

This time the Browns gave the White Stockings a real licking, taking four of the six games and all of the money, which amounted to about $15,000. That winter Spalding recouped two-thirds of the amount by the sale of Kelly, but he was thirsting for revenge against the Browns.

Unable to accept the defeat of his pets as final, Spalding issued still another challenge for a series with the Browns to take place in various cities in April, 1887, before the championship season got under way. This strangest of all world series was actually played, although no history of baseball ever written has mentioned it. It was, of course, the only world series ever played before the season began.

The original plan was for the Browns and White Stockings to clash in six games that April, with three more to follow in October, provided that the Browns and White Stockings repeated as monarchs for the third straight year. Three of the April brawls were to take place at St. Louis, out of deference to the Browns' status of world champions. One more was to be staged at Louisville, still another at Cincinnati, and finally one at Indianapolis.

So eager was Spalding to regain his prestige that he had Anson take the club to Hot Springs, Arkansas for a boiling-out process. All players were then forced to sign a pledge of total abstinence from liquor for the entire 1887 campaign, but an exception had to be made in the case of Harry (Shadow) Pyle, an asthma sufferer who could not even sleep in a chair, much less a bed, without resorting to stimulants. Spalding also arranged that the umpire who would work the set of games would be Herman Doscher, who will be recalled as the blacklisted Cleveland manager.

The Browns were in no shape to meet that sturdy challenge. None of the St. Louis pitchers was ready. Bob Caruthers, in an attempt to get more money, went all the way to Paris, France after the 1886 series, saying that he would remain there until his figure was met. Although he finally yielded to terms before the spring series with Chicago, he was in no shape to pitch well, and because of the unique locale he had chosen for his holdout campaign, he was dubbed Parisian Bob Caruthers by the press, a nickname that stayed with him throughout his life. Nat Hudson, another pitching holdout of the Brownies, missed the series completely. Dave Foutz had to do most of the flinging despite having a sore arm, and because of their disintegrated staff, the Browns had no chance, losing four of the six, the last three in succession.

That early baseball magnates did not hesitate to swindle their players has already been recorded. And now documentary evidence has come to light which shows how club owners cheated each other. Among a collection of papers from the personal file of Aaron S. Stern, president of the Cincinnati Reds in 1887, a collection which is now the property of the Ohio Historical and Philosophical Society, is a message from Stern to the treasurer of the club, Louis Hauck, in regard to the sixth game between the Browns and White Stockings, which was played at Cincinnati, April 13, 1887. Here, in its entirety, is Stern's proposal to shortchange Spalding and Von Der Ahe, and presumably the dirty work was accomplished.

Friend Louis:

Please note the following:

In the game between Chicago and St. Louis use no turnstiles and say nothing about the Hawley[1] tickets — if they ask for our turnstiles, say they are out of order. I want to make all of Hawley's tickets — also all exchange money they are to know nothing about. I may be over and work it myself. If not read this to Niland and let him work accordingly — you had better instruct Oehler[2] to keep the turnstiles away after Tuesday's game. Give the number of tickets to the Chicago and St. Louis men before the game and let them figure themselves. I want to make all I can. You will understand, we are to get twenty per cent of the entire receipts.

I have a chance to sell one of our men and I think well of it. I will see your father on my return and talk it over.

Regards,
Stern

---

1 Hawley's was a downtown ticket headquarters in Cincinnati. By not reporting any tickets sold at that source, Stern was able to steal the entire amount instead of taking only the twenty per cent, to which he was entitled.

2 William (Dutch) Oehler, groundkeeper for the Reds from 1884 to 1894.

Stern's personal papers, which he should have had the good sense to destroy, illustrate beautifully the mental equipment and moral standards of a baseball magnate in 1887 and perhaps many another year. During the winter of 1886, when the fans of Cincinnati were dreaming of a possible pennant and assuming that Stern, owner of the club, was doing likewise, here is what was really on his mind. The following two notes tell their own story.

Southern Hotel,
St. Louis,

March 11, 1887

Friend Louis:
I shall now commence to figure our expenses as low as they can possibly be made and I shall spend as little money as possible in running the Cincinnati club. Shut off the free list and see that every dollar that is in the grounds remains there.

Stern

February 2, 1887

Friend Louis:

Enclosed find contract and check for same. Please enter on books as candy privilege. Have discovered another new privilege to be known as the cushion privilege, allowing the party to sell cushions in the Pavilion Terrace for which we are to get $75. I will retire very early tonight and hope to study up some other new privileges. Perhaps you can think of one. Call on me when you are downtown. With kind regards,

Yours,
A. S. Stern

And so, when the fanatics of the game were walking through the snows of winter, looking forward to the warm magic of another April with its concomitant crack of bat against the ball, the magnates had their dreams too. They were retiring early those nights, dreaming up not new players but new privileges. And still the game survived.

The Brotherhood Boys 9

THERE WAS no way of knowing in June, 1885, that a new organization described by the press as the National Brotherhood of Professional Baseball Players was destined to bring to the game the most bloody and costly war in the pastime's history. Originally the Brotherhood was as benevolent and protective as the Elks, and it became a vehicle for warfare only because the players were able to use the organization to fight new abuses introduced by the magnates.

The movement was started by Billy Voltz, a former sporting editor of the Cleveland Leader but a versatile chap who managed a minor league team at Chattanooga in 1885. By mid-season of that year more than 200 players had signified their intention of joining the organization, and the plan was to assess them five dollars a month, making a reserve fund of $1,000 a month or $6,000 a season to be used during the winter for sick and indigent subscribers to the fund.

That winter, however, a conference committee of magnates from the National League and American Association proposed a strange plan for the grading of salaries, limiting pitchers and catchers to a maximum of $1,800, outfielders to $1,700 and infielders to $1,600. But even before the meeting adjourned the promoters were sensible enough to realize that such a scheme would make every player become a pitcher or catcher, so a compromise was immediately effected whereby all salaries were limited to $2,000. At the same time all clubs were forbidden to pay salary advances to their players.

When news of the salary limit spread, Voltz announced that not one of the New York Giants had signed for 1886 and that the Brotherhood would be heard from. One of those unsigned Giants was John Montgomery Ward, who had started his major league career as a pitcher for Providence seven years earlier. It will be recalled that Ward pitched a perfect game for Providence in 1880, and after a sore arm terminated his career on the mound, he switched his talents to the shortstop position and became one of the league's most brilliant guardians of that post. Ward was an attorney, and his keen, legal mind made him the ideal man to take over the movement founded by Voltz. Ward instantly became the spokesman for the players who wanted to air their grievances. And the grievances were numerous and loud.

The $2,000 salary limit was never enforced. Magnates customarily made out each player's contract for that figure and then entered into side agreements for more, the amount depending on the persuasive powers of the athlete. Not playing skill but oratory became the most important factor in bargaining.

But it was not the maximum salary law but the erasure of salary advances that rankled most with the players. Pitiful letters written by players to their clubs in the winters of the eighties, letters in which destitute athletes, some of them with pregnant wives, begged for advance money, are still in existence today, mute testimony to the heartlessness of the game's operators. These letters are now parts of historical association collections, but letters from the magnates to the players are more scarce, for the pleading communications were seldom answered.

Fantastic charges were made against players and incredible demands were made upon them. In 1886 one newspaper accused members of the Washington team of smoking opium, adding the sage postscript, "You cannot hit the pipe and hit the ball."

There was something slightly berserk about that Washington team of 1886, and it wasn't caused by opium either. John H. Gaffney, the manager, fined one of his players, Frank Gilmore, $100 for not reporting to the park on the day of his marriage. Gaffney was a bachelor. It was with this same Washington club that Connie Mack broke into his first major league box score as a catcher. The Washingtons were hopeless residents of the league cellar, winning 28 and losing 92, which is almost the ultimate in inefficiency. So rare were the club's victories that when the team finally managed to defeat the Giants, 4 to 2, the Washington Critic burst forth as follows:

"Now holler for the Washingtons
And 2 New York give praise
4 kindly giving us a chance
2 win on our good plays.

"We've seldom won a game b-4;
Our luck was hard 2 bear,
And now we thank New York 4 this
Most 4-2-nate affair."

Most club owners made substitute players, even those who were under suspension and not drawing salary, work as gatemen on the park's turnstiles, a practice which gave the hirelings further cause for being disgruntled.

Perhaps the ultimate in effrontery was reached by the operators of one team who appealed to the citizens to send cash donations to the club's management, saying that, after all, cities supported such ventures as art museums, so why not baseball?

In Indianapolis a man named William H. Marsh had a house directly across the street from the ball park, and he soon learned that his roof made an ideal place for fans to watch the games. John T. Brush, the owner of the Indianapolis team, then built a fence thirty feet high to obstruct the view from Marsh's roof. Marsh thereupon erected a scaffold which was even higher than the fence, but offered to stop there if Brush would pay him twelve dollars a month. Now, naturally, Brush was within his rights in objecting to a public grandstand operated across the street from his park, but it is interesting to observe the lengths to which a club owner would go to win a twelve dollar a month dispute.

Then there was the case of Cliff Carroll, a player who traveled around the league with a pet monkey which eventually died and was buried under home plate on the field at Pittsburgh. Fined one hundred dollars on one pretext or another by the Washington management, he refused to sign a contract for 1887 unless the money were returned. Robert C. Hewett, president of the Washingtons, then gave him a check for that amount but stopped payment on it. Carroll eventually got his money only because John Ward and a committee from the Brotherhood attended a National League meeting and prevailed upon the other club owners to force Hewett to act with decency.

Of course, generalizations are never true, and not all magnates were alike. Fred K. Stearns, for instance, who brought the 1887 pennant to Detroit, was not at all like his fellows. Honorable in his dealings both with players and fans, Stearns hired a special train to carry the players and newsmen to the 1887 world series. But he was so chastised for this extravagance by his directors that he soon got out of baseball.

As the Brotherhood gained in power, the magnates spread the word that the union of players was composed of a bunch of drunks and ingrates. This was not entirely true, because the Brotherhood was not open to all players, and several prominent lushes were barred from membership.

The first demand made by the Brotherhood was for recognition. A committee of three players, Ward, Ned Hanlon and Dennis Brouthers, asked that they be permitted to appear at the National League meeting in 1887 and state the Brotherhood's case. The magnates, not knowing what recognition would imply, were hesitant to grant it, but finally did so on the behest of Spalding.

Originally the Brotherhood was not particularly opposed to the reserve clause, but the sale of King Kelly for so great a sum caused discontent among the players, who were beginning to realize that their services had value. But when the Brotherhood committee was asked to suggest a new contract form, one which would replace the obnoxious reserve clause, Ward, Hanlon and Brouthers had to confess their inability to make any improvement.

Despite what was said about him, John Montgomery Ward was not an anarchist. In fact, in an interview in 1887 he said, "In order to get men to invest capital in baseball, it is necessary to have a reserve rule. Some say that this could be modified, but I am not of that opinion. How could it be modified? Say, for instance, that we began the season by reserving men for only two, three, four or even five years. At the expiration of that period players would be free to go where they pleased, and capitalists who invested, say $75,000 or $100,000, would have gained nothing but ground and grandstand. Then again, players have agreed that this could not be overcome by making the length of reservation vary. It could not, and would cause no end of dissatisfaction. It would be unfair to reserve one man for two years and another for five. The reserve rule, on the whole, is a bad one; but it cannot be rectified save by injuring the interests of the men who invest their money, and that is not the object of the Brotherhood."

That is not radical talk by any means, and it appears likely that the Brotherhood would not have continued the fight against the reserve clause had the magnates only made other, slighter concessions such as the repeal of the $2,000 salary limit. But the National League refused to do that, an indication that there was no sincerity whatever behind the claim of the owners that they were willing to adjust whatever differences existed.

In the winter following the season of 1888 Al Spalding led two teams of players to Australia, a junket which was expanded into a tour of the entire globe. This strange caravan included Spalding's mother, a 180-pound lady with snow-white hair; Cap Anson's 300-pound, poker-playing father, and as many prominent players as could be induced to make the trip. The two teams engaged in exhibitions in such strange settings as Ceylon and Egypt, and among the touring players was John Montgomery Ward, accompanied for part of the distance by his lovely actress wife, Helen Dauvray.

During the absence of this party John T. Brush, owner of the Indianapolis team in the National League, forced into baseball a law that provided for a plan of classifying players' salaries, a law so reprehensible that open warfare between players and magnates became inevitable.

This plan provided that the president of the league, Nicholas E. Young, was annually to classify the players, grading them not simply according to skill but according to such qualities as earnestness, habits and special qualifications. Young's classification was to be final, and each player's salary was to be determined by his grading, as follows:

CLASS	SALARY	CLASS	SALARY	CLASS	SALARY
A	$2500	C	$2000	E	$1500
B	2250	D	1750		

The worst feature of this plan from the standpoint of the player was not the limitation upon his salary but the fact that the league president was placed in the position of a schoolteacher grading children according to their conduct and effort. The Brotherhood had agreed to abide by the reserve clause in the absence of any better rule, but when Brush nullified the agreement by forcing this classification plan while Ward was out of the country, the players were up in arms.

But with Ward abroad the players were helpless. And even when the tourists returned it was too late to do anything about 1889. A crowd waited all night for the boat which brought the globe-trotters back to New York. When Ward got off the boat and heard the first news of the Brush plan from the mob, he tightened his lips and gave out only guarded comment, then joined his wife at their suite at the Hotel Marlborough.

A few days later Ward asked for another meeting between the Brotherhood Committee and the magnates. This was refused, Spalding saying, "There is nothing to discuss." That was the straw that broke the camel's back, and those magnates who later became impoverished by the Brotherhood can thank Brush's classification scheme and Spalding's arbitrary attitude. For throughout the summer of 1889 players began plotting for the open revolt they knew must come.

There were at this time throughout the country various capitalists who knew of the dissatisfaction among the ranks of the ball-players, men who thought they saw in the situation an opportunity to form a third major league. And although they, as businessmen, certainly had no permanent sympathy with the players, they thought it possible to capitalize upon the unrest for purposes of immediate profit.

One evening during the summer Ned Hanlon, then an outfielder with Pittsburgh, called upon Albert L. Johnson, a street railway magnate from Cleveland, and asked Johnson if he didn't have a ball ground somewhere along his station line. Hanlon spoke of how the league had broken faith with the players so many times and said that he, Ward, Pfeffer and Jimmy Fogarty, on their trip around the world, had spoken in frequent hushed conferences about ways and means of raising capital in each league city. Hanlon proposed that Johnson influence other capitalists to lend money to the players so that grounds could be built in each city.

Johnson replied that he was acquainted with only a few of the players, and that Hanlon should introduce him to some of the men from the Cleveland team; so Ned arranged a meeting between Johnson and the Cleveland pitcher, Larry Twitchell. After this session Johnson agreed to lend all possible aid, and as each National League club visited Cleveland that summer, Johnson met with one or more of the team's players.

"If it is true," said Johnson, "that the league can hold a man on a contract for any or all time that it may desire, when it simply guarantees to him ten days' pay (for that is everything in the world that it does for the player), why then the laws of our land are worse than those of any nation on earth."

The plan that Johnson worked out with the players provided that the capitalists would build grounds and would retain a fair percentage of the profits for this risk, but that the players would share in the profits of the new league. In fact the players were to retain fifty per cent of any profits, in addition to money provided by a pool, the amount to be determined by each club's finish in the race, as follows:

1st Place	$7,000 to be split
2nd Place	$5,000 to be split
3rd Place	$3,000 to be split
4th Place	$2,000 to be split
5th Place	$1,500 to be split
6th Place	$1,000 to be split
7th Place	$ 500 to be split
8th Place	Nothing

The National League owners sensed that something was afoot, but they had no idea of the enormity of the project, and they openly scoffed at the threatened rebellion, so little had they learned in the five years following the Union Association squabble.

John Tomlinson Brush, the man who was held in so much esteem by his fellow magnates because he had thought of the classification plan, was perhaps typical of his era. Born at Clintonville, New York, June 16, 1845, he was orphaned at four and brought up on a farm by his step-uncle. He went to Utica in young manhood, worked in a country store, saved enough money to open a clothing store that eventually had branches in Troy and Lockport, then settled in Indianapolis, where he expanded his clothing business. He had seen his first baseball at Troy, where he watched the corrupt Haymakers of the old National Association, but his first active connection with the game came when he bought the Indianapolis team. He had been in baseball only two years when he dreamed up his classification scheme.

By November, 1889 the players had completed their plans, and on the fourth day of the year's penultimate month the Brotherhood issued a scathing manifesto, citing all its grievances and boldly announcing the formation of the Brotherhood or Players' League. The pot had come to boil.

A few days later Aaron S. Stern, owner of the Cincinnati Reds, was walking down Wabash Avenue in Chicago when he chanced to meet Henry V. Lucas, the already largely forgotten St. Lucas of Onion fame.

"What do you think of the Brotherhood?" Stern asked.

"It will fail," Lucas replied.

"Why?"

"Simply because the players will not stick together. The average ball-player cannot be relied on to remain with such an organization if he can see more money somewhere else. They will not take chances of sharing visionary profits when they can work for sure money with a regular club."

Lucas knew from bitter experience.

Year of Bitterness

10

"I am a baseball player.

"I support my wife and family on the money I earn on the field. In 1888 I played with Detroit. This year I was sold to Cleveland, and told that I must play in that city or leave a business in which I have spent my life to attain proficiency. All of my interests were elsewhere, yet I was forced to play in Cleveland.

"Now, suppose I were a theatrical manager like George Floyd. I signed a contract with the Aronsons. After I had fulfilled my contract with them, they could say to me, 'You must manage our opera house in Hoboken next year or we will drive you out of the business.' Well, I guess not. No corporation in the world can say 'you must' or 'you must not' to a man except the ones conducted by the present baseball magnates."

Larry Twitchell

THAT WAS the credo of the men who met to issue their manifesto at the Fifth Avenue Hotel, New York, November 4, 1889. To a casual observer the atmosphere of that hostelry would not have indicated that anarchists were in session, although that was the noun applied to the Brotherhood boys by National League magnates. Gentlemen in furlined overcoats and silk hats crowded the lobby and elevators, kid gloves were used to tap the ashes from La Rosa Perfectos and Henry Clays at twenty-five cents a copy, and patent leather shoes, diamond stickpins and gold-headed canes were much in evidence. These were the slaves of baseball, a group of serfs unique in the annals of the class struggle. And just off the lobby, at the bar, sat John Ward, impeccable over a highball, either a great emancipator or arch villain, according to the point of view, planning the strategy of baseball's costliest war.

The Brotherhood Manifesto, a remarkable document of 643 words, made fully known the intentions of the players and announced the formation of the Brotherhood League, recited the history of relations between players and magnates in the National League, attacked the reserve clause and the Brush classification plan, and asked for the support of the public.

A few excerpts:

"There was a time when the League stood for integrity and fair dealing; today it stands for dollars and cents. Once it looked to the elevation of the game and an honest exhibition of the sport. Today its eyes are upon the turnstile. Men have come into the business for no other motive than to exploit it for every dollar in sight."

"Players have been bought, sold or exchanged, as though they were sheep, instead of American citizens. Reservation with them became another name for property-rights in the player. By a combination among themselves, stronger than the strongest trusts, they were able to enforce the most arbitrary measures, and the player had either to submit or to get out of the profession, in which he had spent years in attaining proficiency."

"Two years ago we met the League and attempted to remedy some of these evils, but through what has been called League 'diplomacy' we completely failed. Unwilling longer to submit to such treatment, we made a strong effort last spring to reach an understanding with the league. To our application for a hearing they replied that the matter was not of sufficient importance to warrant a meeting, and suggested that it be put off until fall. Our committee replied that the players felt that the league had broken faith with them; that while the results might be of little importance to the managers, they were of great importance to the players; that if the League would not concede what was fair we would adopt other measures to protect ourselves; that if postponed until fall we would be separated and at the mercy of the League, and that, as the only course left us required time and labor to develop, we must therefore insist upon an immediate conference. Then upon their final refusal to meet us, we began organizing for ourselves, and are in shape to go ahead next year under new management and new auspices."

The National League for 1890 provided for franchises in Boston, Brooklyn, Chicago, Cincinnati, Cleveland, New York, Philadelphia and Pittsburgh. Substitute St. Louis for Cleveland, and that is the National League of today. The Brotherhood, anxious for competition in each city, was able to place franchises in all National League spots except Cincinnati, and Buffalo was substituted for the Queen City.

Brotherhood players signed contracts for three years at their 1889 salaries, which could be increased at the discretion of the individual club, but could not be slashed. Should a player desire to be transferred he could arrange it, and the club which lost his services was not reimbursed. Naturally, there were numerous lawsuits filed, and in almost every instance the courts upheld the player's right to leave the National League.

Among those who jumped their reserve clause to sign with the Brotherhood were Connie Mack, John K. Tener, Kling Kelly, Orator Jim O'Rourke, Roger Connor, Pete Browning, Dave Orr, Buck Ewing, George Van Haltren, Jake Beckley, Old Hoss Radbourne, Hugh Duffy and Jim Galvin. In fact, almost all players jumped to the Players' League, a conspicuous exception being Cap Anson, who was a stockholder in addition to a player with the Chicago White Stockings.

The situation was much the same as had existed during the war with the Onions in 1884, with players jumping and, in some instances, jumping back again, with lawsuits being filed and injunctions granted, and with threats and counter-threats being made. Prominent people in all walks of life made public statements about the situation, including the famed attorney and agnostic, Robert G. Ingersoll, who told the Brotherhood that the reserve clause wasn't worth the paper it was printed on.

The National League purposely arranged a schedule that would be in conflict with the Brotherhood's card of contests, and the public reacted by staying away from both games in most cities, and from American Association games too. All three leagues lost money in 1890, the most dismal year in the game's history from the standpoint of the gate, and all brought on by the war.

Newspapers around the country chose sides and printed attendance figures that were slanted one way or another in an attempt to favor one circuit at the other's expense. It is not likely that completely accurate attendance estimates will ever be known, although the following table was compiled by Clarence Dow, an unbiased observer, and is probably as near the truth as any:

NATIONAL LEAGUE		BROTHERHOOD LEAGUE	
Boston	147,539	Boston	197,346
New York	60,667	New York	148,197
Brooklyn	121,412	Brooklyn	79,272
Philadelphia	186,002	Philadelphia	170,399
Cincinnati	131,980	Buffalo	61,244
Chicago	102,536	Chicago	148,876
Pittsburgh	16,064	Pittsburgh	117,123
Cleveland	47,478	Cleveland	58,430
	813,678		980,887

This would indicate that the Brotherhood slightly out-drew its more respectable rival, but the Players' League season was by no means a howling success. An extremely lively ball was used by the Brotherhood, and the public got the idea that the high scoring games indicated inferior baseball. Actually, that was not the case at all. The Brotherhood had the best players in the country but, like the old Union Association, lacked the executive brains to manage the affairs of the players.

However, the hitting in the Brotherhood League was terrific, Pete Browning leading the pack with a mark of .391, compared to Jack Glasscock's league-leading .341 in the National. Glasscock's case was a strange one because he had been one of the original jumpers, making the leap when President Young classified him as a "B" player despite the fact that he was the greatest shortstop in the land. But Glasscock was induced to jump back and he landed with the New York Giants.

Probably one million dollars was lost in all by the three leagues during that one season. But the National League, carrying the rather trampled banner of the reserve clause, was the only one to survive. Oddly enough, the Brotherhood had the National on the ropes and didn't know it, failing to press the advantage because of the lack of business acumen. Towards the end of the year the Brotherhood acquired the Cincinnati franchise from Aaron S. Stern, the owner of the Reds. Stern had opposed the Brotherhood all season, but after losing $15,000 on the Reds that year despite the absence of any local competition, he glibly sold out the club, lock, stock and barrel to his hated rivals, which was certainly a demonstration, if any were needed, that business, like politics, makes strange bedfellows.

The sale of the Reds practically left the National League with only six clubs, for the Pittsburgh team was moribund. With their proud league in such a pitiful condition, the magnates then became willing to sit down and talk things over with the players. And that is where the Brotherhood was outsmarted. Frankly stating the extent of their season's losses, the Brotherhood, without knowing how badly off the National League was, agreed to a merger of their strongest clubs. Al Spalding had spent most of that summer in England, but he got in on the kill. With John B. Day and Charles H. Byrne of the National League, Allen W. Thurman, Albert L. Johnson, Wendell Goodwin and Edward B. Talcott of the Brotherhood and Christ Von Der Ahe and Bill Barnie of the American Association, Spalding took charge of a conference held in Room 439 of the Fifth Avenue Hotel, New York. After each league presented its views without the National tipping its withered hand, Spalding arranged for the National and Brotherhood teams in New York, Pittsburgh and Chicago to consolidate, bringing an end to the war and causing the Brotherhood to disband.

Little attention has been paid to the late history of the American Association, because by the late eighties that picturesque circuit had become a carbon copy of the National. Weak executive leaders were the chief trouble. In 1885 and 1886 the Association was superior in every way to the National League and infinitely more popular with the public. But trouble started because of a player named Sam Barkley.

A second baseman with the champion Browns of 1885, Barkley was released by Von Der Ahe that winter, and he had offers from Pittsburgh and Baltimore. Those two Association teams fought over his services, and Denny McKnight, the loop's president, told Barkley he could sign with either team. So he signed with Pittsburgh, but the other American clubs ganged up on Pittsburgh and its president, W. H. Nimick, and blacklisted Barkley. Sam went to the courts, sued the Association for reinstatement, and won his case. The Association then demanded that McKnight resign.

Thirsting for revenge against Baltimore and the rest of the Association, Nimick placed his Pittsburgh team in the National League. Two years later, in 1889, Cleveland also deserted the Association for the National, and when Cincinnati and Brooklyn followed in 1890, the colorful circuit of Von Der Ahe was doomed.

After the Brotherhood was licked, or thought it was, the Association still managed to go through its tenth and final season in 1891. But still another squabble then brought on defeat.

Two players who had jumped to the Brotherhood from the Athletics, Outfielder Harry Stovey and Second Baseman Louis Bierbauer, should have reverted to the Philadelphia team when peace was declared. But the Athletics failed to reserve these men, so Boston of the National signed Stovey, formerly one of baseball's great home run hitters and base-stealers, and the Pittsburgh Nationals claimed Bierbauer. Although Boston and Pittsburgh were technically justified from a legal standpoint, their piracy of these players from the bankrupt Athletics was considered unethical, and the event led to more warfare between the National and Association in 1891. As an aftermath of that incident, Pittsburgh's team became known as the Pirates, a nickname that has clung to the Smoketowners ever since.

That last bit of warfare finished off the crumbling Association. Deserted by its strongest franchises, the National's most successful rival was forced to sue for peace, and in October, 1891 the strongest teams in each league were merged. This gave the National League a twelve-club circuit which was to operate as a monopoly for eight years starting in 1892, with the original clubs located in Baltimore, Boston, Brooklyn, Chicago, Cincinnati, Cleveland, Louisville, New York, Philadelphia, Pittsburgh, St. Louis and Washington.

But in the ten seasons that it did last the American Association was a good influence on the game. It established the principle that baseball could be played on Sunday, a practice which was copied by the National League in 1892 and which became a permanent tradition of the game despite the occasional opposition from Sabbath societies and other such organizations. The Association was closer to the people than the National, a situation which forced the latter organization to adopt a more liberal attitude.

One innovation begun by the Association was the rule giving the batter his base when hit by the pitcher. This legislation was put on the books in 1884, and the National copied it three years later. The "hit batsman" department has become a very minor statistical feature of box scores, but in the early days pitchers plunked the batters with much more frequency, and the rule was a good one.

In its latter years, though, the Association seemed content to ride along with any practice the National League introduced. When the National gave a base hit to a player who received a base on balls in 1887, the Association agreed to do the same thing. This practice lasted for only that one season, but it proved to be the most unpopular scoring innovation ever made. It also made possible baseball's highest recorded batting average, Tip O'Neill's .492 mark with the St. Louis Browns. How often Tip walked that year isn't known for sure, although Ernie Lanigan, the game's greatest statistician, estimates that O'Neill's true average was around .400. That same year Cap Anson led the National with a .421 figure, which was similarly caused by the new rule. Obviously, it isn't fair to the few players who have managed to hit .400 to include in their ranks those who reached the lofty perch by being given credit for safeties on walks. However, Tip O'Neill was a fine hitter. He repeated as champion in 1888, although his mark dwindled to .332. Anson also repeated with a .343 record, the fourth and final time he was to win the batting crown. Not until the immortal Honus Wagner was the National League to produce a batting king who won the title more times than that.

The real cause of the Association's decline, lack of executive leadership, was demonstrated by the work of Denny McKnight and his successor, Weldon Wikoff. They were not strong men, and often did the National League's bidding. As league presidents they confined their activity to the compiling of averages, notifying umpires of their assignments, and informing clubs of signed contracts and releases. Whenever a fair question was put to them by sports writers of the day, they maintained an owl-like silence that was misinterpreted as wisdom, a situation that is not entirely unknown today.

Unlike Abraham G. Mills, the National League president who indignantly quit his job when the Union Association players were readmitted to league ranks, Nicholas E. Young, National mogul at the time the Brotherhood players were welcomed back into the fold, hung onto his. In fact Young, whose career dated back to National Association days, was to remain at the helm until 1902.

Pietro the Gladiator 11

IT IS extremely doubtful if any player who ever lived, including Ted Williams of the modern Boston Red Sox, enjoyed hitting a baseball more than Lewis Rogers (Pete) Browning, champion batsman of the American Association with a mark of .382 during the first year of that loop's existence. That Pete's eyes, or, as he called them, "lamps," were still sharp eight years later was proved when he won the batting crown of the Brotherhood with a .391 figure, and when Browning finally left the big show after 13 campaigns, he deposited a lifetime average of .355.

Totally forgotten today, save by the oldest fans, Browning's contribution to baseball's colorful fabric was not so much the fact that he was a great hitter as the way he delighted in talking about his numerous achievements. Pete chattered about his hitting incessantly, in a picturesque language all his own, to anyone who would listen. And just as five decades later another player who oozed color, Jerome Herman (Dizzy) Dean, was to back up his fantastic claims with his performance, Browning invariably did on the field what he claimed for himself of an evening.

A native of Louisville, where he was to die in an insane asylum at the age of 44 in 1905, Browning had more nicknames than any player who ever put on a spiked shoe. In the newspapers he was called Pete, Petie, Pietro, Glad, Gladdy, and the Gladiator, in addition to numerous less dignified appellations which related to his nocturnal tendencies. Because Browning never objected to anything written about him, no matter how scandalous, one paper used to refer to him as Pietro Redlight District Distillery Interests Browning. Not only did Pete consider such references flattering and charming, he customarily bought newspapers from every city in the league, and faithfully clipped every mention of the Gladiator, pasting the accumulation in huge scrapbooks. Sports writers got so they would take any story, no matter how apocryphal, and hang it on Pete, who would just grin and clip it out along with the others.

In his early days Pete liked the bottle, and at times it interfered with his playing. Each winter, back in Louisville, he would maintain a rigid schedule of training; but in the spring he would become so overwhelmed at the excitement of meeting his mates, that he would go on one prolonged spree after another. But as he grew older, these excursions became more infrequent, and in the sunset of his career it was claimed that he had gone for over three years without a drop. Because of an interview he had with Harry M. Weldon, baseball editor of the Cincinnati Enquirer, Browning's exact words about the liquor situation have been preserved, as follows:

"No, I ain't blowed one off since a year ago last August, and you can bet it will be many more years before I touch another. There is nothing in it. Just look at me now, I am linin' 'em out. It don't take old redeye to give you courage to go up agin' 'em. I could have had a saloon to play in Louisville this year, but what's the use. You can get your kite out once in a while, and after you've been in this business a few years you're lucky to get change for a half. I have got the stick now. Manager Loftus give it to me today, and I lined out that 'soaker' that brought in our two runs. Reilly used it too, and liked to killed the Bostons' left-fielder."

This conversation, like all of Pete's conversations, ended up with a discussion of hitting. He was constantly sending the team's batboy to the nearest drugstore for a bottle of sweet oil, which he rubbed on whichever of the several hundred bats in his possession he was going to use that day.

"I never stole a bat in my life," Pietro told Weldon on another occasion, "No I didn't. Them Brooklyns won't take a bat. No, they won't. We had 44 bats when they drove out there today, and when they left we could find only ten. I don't say the Brooklyns took 'em, but somebody made a wholesale swipe of a lot of good sticks. Pietro buys all his bats, you can bet he does. That's right. I've got 205 bats if you want to know. I only use one of them now, but I like to carry bats for the other fellows. I never run across a fellow like Reilly. Every bat you pick up has a "R" on it. He won't even let me carry one of his bats. There is only one stick that I want. Big Darby O'Brien has got it. If Pete could make a trade with him, he could lead the league in hitting, you can gamble on that."

If Browning went hitless in a game, and that happened sometimes, none of the players ever saw him at night. But if he had made two or more safeties that day, no hotel lobby or sidewalk was big enough to contain him; and on those nights you could find him on the street in Louisville, or Cincinnati, or St. Louis or Baltimore, or any other city in the circuit, his shoes neatly shined and his face adorned with a smile as big as the great outdoors.

The other players and the fanatics who followed the pastime always liked to kid Pete about his hitting. He was a little deaf, thought everyone else was, and conducted his conversations in the manner of an auctioneer. He had utter disdain for the batting averages that were published in the papers and always claimed they cheated him by forty points or more. Since the Gladiator always figured his own average on his cuffs, players circulated the story that Browning always led the league but couldn't prove it because a chambermaid mistakenly had his shirts sent to the laundry.

Harry Walker, an outfielder who blossomed in the 1940s with the Cardinals, Phillies, Cubs and Reds, attained a certain aura of celebrity through his batting habit of taking off his hat between pitches, a practice which annoyed enemy hurlers so much that it became a fetish with Walker and ended up by his being dubbed Harry the Hat. And although fans who have watched Walker may have thought that they were witnessing a nervous habit unique in the pastime, apparently Pete Browning anticipated Harry by more than fifty years.

For one day a writer asked Browning why he always removed his hat while batting and Petie explained, "It's business. I put my mitt to my eyebrows and push the hair out of the way of my lamps. You can't line 'em out unless you have good peepers. Old Pete knows that, and he takes good care of 'em. He never washes 'em with soap and water. It don't do. It will ruin the best lamps in the world. Pete closes 'em up when he is washing. Then he waits 'til about ten o'clock when he goes out in the streets and looks right up at the sun, two, three times. That opens 'em up good, and then he can line 'em out."

Aside from batting, the Gladiator was not too good a performer. He was fast on the bases and customarily got a good lead, but he didn't like physical contact, and he was afraid to slide. This timidity, strange in so good a hitter, even showed itself at bat, and he was so adept at dodging pitches that he was seldom hit. Defensively he could perform with skill on an open field, but if a ball were hit anywhere near the stands he would fall victim to a claustrophobia that made him play it safe and take it on the rebound off the fence. One story which has been given wide circulation claimed that Browning drew his last release when he failed to make a catch because timidity prevented him from crossing a small mud puddle in the outfield to reach the ball.

Pete probably could have been a good fielder, but he cared nothing about that phase of the game and passed it up. Hitting was everything there was in life for him, and you couldn't ask his opinion on any subject whatever that he didn't explain in relation to meeting the ball with the bat.

One day, when a writer noticed Pietro borrow a cigarette from a sport in the grandstand, he asked him what he thought of cigarettes. The Gladiator puffed out clouds of smoke, and as he caressed his window-sash bat, he soliloquized:

"I never did think it right to smoke these toys. It gives people an idea that you ain't strong enough to smoke a real cigar; makes you look like a dude. I don't care though. I see Bug Holliday and John Clarkson smoking cigarettes and I sees 'em both get hits. Says I to myself, them things help the lamps. They're just the proper caper for Glad, so I tries 'em and they roll bully for me. I only want two hits this afternoon. If the Gladdy can keep up that lick, he will stay up with the .300 boys."

Browning is not so well known today as others of his era, as King Kelly or Cap Anson or Old Hoss Radbourne. He was not quite so good a hitter as Anson, didn't last as long, and never the equal of Kelly in the field when the King was sober, but he had a charm that made him unique. He was the walking personification of life, in the American Association, a Christ Von Der Ahe with a bat, just as Anson, the walking personification of life in the National League, was Al Spalding with a bat.

The best way to visualize players of an era so far removed from modern times is to consider how their personalities, not their batting averages alone, compare with players of today. Browning had a touch of Dizzy Dean in him, a touch of Ted Williams in his fondness for hitting, a touch of Bobo Newsom in referring to himself in the third person and perhaps a touch of Paul Waner. Anson, on the other hand, had the outspokenness of a Rogers Hornsby and that same great player's honesty, the unimaginativeness of a Lou Gehrig, the almost mystic managerial skill of a Joe McCarthy. Anson, like Gehrig, was an iron man.

Browning was like the league he represented, and like the league he declined and passed from the scene, a victim of the fight between two tendencies in the game. The National League and Anson survived; the Association and Browning disappeared. And when they left they took with them an informality and charm that baseball was never to know again.

Anson, who began playing professional baseball with Rockford in the first year of the National Association's existence; was still on the job 27 years later. Like the National League he played for he survived wars with the Unions, the Brotherhood and the American Association. But, unlike the National League, he eventually lost out too, just as Browning did. In his autobiography, a strange combination of good sense, outspokenness and conceit, Adrian Anson claimed that in the end he was betrayed by Al Spalding after all his years of faithfulness and loyalty to the Chicago club, forced off the team in a stock deal that prevented him from acquiring control. Be that as it may, Anson too was defeated eventually, defeated by the years.

Baseball players take a lot of punishment. The average fan has no idea of the strain of playing an annual schedule of 154 games. Great players have to punish themselves to attain that greatness in most cases, one notable exception having been Babe Ruth. In an era when the great majority of players customarily caroused at night, Anson never ate potatoes, drank nothing but water and went to bed alone and hungry every night during the season.

On the field he was a snarling, tough competitor, asking no quarter and playing the game according to his code. He would always try to intimidate a new umpire or new player as a matter of policy, and if they survived he accepted them as worthy of the league. Umpires hated him, much as they were to hate Leo Durocher years later, but, as in the case of Durocher, they privately admired his skill and the way he played the game. He badgered them because he thought it good strategy to do so. As one newspaper observed in verse:

"There is no team, however watched and tended,
But some old bum is there;
There is no umpire, howsoe'er defended,
But calls a 'foul' for 'fair.'

"All games are full of groans and kicks and howling
At some alleged bad break;
But of all teams that win their games by growling,
Chicago takes the cake."

Fans in opposing cities pretended to hate Anson, but after he had been around for so many years, they marveled at the consistency of a career conducted on such a high level and gave him generous applause.

As a manager, Anson was great. When the old guard of the White Stockings passed, his team became known as Anson's Colts, and he watched those colts as a racehorse trainer would nurture a great young thoroughbred. Having seen all the distractions that could tempt young players, Anson expected the worst of every recruit added to his roster. But he watched them for three years after they joined his team, and if they survived that period's temptations he treated them with kindness and consideration.

Before he finally quit the diamond Anson made more than three thousand base hits, the exact figure being 3,081, and that total does not include those he made in five years of National Association play. Anson was the first to make three thousand blows, and of the thousands of performers who have since appeared, only six more have been added to the list.

He could have jumped to the Onions, he could have leaped to the Brotherhood, he could have signed at a fantastic salary with any Association club. But he always remained loyal to the National League. And the league sold him down the river at the finish.

Anson's relations with Spalding had been cordial up until the time of the world tour. But on that junket Spalding brought along a man named James A. Hart to act as business manager until the group reached San Francisco. Spalding then took up a collection from the players to buy Hart an expensive pair of diamond cuff-buttons, and Anson, in his usual gruff manner, refused to kick in. Three years later, much to Anson's astonishment, Spalding resigned as president of the White Stockings, and Hart was named in his place.

At this time Spalding wrote a long letter to his captain, telling him that Hart's nomination would not change things one bit, but when, in 1893, Anson had six years to go under his old contract, he signed a new one and then noticed it called for only five years of his services.

Anson stayed on through the season of 1897, but it became apparent to him that he was being eased out. He claimed that Spalding encouraged him to buy more stock in the club and then made it impossible for him to obtain that stock, finally forcing him out.

When Spalding then proposed a huge benefit game for Anson, one which would have raised thousands of dollars, Cap snorted his refusal, commenting that he was not a pauper. And as he left the National League after a baseball lifetime of devotion to it, here is what he said, "Baseball as at present conducted is a gigantic monopoly, intolerant of opposition and run on a grab-all-that-there-is-in-sight basis that is alienating its friends and disgusting the very public that has so long and cheerfully given to it the support that it has withheld from other forms of amusement."

They have him in the Hall of Fame at Cooperstown now too. Spalding is there also.

Lopsided Loop 12

THE BASEBALL fan breathed more easily with the dawn of 1892, believing that the end of the National League's constant warfare heralded the age of a greater game. The emergence of the twelve-club National League monopoly did bring an end to contract jumping and subsequent court decisions, but there were still problems to plague magnates, players and patrons.

For the first and only time in its history the National, in 1892, provided for a split season. This was done in an attempt to find a substitute for the inter-league rivalry that had previously existed, and it was hoped that the postseason meeting of champions of each half of the schedule would take the place of the world series. The split season idea originated in the minors, and after the Eastern League demonstrated the efficacy of such a plan in 1891, the big league magnates decided to try it. At this time the schedule was first set at 154 games, the same number of contests called for annually today.

The patience of the second division fan is frequently taxed, and followers of the loop's less efficient clubs soon found that the prospect of finishing eleventh or twelfth was more horrendous than the possibility of ending seventh or eighth had been. Twelve clubs made too lopsided a league to prove practical, and yet the circuit was to endure in that form for eight years despite its constant unpopularity.

Salaries were still high as a result of the wars with the Brotherhood and Association, but when the season was less than two months old President Young called a meeting at which the princelings were authorized to slash the players' stipends as they saw fit. Each National League team, with the exception of Brooklyn and Philadelphia, called a conference of its players to distribute the sorry news. The athletes were all signed to new documents at a lower figure, most teams reducing the wages from 30 per cent, to 40 per cent. It was also ruled that any player who refused to ink a new agreement would be given his outright release, and all clubs agreed not to sign a player made a free agent in such a manner. All released players were to be put into a pool and subsequently assigned to teams needing them by the league office. The players quite naturally grumbled, but they signed. The only one who quit baseball for the season rather than comply with the order was Tony Mullane, the Cincinnati pitcher, who spent the remainder of the campaign tossing as an outlaw.

In spite of all this retrenchment the league lost money. Cleveland and Pittsburgh managed to break even, but the other teams found the going hard. The situation was especially bad in New York, where the fans learned to ignore the Giants so successfully the club dropped $32,000. Spectators were of the opinion that baseball was a trust with little genuine rivalry.

The two greatest pitchers in the game that year were Denton (Cy) Young, an Ohio farm boy who had joined Cleveland in 1890, and Charles (Kid) Nichols, who delivered his mysterious twists on behalf of Boston. Inspired by Nichols, the Beaneaters won 11 of their first 13 contests and built up a large early lead, winning the season's first half by a two-and-one-half-game margin over Brooklyn. But in the year's second session the pitching of Young shoved Cleveland to the fore, and the Spiders triumphed. Arthur Soden and his two lesser Triumvirs then hesitated before permitting their Boston team to meet Cleveland for the championship, feeling that cynical fandom would believe the Beaneaters had intentionally let down towards autumn to assure that Cleveland won. But the series took place anyway, and after the first game ended in a thrilling scoreless tie, halted by darkness after 11 innings, Boston took five straight and the crown.

When Soden's team repeated as champions in 1893, it became evident that another great baseball machine had been developed. New names again were crowding out the old in the pastime's ever-changing pageant. Harry Stovey and King Kelly had just about reached the end of the trail, but Manager Frank Selee had built a strong team of youngsters ready to capture the headlines and the public fancy. In addition to Nichols, Jack Stivetts and Harry Staley assured Selee of formidable pitching, and the slants of the trio were received by a master catcher, Charlie Ganzel. Tommy Tucker, Bobby Lowe, Herman Long and Billy Nash formed an exceptional infield, though one seldom recalled today outside of Massachusetts, and the outfield consisted of three redoubtable swatsmiths, Hugh Duffy, Tommy McCarthy and Cliff Carroll.

Interest in this fine club of Boston's restored the faith of the fans, and whereas 1892 had been the most disappointing season in league history, 1893 became the best attended flag chase yet conducted. Demonstration had again been made that nothing could kill baseball.

It might be said with a fair degree of accuracy that modem ball dates from 1893, for it was in that year that the pitching distance was increased from fifty-five feet to its present length of sixty feet, six inches. This move was made in an effort to encourage hitting, and the desired effect was achieved. Not once since has there been any dissatisfaction over the amount of space between batter and pitcher, and the change was the last radical move in the game's evolution. At the same time it was proposed to increase the distance between bases from ninety to ninety-three feet, but that move failed, and in all the years that have intervened there has been no tinkering with the geometry of major league parks except in the outfield, where magnates have frequently erected false barriers to stimulate the home run. But the distance between bases has remained as it was since Alexander Cartwright decided that ninety feet was the proper course for the old Knickerbockers in 1845, and the distance between pitcher and batsman has remained static since the 1893 campaign got under way.

The new pitching distance increased hitting because hurlers had to master their art all over again. It wasn't so much that five additional feet withered their speed; but the new distance did make it difficult for them to control their curves, and the flingers went through a period of adjustment that was relished by the side at bat. And the change was graphically shown by the batting averages of those seasons.

Considering the men who appeared in 15 or more games, only a dozen hit for marks higher that .300 in 1892. This group increased to 65 the following year, and zoomed to 94 in 1894, when Hugh Duffy established a record batting mark of .438. Perhaps Duffy was not helped as much by the new pitching distance as Tip O'Neill had been by the rule which made a base on balls a hit in 1887, but he was helped some, and that fact should be taken into consideration when his work is compared with that of such modern sluggers as Ty Cobb, George Sisler, Rogers Hornsby and Ted Williams.

There was a whole crop of new sluggers in the mid-nineties feasting on the pitchers, not only the formidable boys from Boston but such proud performers as Sam Thompson, Ed Delahanty and Billy

Hamilton of the Phils, and Steve Brodie, Willie Keeler, Hughie Jennings and Joe Kelley of Baltimore.

But all this slugging was not done at the expense of team play, for it was in the old twelve-club circuit that intricate team strategy was developed.

The hit-and-run play is such a routine part of the modern game that fans take it for granted and are not apt to inquire as to its origin. Those few who do give thought to the birth of the hit-and-run usually attribute it to the old Baltimore Orioles, the scrappy gang which was ultimately to end the Boston reign. Others believe that Cap Anson devised the play at Chicago. But it was apparently Frank Selee who brought the hit-and-run into general use in 1893.

John Montgomery Ward, the Brotherhood leader, was still on the job that year as manager and shortstop of the Giants. Ward called the Boston aggregation the best for team play he had ever seen, and described their work as follows:

"Say, for instance, they have a man on first and nobody out," Ward proposed. "Under the old style of play, a sacrifice would be the proper thing. Then the man on first would reach second base while the batsman was put out. The Bostons, however, work this play — the man on first makes a bluff attempt to steal second, but runs back to first. By this it becomes known whether the second baseman or shortstop is going to cover second for the throw from the catcher. Then the batsman gets a signal from the man on first that he is going to steal on a certain pitched ball. The moment he starts for second the batsman just pushes the ball for the place occupied only a moment before by the in-fielder who has gone to cover second base. That is, if the second baseman covers the bag, the batter pushes the ball slowly toward right field; if it is the shortstop, the ball is pushed to left field. Of course, it takes a skillful batter to do this, but they have such hitters on the Boston nine. Now, when the ball is pushed to the outfield, the man who has already started to steal second just keeps right on to third, while the batsman is safe at first. Then the trick is tried over again, and in most cases successfully."

This is exactly the technique employed today, although the runner no longer has to feint to determine whether the second baseman or shortstop will cover second. A beautiful thing to see when properly executed, the hit-and-run must have astonished those fans of the nineties who witnessed it for the first time.

William Chase Temple, a sportsman who hailed from Pittsburgh, became so enthused when the Pirates finished second to Boston in 1893 that he tried to think of some way of honoring the club. The split season had been abandoned, preventing the meeting of each half's champion, and the absence of any competing league made a world series impossible, so Temple conceived the idea that after each season a series should be staged between the clubs which finished first and second. To create interest in his plan he donated a handsome loving cup and provided that the clubs ending up one-two should contest for its possession on a "best four out of seven" basis. For four seasons, starting in 1894, teams struggled for this Temple Cup. The Baltimore Orioles participated in all four of these clashes, losing the first two because of an indifferent attitude toward the games, but rallying to snatch the last two after being stung by taunts from the grandstand throughout each season.

The Orioles, managed by Ned Hanlon, won three consecutive pennants starting in 1894, temporarily replacing Boston as the league's strongest club. Including in their ranks such blistering personalities as John McGraw, Wilbert Robinson, Henry Reitz and Sadie McMahon in addition to Jennings, Keeler, Kelley and Brodie, Baltimore won its games through muckerism of the worst possible type, the berating of umpires, the intentional spiking of opponents and the use of such low tricks as hiding balls in the outfield grass to throw in play at strategic times.

Baltimore's success was made possible because of a league policy of leniency toward such hooliganism, and the sad fact that the other teams, even Boston, copied the Oriole formula and tried to emulate the rowdies from Chesapeake.

When reprobates age, the evils of their prime are often recalled with sweet nostalgia, and today there are veteran fans who wish that baseball could return to the days of the old Orioles. But baseball, which today appeals to people with more than a veneer of culture as well as to swine, can no more return to that over-sentimentalized era of tobacco-chewing profanity than it can to the sideburned age of the underhanded pitch, the seventies. The Orioles were great players and four of them, McGraw, Robinson, Jennings and Kelley were to become great managers in later life, but their greatness stemmed from sheer ability. They were titans in spite of and not because of their titanic boorishness.

But excitement in baseball pays off at the gate, and the Orioles made money for many clubs because of the intensity with which they were hated throughout the league. But there was nothing amusing about their studied viciousness. Listen to this anonymous sports writer of the Cleveland Leader:

"I say it with reluctance, for I have always admired Ned Hanlon's pluck—that the national game never received so severe a setback as it did during the last Baltimore series here. The effort to spike players, the constant flow of profanity and vulgarity, the incessant and idiotic abuse of an umpire all combined to make the Baltimore club thoroughly detested. In ten years' experience in scoring games in Cleveland, I have never seen such a torrent of vulgarity, profanity and brutal senseless abuse heaped upon an umpire as Lynch stood from the Baltimore players upon the field here."

By 1896 attendance had fallen off at Baltimore, where the people came to look upon the nine as invincible. The promoters were to learn, just as Connie Mack was to learn later at Philadelphia, that winning teams do not necessarily pay off at the gate. Success sometimes begins to pall. But the Orioles more than made up for it on the road, where their evil reputation continued to act as a magnet on the populace.

It was the Boston team that finally managed to defeat the Orioles in 1897, with Lowe, Long, Duffy, Nichols and Stivetts still going strong as holdovers from the earlier Beantown champions. Frank Selee was still on the job as manager and he had found sensational new players in First Baseman Fred Tenney, Third Baseman Jimmy Collins and Pitcher Vic Willis.

It was the operation of baseball as a trust more than the lamentations of second division fans that finally wrecked the league as a twelve-club wheel. Frank DeHaas Robison, owner of the Cleveland franchise, branched out by acquiring the St. Louis team in 1899 and moving his best players there, leaving Cleveland in the inexperienced hands of his brother Stanley. That was a break for the fans of St. Louis who saw their pets win more games than they lost in the National League for the first time since 1876, but it was a terrible blight to followers of the Spiders. So terrible were the 1899 Clevelands that they abandoned playing at home early in the year and meandered around the loop as a road club after that, establishing an alltime mark for ineptitude with exactly 20 victories to partially assuage the grief of an unbelievable total of 134 defeats.

That winter the National League abandoned the franchises at Cleveland, Baltimore, Louisville and Washington, leaving a compact circuit of eight clubs, the same eight which have battled each other without a change in franchise ever since.

Here are the composite standings of the National League for the eight years of existence as a twelve-team entente, figures which demonstrate more vividly than words could why the loop was lopsided and why the residents of the lower regions had trouble attracting a following:

TEAM	WON	LOST	PERCENTAGE
Boston	706	400	.638
Baltimore	642	443	.592
Cincinnati	597	504	.542
Philadelphia	598	508	.541
New York	577	527	.523
Brooklyn	562	520	.5193
Pittsburgh	571	530	.5186
Cleveland	568	530	.517
Chicago	546	548	.499
Louisville	419	683	.380
Washington	409	695	.370
St. Louis	399	706	.361

A Graveyard
at St. Paul   13

___

CHARLES ALBERT COMISKEY, the former news
butcher and first baseman for the Dubuque Rabbits,
was unhappy when the American Association
expired following the season of 1891. Not a National
League man at heart, Comiskey had managed the
garish Browns to four consecutive championships for
Christ Von Der Ahe, then had piloted the Chicago
Brotherhood team during the one season of that loop's
ill-starred existence, and finally had returned to St.
Louis for the Association's final year. He didn't relish
the prospect of joining the awkward, twelve-pronged
monopoly that was the National. But baseball was
baseball, and Charlie was induced to sign as manager
of the Cincinnati Reds in 1892, launching a fateful
chapter in his career.

At Cincinnati Comiskey's employer was John T.
Brush, the symbol of National League frugality who
had fathered the salary classification scheme that led
to the Brotherhood revolt, but, strange to say, Charlie
learned to respect and finally admire his new employer,
believing him to be honorable in his dealings and a
master politician though not a student of the game.
Brush, who at this time still paid more attention to his
clothing business at Indianapolis than to baseball, could
judge the quality of cotton goods more readily and a
great deal more intelligently than he could estimate
the worth of athletes, but the political aspects of the
baseball trust fascinated him, and he became expert at

the hotel suite shenanigans that dictated the game's policy. He was shrewd but, in Comiskey's judgment, fair and considerate.

However, Comiskey's opinion of Brush, who operated long before corporations learned the value of good public relations, was not shared by the Cincinnati rank and file. To them Brush was the living personification of National League imperiousness, an opinion in which the populace was encouraged by Byron Bancroft Johnson, a brash young sports writer for Murat Halsted's Cincinnati Commercial-Gazette. The son of a minister and a graduate of Marietta College, Ban Johnson was only 27 when Comiskey came to Cincinnati to manage the Reds in 1892. A thorough reporter and a man of burning ambition, Johnson cordially hated Brush and continually badgered him in print, but he immediately warmed up to Comiskey.

Although their opinion of Brush was by no stretch of the imagination identical, Johnson and Comiskey found so much else upon which they agreed, notably the conduct of baseball, that they became inseparable companions. A dynamo when he was working, Johnson also enjoyed the conviviality of life after the day's labor was done, and frequently of an evening he and the Redleg manager would sit down in the back room of one of the city's numerous parlors of nocturnal refreshment, talking baseball and spinning their gossamer dreams. Veteran Cincinnatians like to believe they can point out the very saloon in which Johnson and Comiskey first discussed the organization of the American League as a rival of the National. The story is probably apocryphal, and yet it is virtually certain that the two men must have discussed exactly such a plan at one time or another.

In the spring of 1893 Comiskey listened to the complaints of various baseball managers of minor leagues of the South, wailings over the lack of patronage and enthusiasm in that area. Charlie pointed out that these men might do well to move north, that various cities around Chicago were begging for good baseball. This advice was heeded, and in 1894 the Western League was formed, with franchises at Milwaukee, Indianapolis, Sioux City, Detroit, Toledo, Columbus, Kansas City and Minneapolis.

Comiskey might well be termed the organizer of the Western League, for it was at his suggestion that the circuit was joined, but he was necessarily only an adviser at first because his contract as manager of the Reds extended through 1894. However, Comiskey told Brush, whose recommendations in such matters carried great weight, that Johnson would make an ideal president for the new league. This made Brush pause and think, for although he welcomed the idea of being rid of Johnson and his constant stingings, he feared elevating him to such a position of esteem. Brush was to have attended the organization meeting of the Western League at Indianapolis with a recommendation one way or the other, but for some reason he missed his train. Comiskey was at the meeting, and when he urged that Johnson be accepted as president the delegates, feeling that Charlie must echo the opinions of his employer, gleefully assented. Johnson, who had attended the conclave as a reporter for his paper, took over then and there.

After the season of 1894 Comiskey turned down a new contract at Cincinnati to cast his fortunes with the rising star of Johnson, feeling that his destiny in the game lay outside National League ranks.

"Where will you go?" Brush asked.

"To St. Paul," Comiskey said. "I'm going to take over the Sioux City franchise and transfer it to St. Paul."

"St. Paul?" Brush thundered questioningly. "Are you crazy? St. Paul is a graveyard."

"That's where I want to go," Charlie smiled.

"All right. I see your mind is made up. Well, when you go broke, come on back. And meanwhile, if you need help there, just let me know."

Help for the Western League from John T. Brush was not to continue long because it soon became clear that Comiskey and Johnson were constructing a circuit that would eventually vie with the National for patronage, and when, later, the American League's labor pains heralded the birth of a major league rival, Brush was not to play the obstetrician.

St. Paul was a graveyard of sorts. Comiskey's team lost 17 consecutive games at one stage of the 1895 race and also was deprived of a park in which to play its Sunday games because of an injunction. But Charlie took the setbacks in stride and remained in the Minnesota setting for five years, patiently working with Johnson to improve conditions, mending his fences, sometimes literally, and biding his time.

The idea of competing with the National League was by no means unique with Charlie Comiskey. Many gentlemen of baseball wisdom nurtured the idea, among them Alfred H. Spink, the baseball editor of St. Louis who had backed the Union and American Associations and whose sympathy had gone out to the Brotherhood boys. Spink, whose baseball greatness presently runs through the veins of his dynamic nephew, J. G. Taylor Spink, who serves as a watchdog of the game from his publisher's chair of The Sporting News, properly recognized in the summer of 1898, when he was sports editor of the St. Louis Post-Dispatch, that National League baseball was on the wane and that new blood and new vitality were needed. Spink was laughed at by the eastern writers, descendants perhaps of those who scoffed at Bill Hulbert, but undaunted he wrote hundreds of letters urging that a new major league be formed, and he was aided in his labors by Ted Sullivan, the legendary organizer who had been midwife at the birth of the old Onions. Sullivan was dispatched in search of cities for the new league, just as he had been for Henry V. Lucas fifteen years before, and finally enough details were pieced together to hold a secret meeting in a Chicago hotel that was off the beaten path.

Among those interested in the venture at this time were Christ Von Der Ahe, who had found the National League too chilly an environment for him, and Cap Anson, who felt that he had been betrayed by the circuit to which he had given the best years of a lifetime.

Johnson and Comiskey knew that Spink was working on plans for such a league and were able to discover where the furtive meeting was being held. They were concerned because they felt that two such attempts to compete with the National would be ruinous. Attending Spink's meeting, Ban and Charlie were greeted in a friendly manner, but at that time they declined to join forces with him.

John McGraw of the Baltimore Orioles became a member of Spink's group and hoped to plant a franchise in New York, but he found that any such move would be thwarted by Tammany politicians who would tolerate no rival of the Giants in the city, and would cut streets through any property selected for a grounds if that were necessary. Then Anson discovered that his Chicago backers had welshed on him. But Spink continued to hope that he could launch his new league.

By this time rumors of Spink's plans reached the public, and it was widely whispered that the National would find itself engaged in strife with a fourth rival in 1900. Ban Johnson knew then that he must either join forces with Spink's followers or out-maneuver them, and he chose the latter course because he wanted to run his own show.

Johnson disbanded the Western League following the season of 1899, then announced that the men who owned the same franchises were forming the American League, which was to be a major circuit. His attitude toward the National was amicable, and it was his hope that the organization could continue without a costly war. He explained that his hand had been forced by the rumored founding of a league by Spink's group, and that he was acting only to protect himself.

So loftily was Johnson dismissed by the National League that he was asked to send in his league's fee under the National Agreement, a practice required of minor leagues. Johnson replied that he had sent in no such fee because his league was a major.

The National League reduced its own ranks to eight in 1900, enabling Johnson to purchase the Cleveland franchise, one of those cities which was dropped. Comiskey was able to place his St. Paul club in the south side of Chicago because James A. Hart, Anson's old cuff-link antagonist, could not dream of any rivalry to his National League team coming from any ramshackle park in that section of the city.

The American League was not a major in 1900, though it professed to be, with teams placed in Buffalo, Kansas City, Indianapolis, Detroit, Minneapolis, Milwaukee, Chicago and Cleveland.

A friendly settlement still might have been possible, but National League treachery prevented it. When Ban Johnson, hat in hand, attended a National League confab late in 1900, hoping to be invited to sit down and explain his aims, he was kept waiting in the corridors, and then, when he stepped outside for a moment, the tycoons had the discourtesy to disband. Here again was the same attitude the National League had shown in its dealings with the Onions, the Brotherhood and the old Association; here was the smugness, the self-satisfaction and the deceit that had soured the public on the game. But this time the National League, instead of dealing with bunglers, was dealing with an enemy that was to give it, fortunately for baseball, the licking of its life.

The stupid but typical rudeness to Johnson at last made him determined to fight, and Ban was now ready to move into eastern territories. When he discovered that the National was trying to stifle him by forming a minor league in the Middle West, he abandoned the cities of Minneapolis, Kansas City, Indianapolis and Buffalo, moving into Philadelphia, Boston, Baltimore and Washington, assuring himself that the American would be a real major in 1901. McGraw, who had originally been a member of the now abandoned Spink combine, joined forces with Johnson at Baltimore; Connie Mack obtained the backing for the Philadelphia team; Hugh Duffy was lured from Boston to manage Milwaukee. Prominent players were by now making the jump, and another costly war was on.

The first three attempts to fight the National League failed because the organizers of the opposition lacked executive ability. But the crowd led by Johnson and Comiskey had brains and energy.

Ban started out by making no unreasonable demands. He would not have even expanded into Boston and other eastern centers had the National League shown the slightest decency toward him.

But after they kept him standing in the hall and then sneaked into adjournment, he barked, "If they want a real war, now they can have it!"

They got it!

And Charlie Comiskey, who never had to return to Cincinnati or to John T. Brush, had come a long way from the graveyard at St. Paul.

Conspiracy
at Red Bank   14

THE LOUDEST and most bellicose magnate who
ever ran the destinies of a major league ball club was
not Leland Stanford (Larry) MacPhail, who carved
out a moderate reputation as a noise-maker during a
turbulent career with the Reds, Dodgers and Yankees
from 1934 to 1947, but Andrew Freedman, a traction
millionaire who owned the New York Giants from
1895 to 1901. It was Freedman who led the group
which urged open war with the American League, and
it was this policy which brought humiliating defeat to
the National.

Only 55 when he died of apoplexy in his apartment
at Sherry's Fifth Avenue, New York City, Freedman
was a lifelong bachelor who received his training
for baseball in Tammany politics and the world of
high finance. Buying the Giants from E. B. Talcott
and J. Walter Spalding, brother of Al, he lost money
consistently before eventually selling the franchise to
John T. Brush. Although New York has always been a
great baseball city, Freedman did his best to ruin it as
such, and his reign marked the low point of horsehide
affluence in that metropolis.

Freedman's baseball career was one continuous
quarrel, and his adversaries included everyone with
whom he came in contact: fans, employees, players,
writers, and even his fellow magnates. On one occasion
he assaulted Brush in the barroom of the Fifth Avenue
Hotel, and in retaliation he was beaten up in public

by a friend of Brush's, one Bert Dasher. On another occasion he so insulted J. Walter Spalding during a chance meeting on one of the city's elevated railway lines that the latter, horrified and disgusted, resigned as a director of the Giants, a post he had retained after selling out to Andrew.

High executive of numerous corporations and the intimate friend of such people as James Hazen Hyde, Richard Croker and August Belmont, Freedman made millions through subway contracts and insurance deals before turning his attention to the national pastime. Not since Boss Tweed had run the Mutuals had New York been plagued with such a baseball administration. Although the game has produced numerous magnates who demonstrated an imperious attitude, most of them confined their contempt of people to the players and public, but Freedman even had contempt for his fellow magnates, and certainly he never hesitated to express it. He was the original "terrible tempered Mr. Bang," and although in a few years the word "brainstorm" was to be introduced to the language by way of explaining the incredible conduct of Harry K. Thaw, the attorneys for that gentleman might have found inspiration for the term more readily had they studied the public and private actions of Andrew Freedman.

Syndicate baseball was a natural development of the National League monopoly that flourished, or at least existed, for the eight years beginning in 1892. Toward this end Harry H. Van Der Horst, owner of the Baltimore Orioles, concerned over slipping attendance in the Maryland city, transferred his best players, including Manager Ned Hanlon, to Brooklyn in 1899. Some of the players wouldn't go; John McGraw, for instance, remained at Baltimore; but enough of them did migrate to assure Flat-bush of the pennant, and that wrecked the famed Oriole dynasty. And it has already been noted that the worst team of all time was made possible for Cleveland when Frank DeHaas Robison made a move quite like that of Van Der Horst the same summer, shuttling players from Cleveland to St. Louis.

But the proposals of Andrew Freedman dwarfed the actions of his fellows, and for cold effrontery and public disregard there was nothing like them in the history of the game. Even so conservative a magnate as Al Spalding was moved to observe while penning his reminiscences for autobiographical purposes:

"Soon after the American sport became established as a National pastime, and was showing its promoters a balance on the right side of the ledger, a certain clique came into the League for purposes of pelf. They at once let it be known by their acts that they were in baseball for what they could get out of it. They were absolutely devoid of sentiment, and cared nothing for the integrity or the perpetuity of the game beyond the limits of their individual control thereof. With these men it was simply a matter of dollars and cents.

"I do not know how better to characterize the monstrous evil which at this time threatened the life of Baseball than to denominate it 'Freedmanism'; for Andrew Freedman ... was the incarnation of selfishness supreme."

This, mind you, was not John Montgomery Ward sounding off in the barroom of the Fifth Avenue Hotel; this was not Henry V. Lucas in an outdoor garden at St. Louis, stimulated after talking to the athletes he loved; this was Albert Goodwill Spalding speaking, Spalding the opportunist whose trail had led from the pitching box to a million-dollar sporting-goods business, and his words sound precisely like the warnings given in the Brotherhood manifesto.

Spalding had fought the Onions, he had battled the Brotherhood with all the resources at his command, and now he was exhorting, like a parrot, the danger of the sad and identical prophecies that the players had made about baseball management. Even the Spaldings got in line to fight Freedmanism.

Across the Hudson in Red Bank, New Jersey, on a baronial estate at which his deeds were plotted, Freedman met one night in August, 1901 with fellow conspirators who represented the St. Louis, Boston and Cincinnati clubs of the National League. Executives of the circuit's other teams, Brooklyn, Chicago, Philadelphia and Pittsburgh, known to oppose Freedman and his plans, were not invited. But with exactly half the league in his corner the New York owner felt that he could control the game. The reduction of the loop from twelve to eight clubs had been instigated by Freedman, and although there was adequate reason for such retrenchment, it seems logical that his interest in the matter was determined by his attempt to prevail over a majority.

Freedman's group, comfortably conspiring in the drawing room at Red Bank, proposed to tear up the National Agreement, the much-discussed document drawn up originally by Abraham G. Mills which provided the rules that governed the relations of leagues, and substitute a monstrous trust divided into preferred and common stock. The game was to be governed by a Board of Regents, and clubs would lose their individual identity. Managers of each franchise were to receive identical salaries from the league, players could be blacklisted without reason, and a small group, associates of Freedman, were to run the game as they saw fit.

This was too much for the rest of the league to swallow, and the anti-Freedman forces determined that the only way to lick the Giant prexy was by using Al Spalding, the most experienced baseball politician still extant. At the National League meeting in 1901 those clubs voted for Spalding for president, while the Red Bank plotters cast their lot with Nicholas E. Young, who was still president of the National and something of a rubber stamp. This hopeless deadlock was not dissolved by 25 ballots, and when further voting seemed useless, the Trust crowd left the council chamber and went to bed. Another ballot was then taken and Spalding was elected president unanimously by the four clubs present, which of course did not constitute a majority.

Spalding, awakened and informed of his election, then proceeded to engage in one of the most grotesque off-the-field tableaux in baseball history, routing poor old Nick Young out of bed at 4 A.M., and trying to obtain from him a trunk which contained the League's official papers, records and correspondence. Young, who knew as well as Spalding that the latter's election was a fraud, quite naturally refused to yield his escritorial treasures, but he did agree that the trunk be held in trust by his son, Robert, whose slumbers had also been interrupted by the nocturnal visit of the former Rockford pitcher. Spalding, however, was too quick-witted for the pair of sleepy gentlemen, and hired a porter to steal the trunk and hide it for him. In his autobiography Spalding quite understandably chortled over this incident of his career, but he failed to explain where he acquired the services of a porter in that gray hour before dawn.

Freedman of course exploded the next day when he learned that Nick Young had entertained a burglar in his bed-chamber, and promptly got an injunction to prevent Spalding from assuming office. For months the National League had no ruling head at all, and

Spalding, scrupulously avoiding setting foot in New York State so that the injunction might not be served, made speech after speech concerning the low estate of National League life, speeches that were almost unanimously applauded by press and public. Young continued to occupy the president's chair, and the preposterous situation was not concluded until Freedman was finally prevailed upon, in 1901, to sell his stock in the Giants to John T. Brush. When that occurred Spalding resigned the office he had never held, and before the 1903 season Harry C. Pulliam, secretary of the Pittsburgh team who had started life at Paducah, Kentucky, was elected as the league's sixth president, although the chronologies of baseball, which skip Arthur H. Soden for no discernible reason, list him as the fifth.

So that was the sordid state of affairs in the National League when it was trying to fight off Ban Johnson's buoyant young rival circuit.

Chicago won the first American League pennant in 1901, but Charlie Comiskey was no longer on the job as field manager. That season he turned over the reins to Clark Griffith, who jumped the reserve clause with the Chicago Nationals to go to the South Side of the world's hog butcher, and remained in the front office, the first major league player to become a major league club owner.

Some idea of the extent to which the National was raided is gained from a study of the 1901 American League roster, which shows that of 182 players who appeared in championship games 111 had previously appeared in the National. Of course not all these were jumpers; some had gone from the four National clubs that disbanded following the 1899 campaign to join forces with Ban's circuit when it was still a minor in 1900. But the list of former Nationals active in the American in 1901 included some of baseball's greatest names: John Anderson, Jimmy Barrett, Roger Bresnahan, Steve Brodie, Jimmy Collins, Lou Criger, Lave Cross, Harry Davis, Mike Donlin, Jiggs Donohue, Hugh Duffy, Kid Elberfeld, Bones Ely, Clark Griffith, Bill Hoffer, Dummy Hoy, Frank Isbell, Fielder Jones, Nap Lajoie, Ted Lewis, Jimmy McAleer, Joe McGinnity, John McGraw, Sam Mertes, Doc Nance, Fred Parent, Wilbert Robinson, Fred (Crazy) Schmidt, Ossee Schreck, Cy Seymour, Chick Stahl and Cy Young.

Milwaukee finished last in the American's first campaign, and it was found expedient to replace the city in 1902 with St. Louis. More and more, Ban Johnson's league was approaching the proportions of the National.

Naturally, the National fought back. The greatest coup was scored in July, 1902, when John T. Brush prevailed upon John McGraw to resign as manager of the Baltimore Americans and jump to the Giants. With him went such renowned players as Joe McGinnity, Dan McGann and Roger Bresnahan, with two other Orioles of note, Joe Kelley and Cy Seymour, leaping to Cincinnati. This defection virtually ruined the Orioles, but so stupid was the National League in thinking that the job was done simply by wrecking the club that Johnson quickly assembled a makeshift team to fill out the schedule. That protected the franchise and permitted Johnson to move the players that winter to New York to become the progenitors of today's great Yankees. The assembling of the American League was complete.

By then the National League knew it was licked, and was ready to sue for peace. The boys didn't keep Ban waiting in the corridors this time, nor sneak into any adjournment behind his back. A committee consisting of Frank DeHaas Robison, James A. Hart and August

(Garry) Herrmann, Cincinnati's new president, met on January 5, 1903, with Harry Pulliam, the recently elected president of the League, acting as chairman, and Johnson, Charles Somers and John F. Kilfoyle of Cleveland representing the American.

Assuming that their new contestants were as compliant as the old Association magnates had been or as naïve as the Brotherhood delegates, the National barons first proposed that the best clubs in both leagues be merged, which would have restored another twelve-club monopoly that would have retarded the game's development for years. Johnson refused pointblank, and the American delegation scuttled the conference, much to the amazement of the National League crowd.

But four days later they sat down again, and when Johnson promised not to invade Pittsburgh, the National declared itself agreeable to the two-league idea.

Then came the drawn out business of details, the settlement of cases involving disputed players and the withdrawal of court actions. It was then provided that a National Commission be created to settle the game's executive problems with Garry Herrmann of Cincinnati as chairman, and the two league presidents sitting in as members. This commission was to supervise play in the majors and serve in an advisory capacity towards the various minor leagues that were now springing up indiscriminately. Joined together by a new agreement, these organized leagues, major and minor, became "Organized Ball," a structure that has continued to this day.

And so, ten years after baseball achieved maturity from the standpoint of technique in 1893 with the establishment of the pitching distance at sixty feet, six inches, the game attained legislative maturity with the acceptance of the two major leagues as equals. Fandom, always bored with the game's executive difficulties, heaved a sigh of relief and looked avidly toward action on the playing field.

It was a curious prank of fate that made John T. Brush and Charlie Comiskey, who had worked hand in hand at Cincinnati, among the chief antagonists when the two leagues clashed. But even when Brush tried to wreck the American League by breaking up the Baltimore team, Comiskey stuck by his old boss, shrugged his shoulders and said, "That's just his way of fighting." The men remained friends, and Comiskey carried his respect for John Brush to the grave.

Comiskey's entire attitude toward the National was one of friendly spoofing. He once encountered Garry Herrmann, who was sort of a latter day Von Der Ahe, wandering around the lobby of the Fifth Avenue Hotel, complaining that he had just lost his watch.

"What did you expect, Garry?" Comiskey asked. "You just came out of a National League meeting, didn't you?"

But Comiskey was kidding. The days of Freedmanism and thievery were over, and the new class of magnates that was to come along was to bring new glory to the game. Despite the fact that Charlie Ebbets of Brooklyn was to say in 1908, "Baseball is still in its infancy," the game, after a most painful adolescence, was actually ready for manhood, for Ban Johnson had provided the real answer to the conspiracy at Red Bank.

Era of
the Dead Ball   15

MOST OF the accomplishments in baseball during the first decade of the twentieth century had some relation to pitching, with the result that the scoring of a run, such a commonplace occurrence in the see-saw games of the nineties, became something in the nature of an event. The great parks of steel and concrete that big league clubs occupy today were not yet built, and fans huddled in the wooden stands to marvel at the futility of the batters who had to face such stalwarts of the mound as Jack Chesbro, Joe McGinnity, Christy Mathewson, Eddie Plank, Ed Walsh, Rube Waddell, Mordecai Brown and Addie Joss.

Whether the wizardry of the hurlers was brought about by their innate skill, the use of freak deliveries, the dead ball or a general decline of formidable hitters will never be learned; but all of these factors combined to make baseball a pitcher's game. There were still a few great batters. Napoleon La joie, a former hack driver from Woonsocket, Rhode Island, was a mighty man at the plate, and John (Honus) Wagner, an easy-going Dutchman of amazing talents, repeatedly led his league, the National, in hitting.

But it was pitching that decided the games, and a pitcher who couldn't go the distance was not considered worth his salt. Joe McGinnity, for instance, started 48 games for the Giants in 1903, completing 44. Three times in August of that year he pitched both games of double-headers, winning all six contests and gaining the title of "Iron Man." In the following year Jack Chesbro of the Highlanders, now the Yankees, worked even harder than McGinnity, starting 51 contests and completing 48. Chesbro won 41 games and lost 12 that season, but as luck would have it a wild pitch from his overworked right arm cost his team the pennant. That same year Cy Young, pitching for the Red Sox against the Athletics, hurled the American League's first perfect game, duplicating the 1880 masterpieces of John Lee Richmond and John Montgomery Ward. And Waddell, the eccentric lefthander of Connie Mack's club, fanned an estimated 352 men, that figure being approximate because box scores differed. When Bobby Feller of Cleveland approached the mark in 1946, statisticians were thrown into a turmoil trying to ascertain Waddell's correct total, but the American League simplified the matter by merely accepting Feller's final total of 348 as a record, without doing any research at all.

George (Hooks) Wiltse, though perhaps not to be mentioned in the same breath with those already described, also found pitching for the 1904 Giants a pleasant chore. McGinnity won 35 games for the New Yorkers that season while Mathewson copped 33, their twin total of 68 making them the greatest pitching pair for a single year the game has ever known, but Wiltse, just starting his major league career and pitching only on the rare occasions when Matty and McGinnity didn't labor, managed to win his first 12 decisions. Ten years later Guy Morton of Cleveland must have wondered how Wiltse had done it, for Guy was on the short end of his first 13 major league verdicts.

Batting became such a lost art that by 1905 Elmer Flick of Cleveland led the league despite hitting for the anemic percentage of .306, understandably the lowest figure for a monarch in the game's annals; and the runner-up that year, Willie Keeler of the Highlanders, batted only .302. That season home runs became almost extinct, Harry Davis of the Athletics leading his league with eight, and Fred Odwell, an obscure outfielder who drew his pay-check from Cincinnati, pacing the National with nine.

Offensive play reached its nadir in 1908 when both leagues established records for ineffectiveness at the dish, the National hitting .2389 as a league, and the American, .2391. That year the Brooklyn Dodgers as a team hit .213, the lowest mark recorded by a club in modern times, and the White Sox, anxious to add their bit to the non-hit department, connected for only three home runs all season long, the culprits being Fielder Jones, who managed the club, Frank Isbell and Ed Walsh.

The use of questionable deliveries undoubtedly aided the pitchers. The greatest exponent of the spitball was Walsh, who worked the staggering total of 464 innings in 1908, winning 40 games and losing 15. Walsh learned about the pitch from a team-mate, Elmer Stricklett, in the spring training camp of the Pale Hose at Marlin, Texas in 1904. Stricklett had picked up the delivery several years previously while toiling for Newark from a pitcher named Corridon.

Through the years pitchers have wrapped their fingers fondly around a baseball, gripping the cover tightly and picking at the seams, wondering if there weren't some new twist they could give it to make it dazzle the batters. But human beings and baseballs being what they are, there are certain limitations. Pitchers working in 1950 could do no more with the ball than those who struggled in 1900, and some fans have been found unkind enough to suggest they could not do as much. Arthur Cummings is believed to have discovered or at least perfected the curve while pitching for the Stars of Brooklyn in the late sixties. The inshoot, a term no longer used by professionals, but a pitch which is a fast ball, was discovered by a college pitcher, Avery of Yale, in 1872. Fred (Tricky) Nichols developed the drop in 1875, and the pitch is now known as a sinker. Bobby Mathews threw what he called a "raised ball" in 1869, which is nothing but a fast ball with a good hop; Charles Sweeney added the screwball in 1880, the pitch which Mathewson was later to call a fadeaway; Edward (The Only) Nolan added the overhand curve in 1876; and Al Spalding first used the change of pace in the early seventies.

But the spitter was something new, and hurlers who employed the moist delivery found that it gave a tremendous break to the ball; the only trouble was it would break one way one day and another way another, and it was also difficult to control.

But even pitchers who couldn't learn to control the spit-ball learned to scuff the ball's cover, or tear it with a knife, or rub it with sandpaper or paraffin, or dirty it to gain an advantage over the batter. And yet the Wagners and Lajoies, and later the Ty Cobbs and Tris Speakers, looked at all those trick deliveries and continued hitting.

The two leagues still hated each other in 1903 even though peace had been made by their executive heads, but the magnate who found it easiest to forgive and forget was Barney Dreyfuss of Pittsburgh. Least hurt by the war between leagues because his territory was never invaded, Dreyfuss won the National League pennant in 1903, then challenged the Boston Red Sox, champions of the Johnson wheel, to a post-season series to determine the world's championship. When the Red Sox defeated the Pirates, five games to three, despite heroic pitching by Pittsburgh's Deacon Phillippe who won all three of the Smoketown victories, the other

National League magnates were furious at Dreyfuss for permitting his team to fraternize with American League players.

That was why, when the Giants won the flag in 1904, they refused to meet the Red Sox, who had repeated as champions. John McGraw's hatred of the American League was especially intense because the circuit had finally invaded New York and because Ban had never forgiven him for deserting the Orioles. But such a lambasting did the Giants take in the press that in 1905 the world series was established under National Commission auspices as a fitting climax to the pennant races, and the stage was set for one of the nation's foremost sporting events. Not since 1904 has the American public had to do without a world series, and the American League has continued to supply the superiority established with the first victory in 1903.

Naturally, the absence of hitting that was noted throughout each championship season extended into world series play. In the 1905 classic the Giants and Athletics met five times in six days, with every game ending in a shutout and Christy Mathewson pitching three of them, yielding only 14 hits and walking only one man in the three games. Rube Waddell, the Athletic ace, missed action because of a shoulder injury he acquired in a friendly wrestling bout after winning twenty-seven games during the regular year. But it is doubtful if even the presence of Waddell would have helped the Athletics, certainly it would not have enabled them to cope any more effectively with Matty.

The hitting famine continued throughout 1906, with the American champions of that year delighting in their recognition as "the Hitless Wonders." Those White Sox won the flag despite a collective batting average of .228, the lowest in the league, principally because of an August string of 19 successive triumphs in which the opposition scored only 28 runs. Eight shutouts were included in the 19 wins, four of them pitched by Walsh, who won seven of the games. So capable were the White Sox that they were not at all impressed with the reputation of their intra-city world series foes, the Cubs, who had just won 116 games, a season's record that still stands; and they demolished the highly favored Bruins, four games to two.

Naturally, with runs at such a premium, clubs would go to any strategic lengths to score. This led to increased base-stealing, the more liberal use of the hit-and-run, and the sacrifice. Every close decision was greeted with a violent argument, for every run counted, and umpires found that usually they could please neither side.

It was in the American League that the umpire was first elevated to a position of dignity, and Ban Johnson made certain that the men in blue were absolute masters of the field of play. No longer did the job of officiating go to former players who were down on their luck. Ban clothed his arbiters with authority, backed up their decisions with fines and suspensions from the league office, and made their word the law. This did away with the senseless wrangling introduced to the pastime by the old Orioles and speeded up the games.

But one old Oriole who refused to have his wings clipped was John McGraw, and perhaps that led in part to his decision to desert Baltimore and the American League. McGraw got nowhere in his arguments with Johnson, who stubbornly backed up every umpire who removed McGraw from the game. But once a member of the National League McGraw did about as he pleased, going to any lengths to win a game, inciting crowds in every city in the circuit, and bullying the magnates of opposing clubs and even the beleaguered president Harry Pulliam. All the rowdy tactics of the

Orioles were retained by McGraw until he mellowed with middle age, and worse, they were copied by other teams throughout the league.

But McGraw got results, and he was absolutely without fear. When his Giants were able to repair the National's prestige by winning a world series, he became grudgingly respected by fans who had been hostile to him previously, and who would soon be hostile to him again. And the magic of McGraw's management restored the love for baseball in the hearts of people in New York, fans who had abandoned the game entirely while Andrew Freedman ran the Giants.

McGraw used methods that were in keeping with his times. Many of his players were crude and ignorant, and he did their thinking for them. But if he operated today he would learn, as that lesser manager but quite similar character, Leo Durocher, came to learn that it does not pay to be an anachronism. Had Leo Durocher played for the Orioles in 1895, he would have been considered a model of deportment. His crime, if it can be called such, was in applying McGraw's methods to an age that rejected them.

Principal rivals of McGraw's Giants were the Cubs, who soon imitated the boisterous conduct that blossomed under Coogan's Bluff. Managed in their golden years by Frank Chance, Chicago won four pennants in five years beginning in 1906, missing out only when Pittsburgh nosed ahead of the Bruins in 1909.

Much of the credit for the fine showing of the Bruins was given to the double-play trio of Shortstop Joe Tinker, Second Baseman Johnny Evers and First Baseman Chance, but the belief that this trio made more twin-killings than any other combinations is one of baseball's most extraordinary misapprehensions.

In the first place, teams which make the most double plays are not good ball clubs. The Boston Red Sox made more double plays in 1945 than any aggregation in major league history up to that time, 198, and finished seventh. In the National League the mark of 194 is held by the Reds who did it twice: in 1928, while finishing fifth, and in 1931, while snoozing in the league basement. Losing teams have more opportunity for completing double plays because they have more base-runners to contend with.

Furthermore, the era in which Messrs. Tinker, Evers and Chance flourished was not one which tended to make numerous double plays possible. Infields played in, teams sacrificed frequently, runners were apt to steal; it was an age that did not lend itself to records for the play at all.

As if that were not enough, double plays were not included in the official averages until 1919 in the National League, so that it is impossible to find out how many doubles Tinker, Evers and Chance participated in without going through hundreds of box scores.

But because Franklin P. Adams, a Giant fan, was so disturbed after seeing Tinker, Evers and Chance make a double play that cost his pets a game, or perhaps a flurry of them in several games, and wrote a little jingle about it for his column in the old New York Mail, fans everywhere believe that as a double play combination the trio was without a peer. The jingle, which was called "Baseball's Sad Lexicon," follows:

"These are the saddest of possible words–
Tinker to Evers to Chance.
Trio of bearcubs and fleeter than birds,
Tinker to Evers to Chance.
Thoughtlessly pricking our gonfalon bubble,
Making a Giant hit into a double,

Words that are weighty with nothing but trouble–
Tinker to Evers to Chance."

Despite their undeserved reputation for double play supremacy, Tinker, Evers and Chance were among the best players in history at their positions, and their place in the Cooperstown shrine, which they entered as a unit, is certainly deserved.

The rivalry between the Giants and Cubs culminated in the famous game of September 23, 1908, the game in which Fred Merkle of New York failed to touch second base at the Polo Grounds. When Al Bridwell hit a single that apparently brought victory to the Giants in the ninth inning, Evers, who had anticipated the play for weeks and who had executed it ten days previously against Pittsburgh, called for the ball and touched second forcing Merkle, who had left first to run for the clubhouse in accordance with the custom that was current. Umpire Hank O'Day, who had previously told Evers that such a play was legal, ruled Merkle out, and that was that. But the game did not mean that the Giants finished in a tie with the Cubs for the pennant as is popularly believed. The game, however, had to be re-played, and when it was, Chicago won the contest and with it the pennant, by a full game.

The season of 1908 was a hectic one in the American League also, the issue not being decided until the final day of the season when Detroit defeated the White Sox and finished one-half game ahead of Cleveland.

The Merkle play brought to a close the era of the dead ball, for in the following seasons concessions toward the batter originated, compromises that were not to cease until batting dominated the game to a degree beyond anything that had ever been known, but the change was to be a gradual one.

The ball may have been dead from 1901 to 1908 or thereafter, it may have been dirtied and spit upon and torn, but the fans loved to watch what the pitchers could do with it, and they poured out with a regularity that was to enable each major league team to construct a palace that would hold them. Here are the attendance figures for the majors in the first eight years of their joint existence:

NATIONAL LEAGUE	YEAR	AMERICAN LEAGUE
1,920,031	1901	1,683,584
1,681,212	1902	2,200,457
2,390,362	1903	2,345,888
2,774,301	1904	3,094,559
2,734,310	1905	3,070,752
2,781,213	1906	2,938,076
2,737,793	1907	3,398,764
3,634,988	1908	3,611,366
20,654,210 (Total)	(Total)	22,343,446

Cooperstown
Pastoral   16

BASEBALL GREW SO much in public favor in the
years that followed the peace between the two major
leagues that fans everywhere began to ask how it all
had started. The game was played on every vacant lot,
not only in the great cities of the land and in the towns,
but on farms and in the backwoods of the nation. Major
league attendance consistently climbed to new annual
peaks; there was scarcely a state in the union that did
not have its own minor professional circuit; and in the
hamlets town teams were formed to contend against
each other before huge crowds of gawking rustics.
Children learned to play ball soon after they learned
to walk, and they played whenever the weather
permitted and until it got so dark they could no longer
see the ball. Competition from such sources as golf, the
automobile and the movies had not yet developed, and
baseball enjoyed an unmolested adulation that knew
no bounds. Where had it all begun? No one seemed to
know.

Albert G. Spalding, writing in his annual Official
Base Ball Guide for 1905, proposed that the matter
be settled once and for all. Henry Chadwick, the
great pioneer writer of the game who was still alive
though in his eighty-first year, had always maintained
that baseball was descended from the British sport of
rounders. But Chadwick was a native of England, and
there was enough jingoism present in the personalities
of baseball's devotees to make them reject any alien

theory regardless of how meritorious it might be. Chadwick could offer no documentary proof. All he knew was that the games of baseball and rounders were similar and that the latter had been played in England for two centuries. So Spalding suggested that a commission be appointed to clear up the matter, and that the findings of that commission, however silly, be accepted.

The commission agreed on Abraham G. Mills, fourth (not the third, as credited) president of the National League who resigned in a huff when the Union Association jumpers were reinstated and who then devoted his life to the affairs of the Otis Elevator Company; Nicholas E. Young, fifth (not the fourth, as credited) president of the National League whose career had started as a player at Washington in the sixties; Arthur Pue Gorman, a Senator who had played the game in Washington and who later organized teams in that city; Morgan C. Bulkeley, first president of the National League and later Governor and Senator from Connecticut; George Wright, pioneer shortstop and manufacturer of sporting goods; Alfred J. Reach, early second baseman and iron molder who later headed a sporting goods firm also; and James E. Sullivan, a New York citizen who served as president of the Amateur Athletic Union.

This was a distinguished gallery of successful business men, but only one of the seven, Young, had remained in the game more than a few years, and not one of the seven was a historian, antiquarian or scholar.

Gorman died while the commission was presumably making its findings, and of the others apparently only Sullivan and Mills did any work. People in all walks of life were invited to send in any evidence they might have as to the game's origin.

The report of the Mills Commission, which was finally made and dated December 30, 1907, flatly stated that baseball was not an evolution but an invention, that the inventor was Abner Doubleday, later a Major General in the United States Army, that the place at which he invented the game was Cooperstown, New York, and that the time was 1839. On what evidence was this astonishing conclusion based? Well, Mills and Doubleday were members of the same military post in the G.A.R., and, besides, "a circumstantial statement from a reputable gentleman" said so.

Who was this "reputable gentleman" not even dignified by name in the Mills report? He was a mining engineer named Abner Graves, a boyhood friend of the other little Abner, Doubleday, who was dragged into the comic-strip situation. Graves had written to Spalding, telling him that he had been present when Doubleday invented the game, that Doubleday had made the diagram of a diamond in the dirt with a stick and that later this diagram was put on paper.

Although it was Spalding who was responsible for the Graves letter and who stood to gain the most from the commission's findings, apparently he had some misgivings about the decision, for in his autobiography, published in 1910, he suggested that any further discussion of the matter would be unfair to the commission, which was the equivalent of saying, "I don't believe this nonsense any more than you do, but it's done, so let's skip it."

Few people today care to read old baseball guides, and it is likely that the astounding findings of the Mills boys would have died an early death had it not been for the work of those who stood to benefit by the conclusions reached. Naturally, the citizens of Cooperstown, surprised and pleased with the news that baseball had been "invented" there, took an understandable pride in the myth and began to make plans to memorialize the occasion and the man. And later the National League, saddened and puzzled by the slump in attendance that naturally accompanied the great depression of the thirties, saw in the Mills report a chance to ballyhoo the game. Without obtaining a shred of evidence that the Mills report was anything but unverified malarkey, baseball accepted it as gospel and hired a high pressure publicity firm to beat the drums of ballyhoo. Money was raised, the Cooperstown shrine was constructed, and, among those selected for immortality, were a few phonies.

Bruce Cartwright, grandson of Alexander Cartwright, who organized the Knickerbockers of New York in 1845, threw a monkey wrench into the proceedings when he wrote a letter calling attention to the contributions made to the game by his grandfather, and suggesting that his grandsire, not Doubleday, should be the man honored. It is impossible to determine to what degree this embarrassed the Centennial Committee, which placated young Cartwright, or at least tried to, by setting a day aside as "Alexander Cartwright Day." But Doubleday was the recipient of most of the reverence and declared the game's patron saint.

Fortunately for posterity, a man named Robert W. Henderson, author, staff member of the New York Public Library and librarian of the Racquet and Tennis Club of New York, cared enough about the truth of the matter to conduct a scientific investigation of the game's origin, a search such as the Mills Commission had been authorized to make but did not. Henderson's findings are preserved in his "Ball, Bat and Bishop," a work published in 1947 which traces the origin of all games played with a ball.

Henderson has so successfully exploded the theory about the twin misapprehension of Doubleday and Cooperstown that there is no longer any doubt that baseball was known before 1839 at places other than Cooperstown, but if this establishment of truth has endeared him to the people who run baseball, they are slow in expressing their appreciation. Instead, they cling to the tattered banner of the discredited legend and complain testily that people who want the facts set straight are bitter.

It has been demonstrated by Henderson that the name, "baseball," existed as early as 1700; that printed rules for the game, descended from rounders as Chadwick correctly claimed, existed as early as 1834; and that the diamond-shaped field was in existence by 1810.

So then, what did Doubleday do for baseball? As far as can be ascertained, nothing. If Doubleday was present at Cooperstown in 1839 he must have been A.W.O.L. from West Point, and that seems unlikely in view of his subsequently fine military record. Besides, Dr. Oliver Wendell Holmes, perhaps as reputable a person as Abner Graves, stated that baseball was played by students of Harvard, which institution he attended, and Dr. Holmes was a member of the Class of 1829.

Doubleday lived until 1893 and in his last years he wrote voluminously on many subjects, but not once did he make any reference to baseball. For thirty years he was a friend of Abraham G. Mills but certainly never claimed any connection with baseball in conversations with him, for when Mills sought evidence of such a relationship he could not quote Doubleday but had to refer to the flimsy circumstance of the letter from Graves.

Cooperstown is a pleasant place, and baseball's Hall of Fame might as well be in the sylvan Leatherstocking country as anywhere else in the nation. But it must be remembered that Mills rendered his decision because he was pressed for a statement of any kind after his group had "studied" the evidence for three years, and that launched the myth. Mills could have pleaded the ignorance that would have excused him. But what possible excuse is there for baseball people today to ignore Henderson's findings? Only disinterest. It is extremely doubtful if three of the sixteen men who own major league ball clubs today have read Henderson's book. Or two.

But it is only fair to mention that the American League had no part in the myth and has not been a party to the deception. Not one American League official was represented on the Mills Commission.

This neglect of the national game's splendid past by the people who run major league ball may seem incredible, but, remarkably, it is only typical. The official averages of the game's early days are incomplete, and in many instances incorrect. There has never been an official attempt to correct them, which could easily be done. Neither major league has a list of the men who have played on its clubs. Anyone who wished to know if his grandfather played major league baseball and who wrote to the club he suspected might have employed the old gentleman, would receive word, if he were fortunate enough to obtain a reply of any kind, that the information was unavailable, a statement which is palpably false. Today, however, a small group of people is preparing the first alphabetical list of major league players ever compiled, preparing it without the slightest assistance from the major leagues that it will glorify.

Baseball has no central office for its records. Individual statisticians and historians compile their own, and work at cross-purposes, never knowing when their work is being duplicated by others. Such important and fundamental questions as how many games were won by Cy Young, the game's winningest pitcher (the figure is either 510 or 511), have not been officially answered because there is no one with the power to make rulings about such matters. Players are honored on plaques that spell their names incorrectly or give erroneous information concerning their birth data.

This situation was brought about because in the early days of the game the magnates had no time for such frills as public relations departments. For instance, in the first ten years he was at Chicago Charlie Comiskey did not even employ a bookkeeper, relying on his nephew, Charles Fredericks, who served as club secretary, to keep the books in his vest pocket, just as old Pete Browning used to figure his batting average on his cuffs. Other magnates threw away letters received without even considering the result of their discourtesy, but that was a minor offense for men who locked the ballpark office doors in the face of standees clamoring for refunds and who cheated players and each other, as has been shown by documentary evidence.

Today the situation is getting better. A new class of magnates has been born which plays fair with player and public alike. Some, of course, are more progressive than others in this respect. But, in the main, the men who run baseball today are intelligent enough to see the wisdom of honesty and courtesy, and some even go so far as to answer their mail promptly.

However, the sad plight of baseball's archives has not improved. The game has no depository for the lifelong labors of those who love it and compile information about it. Some records are kept at Cooperstown where Ernest J. Lanigan, the greatest statistician in the game's history, is still hard at work. Others exist in the office of J. G. Taylor Spink's The Sporting News at St. Louis, and Spink, carrying on nobly the tradition of his father and uncle, sees to it that his paper prints facts and not fiction.

But what the game needs is a central bureau empowered to rule concerning such matters as how many men Rube Waddell struck out and how many games Cy Young won. If such a system were in force, individual archeologists of the game could obtain official rulings and record books would agree at last.

Judge Landis, in the 24 years he ran baseball, did nothing to provide such a bureau, which would have been a monument to his administration, and whether A. B. Chandler, his successor as Commissioner, will do so remains to be seen.

But in the light of baseball officialdom's neglect of its own proud history, is it any wonder that the Cooperstown myth was created?

Cork, Cobb
and Controversy 17

BASEBALL PLAYERS have long been reactionary in regard to adopting new equipment, with the result that innovations of impedimenta have occurred with great infrequence. When James Alexander Tyng of Harvard appeared on the field with a catcher's mask designed for him in 1875 by Fred W. Thayer, the sensitive young catcher's anxiety to protect his facial topography was greeted with nineteenth century raspberries. His brother receivers donned the mask later with reluctance, but eventually the use of Tyng's tool became universal. The chest protector followed about a decade later, and it too was greeted with guffaws. Players jokingly called the protector a "sheepskin," and thought it very amusing. One of the first major league catchers to wear it was Jack Clements, most prominent of the game's few lefthanded backstops, who started appearing on the field with it in 1884, when he was a member of the Keystone club of the ill-fated Union Association. Paul Hines, outfielder of disputed unassisted triple play fame, apparently was the first gardener to wear sun glasses, and, again, his use of them was considered effete. Today, however, all outfielders protect themselves against solar interference in such a fashion and even infielders, on days when there is a high sky, wear glasses, or at least smear the region under their eyes with lampblack, which gives them the appearance of minstrels.

Even the glove was disdained by the more hardy of the athletic species. Catchers were quite naturally the first to require a glove, then infielders, and finally outfielders and pitchers. But many players were stubbornly opposed to gloves, and John (Bid) McPhee, the great second baseman who played for Cincinnati for 18 years starting in 1882 did not acquire the leather habit until 1896. Up until the time of World War I there were still players who liked to cut the centers out of their gloves.

But baseball's traditional hostility to innovations was absent when Roger Bresnahan of the New York Giants introduced shinguards for catchers in 1907, and there were no cries of derision. Had a lesser player introduced the protection against fouls and flying spikes there would undoubtedly have been derision, but Roger was known as one of the most courageous competitors in his craft, and the shinguard was widely and immediately copied and improved. This device was a natural consequence of the dead ball era, for receivers were tired of the battering their legs received from crazily breaking spitters and other trick deliveries. Bresnahan's new protection brought to completion the standard raiment for a catcher, and poetical players ever since have referred to the mask, protector and shinguards as the "tools of ignorance." Catching was a lot tougher job in Bresnahan's day than it is now.

There was no announcement that the era of the dead ball was ending, but a change set in with the season of 1909. That year cork was added to the rubber center of the baseball, a circumstance that encouraged hitting, and two years later the entire center of the ball was constructed of cork. This gave a resiliency to hits that had previously been lacking, and the crack of the bat became more audible. Such an increase in batting was so noticeable that the Spalding Official Guide conducted a poll of National League players surveying opinion as to whether the ball was too lively, a question which has been asked from time to time ever since.

But before hitting was to come into full flower there was an era in which the art of base-stealing reached its highest development. This epoch extended roughly from 1910 to 1912. Every major league club reached its pinnacle of pelf between 1904 and 1917, with the majority of teams reaching their base-running high midway in that period. The Giants swiped 347 bases in 1911, a record that is unsurpassed, after the Reds had set the mark at 310 in 1910. The entire National League stole on 1691 occasions to set a record in 1910, and the following year American League athletes committed 1810 larcenies. Today teams steal with only one-fifth of that regularity, ample evidence that the stolen base is virtually extinct.

The individual creators of this terror on the paths included National League players for the most part, such greyhounds as Bob Bescher of the Reds, Larry Doyle, Fred Snodgrass and Josh Devore of the Giants, and a young outfielder who began with the Pirates in 1910 and who was to surpass them all, Max Carey. Bescher's mark of 80 steals in 1911 is still the National League high.

But that the American League was not averse to burglary was demonstrated by the man usually acknowledged as the greatest player of all time, Tyrus Raymond Cobb of Detroit. Cobb stole 96 bases in 1915 by way of closing the books on the era, only one of dozens of records he was to splash indelibly on the pastime's annals.

In any history of the game there is little room to dwell on the accomplishments of individual players except as they relate to the general pageant, but to ignore the achievements of Cobb in any book about baseball would be both criminal and foolish and rather like writing of the cough-drop without reference to the Brothers Smith.

Today if a player makes 200 or more hits in a single season, the feat is considered extraordinary. Before Ty Cobb laid down his bat he had hit safely 4, 191 times, which is roughly 200 hits a year for more than two decades. Cobb played in more games, went to bat more times, scored more runs, made more hits, had more total bases and stole more bases than any player who ever lived. His lifetime batting average of .367 is still the game's top challenge.

Cobb played for 24 seasons and led the American League in batting 12 times, nine years in succession starting in 1907. He played through the era of the dead ball and then gleefully met the arrival of the lively pellet, excelling at the game consistently regardless of the style of play in vogue. His swan song was an average of .323 at the age of 42 in 1928. Ty possessed the most fierce competitive instinct that any player ever brought to the diamond, a burning zeal to excel that could not be quenched. Genially hated not only by opponents but by his own team-mates, he seemed driven by a bonfire that blazed in his recesses. Baseball has never seen his like, just as, in a different way, it has never seen another Ruth, and probably never will. Perhaps if he had it to do over Cobb would play the game differently, but that does not appear probable. He was jet-propelled if ever a player was, and that is not the sort of energy that is easily dammed. The roaring avalanche that was Ty Cobb scared the living daylights out of half of his opponents; he was absolutely without fear.

Ty reached the heights when he hit .420 in 1911 and .410 in 1912. No player in history ever put together two years at bat like those, although Rogers Hornsby of the Cardinals hit .424 and .403 in 1924 and 1925.

Naturally, a player of Cobb's disposition was involved in one scrape after another, on and off the field. He was a favorite target for hecklers, most of whom operated behind the comparative anonymity of a grandstand seat. Cobb had fights with fans, players and umpires, and although he did not win them all, he never ran from one.

The dispute of Cobb's that had the most far-reaching consequences was a rhubarb engineered by an inconsequential politician named Lueker at the old Hilltop Park at New York on May 15, 1912, when the Tigers were making their first swing through the East.

Lueker gave Cobb a good razzing all through the early stages of the game, and when the Tigers came to bat in the fourth inning, Tyrus leaped into the stands with both fists flying and gave his tormentor a thorough thrashing. Umpire Silk O'Loughlin thumbed the fiery Bengal from the premises, as is usual in such cases. At this time Ban Johnson was at Boston attending the formal opening of Fenway Park, and when word of the Cobb incident reached him, he suspended Ty indefinitely.

Detroit was to play at Philadelphia the next day, and in a pre-game meeting the Tiger players jointly signed a telegram to Johnson threatening to strike if Ty were not instantly reinstated. That was the sort of a challenge Ban liked, and he ruled that if the players went through with their threatened layoff, the Detroit club would be fined $5,000 for each game that was not played.

This made it necessary for Manager Hughie Jennings to dig up substitute players for the game of May 18 with the Athletics. The two coaches, Joe Sugden and

Jim McGuire volunteered for duty in that game, and Jennings even used himself as a pinch-hitter. For the other positions Hughie induced a group of amateurs from St. Joseph College to wear Detroit uniforms.

The game turned out to be a farce, and the Athletics enjoyed a field day at the expense of their sandlot opposition, winning 24 to 2. But the strange situation attracted a curious crowd of almost 20,000 fans who rocked with laughter as their Athletics pounded out 17 singles, three doubles and six triples, drew seven bases on balls and executed ten successful steals.

Another game, scheduled for May 20, was canceled, and Johnson raced to Philadelphia to read the riot act to the obstinate Bengals. They finally agreed to resume their schedule at Cobb's urging. Each player who signed the telegram to Johnson was fined $100, but Ty himself emerged from the battle with a fine of only $50 and ten days of enforced idleness.

That was the only time in major league history that players actually went through with a strike, although there have been numerous threats to strike. And out of the incident grew another brotherhood of players, the Ball Players' Fraternity of Dave Fultz.

Fultz was an outfielder who had started with the Phillies in 1898 and whose career had ended abruptly in 1905 when he had a collision on the field with Norman (The Tabasco Kid) Elberfeld. A graduate of the Staunton Military Academy and Brown University, he then became an attorney. Considering the rights of players as a result of the Cobb strike he organized a union of major leaguers in the winter of 1912-13, charging them an initiation fee of $5 and annual dues of $18, payable in six installments.

The Fultz movement was inspired in good faith, and its chief purpose was to correct abuses in the clubs' contractual arrangements with players. It succeeded in forcing one important reform on the magnates: it established the principle that no player could be sent to a minor league club of low classification unless intervening clubs had a chance to refuse the athlete's services.

Fultz also called a strike, a general walkout of all players in the majors and minors, but it never came off. This incident came about when Brooklyn sent a first baseman named Clarence Kraft to Nashville although the Newark club (higher than Nashville in minor league hierarchy) claimed him. But when Charlie Ebbets, the Dodger president, repurchased Kraft and allowed him to remain at Newark, the threatened strike was aborted.

Still alive and practicing law in New York City in 1944, Fultz took a dim view of the union movement applied to baseball, in the feeling that most of the rights he fought for had become the property of the players.

"Judge Landis was the best friend the ball-player ever had," said Fultz at this time. "Most of the concessions we wanted in 1912 were given to the players by Landis. I don't think there's much chance for a union in baseball now, because there's no longer any need for one."

The first decade after the peace pact between the two majors might have been featured by a few changes: the gradual change in the ball, the rise of base-stealing, the completion of a player's equipment, and the brief flurry of revolution caused by the Cobb strike. But it was largely a period of building, and an era of great prosperity for the game.

The flinty individuals who operated ball clubs still might have sent their gate receipts to the bank in old leather bags, but their savings were beginning to pile up; and the magnates poured the money back into the game by erecting modern grandstands of steel and concrete as monuments to their economy and vision.

Forbes Field at Pittsburgh and Shibe Park at Philadelphia were both thrown open to the public in 1909. Pittsburgh's plant was a tribute to the acumen of Barney Dreyfuss, who had moved the franchise there from Louisville in 1900. The Philadelphia story was the work of Benjamin F. Shibe, who was the man behind Connie Mack.

Three more great structures improved the real estate of the game in 1910: Comiskey Park at Chicago, Griffith Stadium at Washington, and League Park at Cleveland. Comiskey's place was a "dream park," perhaps the finest field ever built from the standpoint of the player, but today it reclines in a wretched slum, as the world has moved around it.

A fire destroyed the old wooden stands at the Polo Grounds in April, 1911, but President John T. Brush immediately wired engineers and the modern plant on Coogan's Bluff was built that summer. And then, in 1912, Redland Field in Cincinnati, Navin Field in Detroit and Fenway Park in Boston were all opened. Two of these places were to change their names to publicize new owners later, Navin Field becoming Briggs Stadium and Redland Field undergoing a rather prosaic metamorphosis to Crosley Field.

Ebbets Field opened its gates to the frenzied citizenry of Flatbush in 1913; Wrigley Field admitted its first horde of grateful gum-chewers on Chicago's north side in 1914; and Braves Field began to admit its cultured clientele in 1915. Major league properties came to fruition with the erection of mammoth Yankee Stadium across the Harlem from the Giants in 1923; and Cleveland's municipal and munificent oval, which replaced League Park, in 1932.

The only park not referred to is Sportman's at St. Louis, occupied today by the Browns and Cardinals. Those earlier Browns, representing St. Louis when the National League was organized, played on this very site, where Grand and Dodier avenues now intersect. Both Browns and Cardinals have moved around a bit in the intervening years, but are now back where they started, and Howard Pollet now works his lefthanded magic off the same slab, roughly speaking, that George Washington Bradley employed to mystify the mustached enemy with his underhanded trickery in 1876.

Feud with the Feds 18

THE FEDERAL League war, baseball's fifth excursion into the possibilities of annihilation, was the Brotherhood scrap all over again but with reverse English. Whereas the initiative for John Montgomery Ward's unfortunate uprising of 1890 had come from malcontent players who sought capital, the Federal feud was caused by capitalists who sought players. Observing year after year that baseball had become a profitable business, many men of wealth, excluded from the monopolistic gravy by the National Agreement, wanted to get in on the profits, and they assumed that there was room for a third major league. It was the third such erroneous assumption in baseball history, because what the Federals did not know was that interest in baseball was actually declining. Public enthusiasm started to slacken in 1910 for reasons that were not quite clear. The trend was gradual but distinct, and each of the succeeding years proved less profitable than its immediate predecessor. The Federal League crowd picked the worst possible time to launch a third major, but when they proceeded with their plans, the magnates of the National and American conveniently laid the blame for all their troubles at the door of the Feds, overlooking the real causes.

The reasons for the slump in public response to the game were numerous and complex. Baseball had become big business, and those gigantic new grandstands that were built throughout the land offered visible proof that the game was profitable. But they were built with profits that accrued before the decline set in. And the construction of all those parks focused attention on the fact that baseball was a business, perhaps more so than it was a sport. For the first time the public came to recognize it as a business, and that fact alone caused a depression in interest. Baseball also discovered that new amusements had been invented or old ones had so changed in nature that they would now compete as rivals, such things as the movies, the automobile and, of all things, the motorcycle, and such a sport as golf, which had previously been the monopoly of the enfeebled or infirm. There was also the nuisance competition of newspaper scoreboards on the streets and ticker service to saloons and poolrooms.

Baseball had always been its best advertisement, and not until young people discovered that the automobile (preferably the back seat) and the movies (preferably the back row) afforded tremendous and exotic possibilities for amusement did baseball find it necessary openly to compete with whatever rivals existed and begin the task of obtaining good public relations.

But the Feds ignored the signs of the times and rallied enough capital to give organized ball a two-year headache of migraine intensity that was finally alleviated, thanks to the nepenthe of arbitration, at a cost of perhaps five million dollars.

The experiment began in an unassuming way with the formation in 1912 of a minor loop known as the United States League. This project was launched at Reading, Pennsylvania, but included in its orbit franchises from such cities as New York, Washington and Pittsburgh. The league blew up in early June of that year, but the Pittsburgh team had made some money and its owner, W. J. McCullough, entered the franchise in a new league called the Federal for 1913. John T. Powers was the first president of the Federal, which was by no means a major in that first year of its existence, although some very famous baseball personalities were included in its ranks. Cy Young, for instance, managed Cleveland and finished second, and two other former major league pitchers, Bill Phillips and Chick Fraser, piloted teams. Phillips won the pennant with his Indianapolis entry, and Fraser bossed the St. Louis club to third place in the six-club standings.

The major league aspirations of the circuit became known with the election of James A. Gilmore to the presidency in September, 1913. Gilmore had made his fortune in the stationery business, but he assured himself of practical baseball help by hiring as league secretary Lloyd Rickart, who had been with the St. Louis Browns in a similar capacity for years.

Gilmore was acquainted with other men of wealth who joined in the fun, such well-heeled backers as Charles Weeghman, a Chicago restaurateur, and Robert Boyd Ward, a self-raising product of the bakery business who entered the picture at Brooklyn. The veteran baseball historian, Fred Lieb, has pointed out that baseball was spared its worst possible nickname when Ward was prevailed upon not to call his team the Tip-Tops, which was the commercial name for a certain type of Ward's bread, although the name which finally was selected for the Brooklyn Federals, the Brookfeds, was possibly the most preposterous appellation ever given a club, an incident which the historians of bizarre Brooklyn baseball have largely ignored.

The strategy used by Gilmore, Ward and Company was to lure established stars with greenbacks, a method that had been found satisfactory in the past. When the Federals proved to the players that they had the money, immediate warfare was inaugurated.

The first player to jump was Joe Tinker, veteran shortstop who had managed the Reds in 1913 but who had been sold at the season's close to Brooklyn. When Tinker failed to induce Garry Herrmann, his club president, to part with a slice of Brooklyn's purchase money, he leaped to the Federal camp, taking over the management of a team picturesquely known as the Chicago Whales.

Then Hal Chase, king of first basemen, jumped from the White Sox to the Buffalo Federals, saying that if the ten-day clause in his contract were just, it should work both ways, and consequently he was terminating his agreement with Chicago by giving his ten days' notice. This case landed in court and was decided in Chase's favor, which made magnates understandably leery of courts, although in the next two years they were to call upon them frequently for injunctions restraining their defaulting players.

With Tinker and Chase in the Federal camp the avalanche began rolling in earnest, sweeping along with it such noted virtuosos of the diamond as Mordecai Brown, Russell Ford, Danny Murphy, George (Chief) Johnson, Mickey Doolan, Jack Quinn, Ward Miller, Armando Marsans and Otto Knabe.

Even Walter Johnson, the great Washington pitcher, agreed to Federal terms but was finally prevented from making the leap when his club owner, Clark Griffith, managed to meet the competition by increasing his stipend.

The achievement of Jim Gilmore in preparing his Federal League for the 1914 season was one of the most remarkable executive jobs ever witnessed by the game, but because he and his brainchild were outlaws they have never received proper credit for it. Eight new ball parks were constructed in a period of three months, and the capital flowed so freely that the league went through its schedule without a single shift in franchises. A card of 154 games was arranged, an exact duplicate of the major league slate, and the Federal staged a thrilling race, Indianapolis nosing out Chicago by a margin of a game and one-half. Only 25 games separated the eight clubs. Gilmore had staked everything on his faith that there was room for a third major, a question on which the press and public were sharply divided.

When the Indianapolis champions were moved to Newark in 1915 for the Feds' second season, Harry Sinclair, not yet smeared with the oil of Teapot Dome, took over as the team's president. Sinclair, of course, had all sorts of money, and before long he was paying the bills at Kansas City and Buffalo in addition to Newark. More stars fell from the orthodox heavens, players such as Chief Bender and Eddie Plank of the Athletics, Leslie Mann, Ed Konetchy and Mike Mowrey.

Before the 1915 season got under way the Federals filed suit in the United States District Court at Chicago under the Sherman Anti-Trust Act, directing action against all major league teams, and charging that the National Agreement was an illegal instrument, asking that any acts of the National Commission be declared void, declaring that the baseball contracts employed by the National and American were no good and ordering organized baseball to dismiss all court litigation against its players.

That was a whopping blow to the game, and threatened to topple baseball's structure once and for all. The case was heard by Judge Kenesaw Mountain Landis, and what his decision was to be was the $64 question of 1915. Actually, the decision was never made, for peace between the leagues was declared before Landis announced his opinion. There is reason to suspect that this is exactly what Landis hoped would happen; all during 1915 he reserved judgment despite all kinds of pressure, and it is logical to deduce that he hesitated because he hoped to avoid a decision that would have wrecked the game. At least when Landis became the Commissioner of Baseball he showed a sympathy for the player and an antipathy for the contract under which he worked that indicated how his sentiments ran.

The Federal League pennant race of 1915 was even more extraordinary than the first one, only 16 games separating the first seven teams, with Baltimore being a hopeless tailender. Chicago, which won one game less and lost one less than St. Louis, was awarded the championship by a single percentage point. And Pittsburgh, in third place, was only one game behind.

By this time Organized Ball was really in a sweat. And when Harry Sinclair announced that he was going to move the Newark team to New York in 1916, the National and American league nabobs began thinking in terms of compromise. Meetings between executives of the two leagues and the Federals took place as early as October, 1915, at the time of the world series between the Phillies and Red Sox. And they continued without interruption after that.

A secret meeting was held at the Elks Club in New York on December 15, 1915, with John K. Tener, president of the National League, and a group of his club owners meeting with Jim Gilmore. The American League was not represented at this session, but Barney Dreyfuss, the Pittsburgh chieftain, was dispatched to tell Ban Johnson the terms on which the Feds would call it quits. Johnson had always opposed the Federals more sternly than had the National League, and he wanted to walk out on the peace agreement rather than assume

$385,000 worth of Federal League player contracts, the chief barrier to peace.

But the Feds insisted that their contracts with the players be honored. More than 200 athletes were in the Federal camp, and 48 had ironclad contracts through 1916 and 36 of these had inked documents which extended through 1917.

The final settlement was worked out in a meeting at Cincinnati on December 22. By the terms of the treaty the Ward interests were to get annual payments of $20,000 for twenty years, Sinclair was to receive $10,000 annually for ten years, and Pittsburgh, $10,000 for five years. Organized baseball also acquired the Federal ball parks in Newark and Brooklyn. By dropping all claims to disputed players, the National and American moguls were spared the embarrassment of proving their contracts were sacrosanct in court, and the Fed players were thrown on the open market.

The Giants paid $35,000 for Outfielder Benny Kauff, called the Ty Cobb of the Feds. Kauff led the outlaw circuit in batting during both years of its existence, with a mark of .366 for Indianapolis in 1914 and .344 for Brooklyn in 1915. The New York Americans laid down $22,500 on the counter for Infielder Lee Magee. But both Kauff and Magee were destined to have their careers terminate under a cloud, and it developed that the greatest player to come from the Feds was Outfielder Edd Roush, a remarkable player for fifteen years to come and one whose purchase was arranged by the Giants for only a fraction of that expended for Kauff. It was also in the Federal League that Bill McKechnie, later an extremely able manager for numerous teams, first piloted a club. He handled the reins for Sinclair's outlaws at Newark.

It is likely that the Federal war would have continued its internecine course for another costly year had it not been for the death of Robert Ward, who expired of rheumatism at his New Rochelle, New York estate, October 18, 1915. With Ward died the Federal dream: the theory that there was room for a third major. He was the richest and the most devoted of the Fed magnates; he had agreed to split with Sinclair the cost of moving the Newark franchise to New York in 1916. His death placed the burden upon Sinclair, but when the time came to make the move, peace appeared to be the better course.

The Federals failed for various reasons, but principally because the backers were inexperienced, and the imminence of World War I made them curtail their activity.

And although the strife temporarily weakened the general structure of the game, two major league franchises were considerably helped. Charles Weeghman, who had owned the Chicago Whales, was permitted to acquire the Chicago franchise of the National League. It was Weeghman who built the park on Chicago's north side which is now Wrigley Field. Phil DeCatesby Ball, an ice dealer who had operated the St. Louis Feds, was likewise allowed to enter the majors, as generalissimo of the American League Browns. Weeghman and Ball, especially the latter, were destined to lend executive vigor to the game, and baseball was better off for their presence.

Except for the guerrilla warfare in Mexico in 1946 baseball has known no battles since the Federal invasion. With real estate properties as valuable as they are today, it is inconceivable that an outlaw rival of the National and American leagues could now be formed. Whatever strife baseball suffers in the future will be civil, a disturbance in its own ranks. But baseball will recover as it always has.

Baseball and
World War I

THE FEDERAL League war began appropriately enough in 1914, a year of upheaval throughout the world, and the virus of war infection suffered by baseball was only a fraction of the turmoil brought to a head when Archduke Francis Ferdinand of Austria-Hungary and his wife, Countess Sophie Chotek, were slain at Sarajevo by Gavrillo Princip. This was to be the first war engaged in by the United States which hurt baseball to any great degree. The Civil War had actually helped the growth of the game, for it was in Union Army camps that baseball was introduced to numerous young men who had never before participated in or seen the sport. The Spanish-American War hit baseball a glancing blow at the gate, but that was all. But World War I, and, later, to a much greater extent, World War II, were to disrupt baseball seriously, and force magnates to the conviction that although they might survive any intra-mural struggle, they well might not survive if the nations of the planet persisted in blowing each other up.

There were other baseball happenings of 1914 aside from the Federal League trouble that were revolutionary in character, notably the subversive activity of the Boston Braves. For three years prior to 1914 the National League pennant had been a monopoly of the Giants, with John McGraw and his club doing about as they pleased. The Braves, ugly ducklings of the circuit, had finished at the absolute bottom four years in a row starting in 1909 and had climbed to fifth in 1913. But in 1914 they slumped back to eighth early in the year, winning only four of their first 22 games. They were still last on July 19, but when they twice defeated the Reds on that day, the cellar door opened and the strangest ascent in baseball began. So closely packed was the National League field in 1914 that three days after vacating the cellar tenement, Boston found itself fourth, and by the time August was one-third gone, the Braves were second, trailing only the Giants, who were gunning for their fourth consecutive flag.

George Stallings, a superstitious tyrant of the dugouts who drove his charges as if they were cattle and whose nervous will to win made him fly into violent rages, has been hailed as the Miracle Man of the game because that Boston team of his eventually beat out the Giants and won the bunting. But it was not so much the working of a miracle as it was the use of pluck by a team of game opportunists. The Braves were not great individually, but as a group they fought for every game that one brief summer in a happy demonstration that, on occasion, effort could compensate for the lack of greatness. Boston had three brilliant pitchers that year in Dick Rudolph, George Tyler and Bill James, and an inspirational catcher in Hank Gowdy; but the player who possibly contributed the most was the veteran second baseman, Johnny Evers, middle man of the double play triumvirate. Evers served as Stallings' captain, and he was still the whining, jaw-jutting ball of fire that he had been for Chicago.

Upset though it was, the achievement of the Braves in winning the flag race was not half so impressive as their four straight world series triumphs over Connie Mack's Athletics. Dominating the American League as the Giants did the National, the A's won pennants in 1910, 1911, 1913 and 1914, being nosed out by the Red Sox in 1912. But that apparently invincible Athletic team with its $100,000 infield of John (Stuffy) McGinnis, Eddie Collins, Jack Barry and J. Franklin (Home Run) Baker and such stout pitchers as Charles (Chief) Bender, Eddie Plank and Jack Coombs was humiliated four times running by the incredible Braves, who used tactics similar to those employed by the old Orioles in making certain their destiny was fastened. So distraught was Connie Mack by the setbacks that in the winter following, largely because the residents of Philadelphia no longer supported his formerly invincible nine, he completely broke up the squad, selling his stars to rival clubs. In 1915 the Athletics employed 56 different players, more than any team has ever used in a season, but most of them were rank amateurs and the A's almost dropped out of the American League, losing 109 games compared with 53 in 1914 and finishing eighth for the first of seven successive seasons in that abyss.

There were other disturbances in the baseball bedrock during the years that World War I provided an infinitely more important upheaval for the nation to consider, tremors that were recorded in the annual seismographs of the official averages. In 1915 the Phillies finished first in the National League for the only time in their history, and the Giants ended up last, but McGraw's club won 69 games and lost 83 for a percentage of .454, the highest figure ever attained by a tailender. Then, in 1916, the Giants defied all laws of gravitation by finishing fourth despite two of the most remarkable winning streaks in baseball history. Early in the campaign McGraw's forces won 17 straight tilts on the road, a record for consecutive wins in hostile territory, and in September the team took 26 in a row, all of them at home, the greatest accumulation of successive victories in the game's annals.

But all of these diamond doings were dwarfed by the struggle for world supremacy. The game had recovered quickly from the Federal League dispute, more quickly than it had after any previous disturbance in its own ranks. But a world war was something new, and the men who ran ball clubs felt that if the United States should be drawn into the conflict, baseball would become only a memory. However, when Congress declared, on April 6, 1917, that this nation was at war with Germany and her satellites, baseball went right on as usual. Major league attendance held up fairly well, and the minor circuits which abandoned play did so because of the strangest of possible reasons, prosperity. Harvest hands and city workers were all too busy making money because of the war to take in ball games.

By 1918, though, the major leagues were in for an unpleasant, unprofitable and unsatisfactory season, mostly due to the "business as usual" policies of the magnates. When Provost Marshal General Crowder issued his "work or fight" order in June, an edict devised to force all men of draft age out of non-essential employment, exceptions were made in the cases of opera singers, actors and motion picture workers, it being held that they provided necessary amusement. Baseball was not made an exception because the magnates did not even bother to present their case in person.

Ball players were not slackers as a general rule, despite the publicity given to a few who were. Hank Gowdy, the Boston catcher, was the first to enlist, and he was followed by a host of others. Before the Armistice about 250 major league players were in the

Army or Navy, 56 per cent, of the active American League athletes and 63 per cent, of the National hirelings. Captain Eddie Grant of the Giants fell at the head of his battalion in the Argonne while acting-major on a particularly dangerous volunteer mission. There is a monument to his sacrifice at the Polo Grounds today. Many others were wounded or gassed. And even such overage baseball personages as Branch Rickey and Jack Hendricks managed to get overseas in one capacity or another. In addition, the Clark Griffith ball and bat fund, which supplied baseball equipment for teams in the armed forces, shipped thousands and thousands of dollars' worth of toggery around the world. Baseball's war record was as good as that of any other industry.

Naturally, though, the "work or fight" order caused demoralization. Cries of "Why ain't you in the Army?" began to be heard from the ignorant occupants of grandstand perches, and though in some instances it might have been a good question, in the main it was impertinent.

Although a few players jumped into shipyards or nitrate plants, most of the athletes remained with their teams, waiting to see how the "work or fight" decree applied to them. Draft boards issued conflicting orders to players, some declaring them engaged in essential work and others warning that baseball was non-essential.

Finally, a committee of magnates did call on the War Department to have their industry classified, and Secretary of War Newton D. Baker told the club owners they had better wind up the season by September 1, with two weeks of grace in which to play the world series. The officials then decided to end the campaign in both majors with double-headers on September 2. All clubs ended the season in that fashion except the

Cleveland Indians, who took the September 1 date literally and failed to show up for their final twin bill with the Browns.

As if the season were not gloomy enough, the National Commission was almost wrecked because of a player dispute which threatened the structure of the entire game. The player in question was Scott Perry, whose name suggests polar exploration but who was instead a pitcher and a cause célèbre if baseball ever had one. Perry pitched for Atlanta in 1916 and 1917, and in the latter year he was sold to the Boston Braves, a transaction which provided that he be given a thirty-day trial. But he did no pitching at all in nineteen days with the Braves, and this inactivity disgusted him so that he jumped the club and finished out the year in an outlaw circuit. Atlanta kept after the Braves to send $2,000 for Perry's services, and though the National Commission disallowed this claim, it was ruled that Boston pay Atlanta $500 and retain the privilege of obtaining title to Perry by paying the remaining $1,500. Perry, meanwhile, remained on the ineligible list of the Atlanta club.

Knowing nothing about this arrangement, Connie Mack, manager of the Athletics, signed Perry in 1918 with Atlanta's permission, and the young pitcher became an instant sensation, winning 21 and losing 19 for the tail-end Athletics. The Braves then entered a claim for Perry with the National Commission, which ruled that the pitcher belonged properly to Boston, the verdict being a split one in which Ban Johnson dissented. Rather than lose the pitcher the Athletics went to court and obtained a restraining order that kept Perry with the A's. This was a sensational development because it was the first time that any club defied the authority of the Commission. John K. Tener, president of the National League, was so horrified by developments that he resigned from the Commission and also quit his job as league president, being replaced by John Heydler, who had filled in during a similar emergency in 1909 following the suicide of Harry C. Pulliam.

With Heydler on the job a compromise was worked out in which the Athletics withdrew their injunction, paid Boston $2,500 and retained title to Perry.

The abbreviated and dismal season concluded with the playing of the world series between the Red Sox and Cubs during the first week of September. Three games were scheduled in each city and the Red Sox won four of the six, with Carl Mays and Babe Ruth each winning two verdicts. For the first time it was decided that first division clubs in both the National and American leagues would share the receipts, a move so resented by athletes on the two pennant-winners that a strike almost took place.

Because of reduced admission prices the receipts were low enough as it was, and the players on the Red Sox and Cubs figured they were entitled to whatever they drew at the gate. Four of the games had already been played before the players were able to express their demands to the National Commission at the Copley Plaza Hotel in Boston.

The players demanded that each performer on the winning team receive at least $1,500 and each losing player $1,000 before taking the field for the fifth game. Garry Herrmann, chairman of the Commission, informed the players that he would reply to their demands before game time, but then later sent word that the decision would be delayed until after the contest. Thousands of fans were streaming through the gates, but the players, angered by Herrmann's indecision, sat morosely in their clubhouses in street clothes.

When time for the game arrived and word of the threatened strike had spread to the restless crowd, the Commission held an informal meeting under the stands, then both Johnson and Herrmann spoke to the recalcitrants, telling them they were lucky there was any series at all. Then Harry Hooper, Red Sox outfielder who seemed to be the spokesman for the strikers, suggested that the entire receipts of the series be donated to the Red Cross. This horrifying suggestion was "not practical," the magnates said.

Finally, rather than disappoint the crowd which contained more than a sprinkling of war veterans, the players took the field and completed the series. Each member of the Red Sox drew $1,102.51 as his winning share, and each losing Bruin snared $671.09. The players then donated ten per cent, of their take to war charities.

Baseball:
Out of Commission 20

THE CLUMSY bungling of the Scott Perry case, the stupid handling of the abortive world series strike and the inability of the game's leaders to make clear baseball's role in World War I were only a few of the ample demonstrations that the game had outgrown the awkward, three-man National Commission. As a form of government it was now archaic, a remnant of the felicitous period that followed the original peace between the major leagues. It might have been expected that Garry Herrmann, being the president of the Cincinnati club, would have sided with his league president in most of the disputed decisions the Commission made. Instead of that Garry usually took the part of Ban Johnson, his convivial crony in the activities of leisure. As a consequence, when opposition to Herrmann and the Commission came, it emanated from John Heydler, the new National League president.

Heydler, a former government printer, had served the game long and well. He acted as secretary under Nick Young and Harry Pulliam, before filling out the 1909 season as president after Pulliam's suicide in July of that year. Then he went back to his secretary post under two more presidents, Thomas J. Lynch, a former umpire who was at the helm for four years starting in 1910, and John K. Tener, who lasted for six years until the Perry case made him quit in a huff, just as

Abraham G. Mills had walked out after the Onions were reinstated in 1885.

Heydler correctly recognized that baseball could not be run successfully by men who had a partisan interest in the game. Johnson was strictly an American League man, just as the National League president, whoever it might be at the moment, would be attached to his own circuit. And Herrmann, being of human clay, was motivated by what would help Cincinnati. Heydler thought that a one-man Commission, with that one man having a neutral interest in the game, would be infinitely better.

There were other events that led to the dissolution of the old Commission. One of the most thorny problems was the George Sisler case, which was decided in 1915, but which had repercussions long afterward. Sisler, a 17-year-old high school pitcher in Ohio, signed with Akron of the OhioPennsylvania League but never reported, being induced to enter the University of Michigan. When he graduated at Ann Arbor in 1915, he joined the St. Louis Browns, managed by Branch Rickey, a former University of Michigan coach. All the time Sisler was at Michigan, the Akron officials, owning his contract, wondered what to do with it. First they sold it to Columbus of the American Association, and then Columbus turned around and peddled the document to Barney Dreyfuss, president of the Pittsburgh Pirates. So brilliant was Sisler's play at Michigan that Dreyfuss figured he had made the discovery of all time, but by this time Sisler reported to the Browns. Later he was to move to first base and become one of the most shining performers of all time, both at bat and in the field, until illness cut him down at the peak of his career.

The National Commission handled the Sisler case as might have been expected, with Johnson declaring him the property of the Browns, Tener saying that he should be awarded to Dreyfuss, and Herrmann going along, as usual, with Johnson. Dreyfuss never forgot that decision and began a one-man attack on the Commission form of government that was eventually to end in the election of Judge Landis. So Dreyfuss was even before Heydler in the attempt to oust Herrmann. Oddly enough, George Sisler today, thirty-five years after the decision, still belongs to Rickey, serving the Brooklyn Dodgers in the capacity of scout.

It is popularly believed that Kenesaw Mountain Landis came into baseball because the game was in such disfavor following the crooked work of the Chicago White Sox in the 1919 world series that the magnates cried out for leadership, but actually the old Commission was on its way out long before word of the White Sox scandal spread. Herrmann did manage to last out the 1919 season as Commissioner because Ban Johnson went to bat for him, but when Ban lost the support of his own league the following year and was no longer able to help Garry, the latter's goose was definitely cooked.

There were two reasons why Johnson became unpopular in the circuit he had founded and had run so well when he was in his prime. The first was a dispute with Charlie Comiskey, the White Sox owner, over the disposition of Pitcher Jack Quinn, a hurler jointly claimed by the White Sox and Yankees and awarded by Johnson to the latter club. Bosom friends for years and co-founders of the American, drinking partners from the days when they sat together as young men at Cincinnati in the nineties and dreamed of a rival to the National League, Comiskey and Johnson finally parted company.

The second reason for Johnson's decline was his decision in the case of another pitcher, Carl Mays, a submarine flinger whose entire baseball life was tinged with unpleasantness of one kind or another. Mays, while pitching for the Boston Red Sox in 1919, walked off the field one day and said he would never again throw a ball in the interests of that club. While he was absent from the team, Boston sold him to the Yankees for $40,000 and two players. Johnson immediately suspended Mays and declared the transaction invalid, saying that Carl would have to be reinstated by the Red Sox before any such trade could be made. But the Yankees, employing the device Connie Mack had found effective in the Scott Perry case, got an injunction to restrain Johnson from interfering, and Mays continued to pitch successfully in a New York uniform. This was a bitter blow to Ban's pride, and conclusive proof that he had lost control of his league.

The first rumors that Landis might become the ruling head of the game were drifting about in 1920, although he had earlier been mentioned as a possibility. Magnates interpreted his action in the Federal League lawsuit, when he sat on the case like an angry hen hatching eggs in silence, to mean that he approved of organized baseball's structure and meant to protect it. How wrong they were! Heydler was one of the first to stump openly for Landis, and another who early recognized the services of Landis to the game was Taylor Spink, the astute publisher of The Sporting News. But Johnson himself, jealous of losing authority and perhaps realizing that a league president would become a mere rubber stamp under the proposed set-up, was never a Landis man.

Before the Judge was selected, other candidates were rumored ready for the position, many of them men who had made military reputations in the war; and so solid a citizen as William Howard Taft was once reported agreeable to taking on the chore of being baseball's czar.

Herrmann was helpless with Heydler, Dreyfuss and Comiskey all against him, and he was eventually eased out prior to the 1920 season. That year baseball existed with no government at all, save such as supplied by the league presidents, a situation everyone agreed was impossible.

When the eight members of the Chicago White Sox attained lifelong ignominy by changing the hue of their hose to black, baseball entered upon its darkest hour. Public knowledge of the scandal was instantaneous when the players were called before a Chicago Grand Jury and asked to explain their peculiar actions in the world series against the Reds the year before. Although Hal Chase, a famous first baseman, had been exonerated of crooked play by Heydler in 1919, found innocent only because the principal witness against Chase, Christy Mathewson, was still overseas with the AEF, the Black Sox tragedy was the first inkling of crooked work in the baseball vineyards since the four Louisville crooks were blacklisted more than forty years before. So well had Bill Hulbert established the National League tradition of honest play, and so well had Ban Johnson applied to the American League the Hulbert theory that the public at large, though frequently disgusted with the stupidity of baseball management, at least knew that the game was as honest as a clock. Then came the Black Sox.

The sordid story of the 1919 world series has frequently seen print, but fact and fancy have been so confused that today it still is not known what actually took place. The White Sox of that year were one of baseball's truly great clubs, with such stars as Joe Jackson, Eddie Collins, Oscar (Hap) Felsch, Ray Schalk, Chick Gandil, Swede Risberg, Buck Weaver,

Eddie Cicotte, Dicky Kerr and Claude Williams. The Reds, on the other hand, were just a run-of-the-mine team that clicked inexplicably for one brief summer, as the Braves had in 1914 or as the Washington Senators would in 1933. And yet, at the time the series took place, the gamblers, incredibly, established Cincinnati as favorite.

There were a few people who suspected that the series was rigged even while the games were in progress; but because this suspicion surrounded every sports event of importance, scant attention was paid to the allegation then. There were always rumors of a conspiracy whenever anything was at stake, but so well had baseball, over a period of years, avoided any connection with the gambler that little credence was ever given to alarmists who scented crooked work.

But eight Chicago players were named in the indictments: Jackson, Cicotte, Risberg, Williams, Gandil, Weaver, Felsch and Fred McMullin, the first seven of whom were regulars, Cicotte and Williams being pitchers. The trial dragged on; appeals were made; witnesses died; papers were stolen. It was impossible to prove anything. Some of the players confessed their complicity and then repudiated their confessions. Witnesses who were subpoenaed fled the country.

Baseball had no ruling body in 1920, the year in which the scandal broke, and the game reached its lowest estate in the weeks that followed. The magnates knew at last that they must clean house as soon as possible and select a strong man of unimpeachable integrity to run their show.

Albert D. Lasker, whose only connection with baseball came about because he was a minor stockholder in the Cubs, then proposed a plan of baseball government that found favor with the pastime's high officials. All the Lasker plan provided for was a three-man Commission of responsible public citizens without any partisan interest in baseball; a board whose qualifications would include integrity but not practical baseball experience. Ban Johnson immediately sensed the folly of having baseball run by outsiders, but Heydler and others thought the Lasker idea was sound.

Baseball proceeded to carry out the idea of the Lasker plan without Johnson's backing, as a majority of the American League officials went along with the idea, but somewhere along the line the three-man Commission proposal was dropped, and one strong Commissioner substituted. It was inevitable that one of the first names to occur to the magnates was that of Judge Landis, and when the eminent jurist was asked whether he would accept the role of baseball's czar, he agreed provided that he should have complete control of the game. So anxious were the club owners to regain public sympathy that they agreed to this policing, yielding all their powers to Landis, who took over as Commissioner on November 12, 1920.

Strangely, Landis did nothing about the White Sox players except to state that regardless of what the jury found, he would never permit them to return to baseball. The fight to convict the Black Sox was largely the work of Ban Johnson, who labored tirelessly to track down witnesses and make the accusations stick. Eventually, all the players were freed by the court, but none has ever been reinstated. Apparently Landis felt that this was all water over the dam, and that nothing could be gained by ex post facto investigations. But if he neglected incidents of the past, he scrupulously probed conditions that were present, and his regime was to be marked by one investigation after another.

The selection of Landis was the final step in the evolution of baseball government. First there was Hulbert, who provided a strong government in one league. Then, after three wars, came Johnson, who firmly established the principle of two rival leagues. It remained for Landis to supervise both circuits and give neutral counsel and leadership. The emergence of Landis also meant that league presidents no longer need be strong men, but merely efficient chief clerks, whose principal duties included the mapping of schedules and the supervision of umpires. Johnson, who completely overshadowed the various National League personages who contended with him during his lifetime, went into decline when Landis took over. Ban did not yet know it, but he was through.

Landis was more than a symbol, the shaggy, white-haired symbol of justice, pounding a gavel into his lean hand and puckering up his lips behind the bench: Landis was the actual instrument of benevolent despotism, and the game, which had been out of commission, now had its Commissioner.

The Sultan
and The Czar   21

"Will there ever be another Ruth? Don't be silly! Oh, sure, somebody may come along some day who will hit more than 60 home runs in a season or more than 114 in a career, but that won't make him another Ruth. The Bambino's appeal was to the emotions. Don't tell me about Ruth; I've seen what he did to people! I've seen them, fans, driving miles in open wagons through the prairies of Oklahoma to see him in exhibition games as we headed north in the spring. I've seen them: kids, men, women, worshippers all, hoping to get his famous name on a torn, dirty piece of paper, or hoping for a grunt of recognition when they said, ʿH'ya, Babe' He never let them down; not once! He was the greatest crowd pleaser of them all! It wasn't so much that he hit home runs, it was how he hit them and the circumstances under which he hit them. Another Ruth? Never!"

Waite Hoyt.

IT IS difficult to imagine two men more dissimilar than George Herman Ruth and Kenesaw Mountain Landis, and yet, working in entirely different ways, they jointly elevated the game from the abyss of public contempt into which it had been mired by the nefarious work of the Black Sox. The recovery of baseball was electric and almost immediate, and it happened because of the carnal Ruth and the intellectual Landis.

Ruth had been spawned on the Baltimore waterfront of the nineties, a favorite haunt for broken down ball players who, unequipped for any other legitimate occupation, sought, or at least found the gutter when their careers were closed. There's no use naming names: there were many of them. They lounged in the poolrooms and tattoo parlors, ate foul bowls of chili in the one-armed lunchrooms, spent the occasional times of their lives in the saloons and foraged through garbage cans on the corners for whatever could be salvaged. And many of them, in their hopeless quest to consume each skid-row day, must have stumbled over a tough, dirty, brawling street arab who was starting life as they were ending it, a kid named George Ruth.

Ruth was not, as popular legend has it, an orphan. At least his father lived long enough to see him pitch for the Boston Red Sox. But at an early age George was removed from the atmosphere of the saloon where his father tended bar and placed in St. Mary's Industrial School, a semi-reform institution that provided a home for boys that was better than any they had ever known. The protective influence of St. Mary's almost certainly saved Ruth from becoming a juvenile delinquent, and also provided him with an opportunity to play baseball on a regular team.

At first he was a catcher, but he threw the ball so hard, it was inevitable that he should end up as a pitcher, which is a more normal position for a left-hander anyway. It was as a pitcher that he was recommended to the Baltimore team, with which club he started his professional career in 1914. It was a coach at Baltimore, a man named Steiman, who gave to Ruth the nickname of Babe, saying, "Well, here's Jack Dunn's newest babe now."

Jack Dunn, owner of the Baltimore club, of course did not know that Ruth was to become the most exciting player in all history. But the young southpaw did look so good that he sold him to his friend, Joe Lannin, the owner of the Boston Red Sox, almost immediately.

Ruth hit his first major league home run off Jack Warhop of the Yankees at New York, May 6, 1915. He was to hit three more that year, another three in 1916, and only two in 1917. The round-tripper business started in earnest in 1918 when he clouted 11, and roared to a crescendo in 1919 when he attracted national attention by thumping out 29. It was then that the game's researchers started leafing through the record books to see what had previously been done in the home run line. They discovered that Ed Williamson of the Chicago White Stockings blasted 27 in 1884, the previous major league record. They also found that Perry Werden of Minneapolis smashed 45 in 1895 in the Western League, a record achievement in the minors. Ruth surpassed Werden when he connected for 54 in 1920.

But oddly enough, the home run, until Ruth, had not been particularly popular. This attitude was due in large measure to Henry Chadwick, so called father of baseball, who continually belittled home runs in the annuAl Spalding guide he edited. Listen to what Chadwick had to say about homers in 1891:

"What is the cost of a home run in baseball and what attractive feature does it add to the game compared with the chances for fielding skill which it deprives the fielder of? Those are pertinent questions in these days (sic) of slugging for home runs with a lively ball to bat with. A home run is made at the cost, to the batsman, of a run of 120 yards at his topmost speed, which involves an expenditure of muscular power needing a half hour rest to recuperate from such a violent strain upon a man's physical powers. Just think of the monotony of a game marked by a series of home runs in each inning."

Father Chadwick may not have liked the home run, but the fans responded to Ruth with an enthusiasm that no previous player, even King Kelly, had aroused, a situation that dulled the painful memory of the Black Sox.

Ruth became an immediate celebrity, and his sale to the Yankees enabled him to strut his stuff before a more cosmopolitan mob of admirers. He fitted perfectly into the New York of the twenties, and like the bullish market on Wall Street he brought inflation to the game: inflated salaries, inflated home runs, and with the years, he added an inflated waistline.

But Ruth's head never became inflated, except in the cocky, self-assurant way that all players must believe in themselves, and the secret of the charm of Ruth was his complete naturalness. Visiting sick children in hospitals was not a publicity pose but a genuine manifestation of his essential warmheartedness and innate decency. His gruff Rabelaisian speech to adults, also profanely decent, was an amusing compound of native intelligence and naïveté. Women were completely captivated by his crude, passionate nature.

During one of the numerous crises in China that marked the era following World War I, the New York Times interviewed a panel of celebrities from all walks of life about the situation Oriental. Caught in the act of picking up a bat in the Yankee dugout and asked what he thought of the Chinese situation, Ruth replied, "The hell with the Chinese," a perfect demonstration of the isolationist mass attitude of America of the times.

The Babe became a familiar figure everywhere in the land, and even in foreign countries his name was as celebrated as that of any American. His tan cap and camel's hair coat, his cigar, his Stutz Bearcat, were all familiar to the mob. He was a man of tremendous appetites, his spending was prodigal, and his earthiness genuine; but his devotion to nocturnal pleasures never kept him from performing. Baseball has produced numerous men who lived as Ruth did off the field. Not one of them was his equal on it.

The Sultan of Swat was interesting far beyond his ability to hit home runs. When he hit a pop fly to the infield, often the ball would go so high it would seem that it would never fall to earth; everything he did was excessive. When he struck out, he struck out so majestically the audience gasped in wonderment. He was all ball-player, and Ed Barrow, the Yankee executive who, like Colonel Jacob Ruppert, often tangled with him over contractual arrangements, said that he never saw Ruth, in all his years, make a mistake in judgment on the field.

The great Yankee teams of Ruth's era roared through the American League like the waters over Niagara, churning up whirlpools of destruction in their wake. The players would leave for a western trip without knowing or caring which city was their first destination. Waiters would board the train with bucket after bucket of home brew and frames of barbecued spareribs ordered by the Babe; and in the Pullman washrooms he would gleefully charge his teammates fifty cents each to join the party. Although always lavish to an extreme and invariably good for a touch, the Babe nevertheless took a fiendish pleasure in charging his little fee of fifty cents for admission to his bacchanals. It made scant difference that the Yankees spent the nights in such a fashion. On the following afternoons they would defeat the White Sox or the Browns or whoever it was by such scores as 8 to 1 or 14 to 3.

Of course, there was a mathematical reason for Ruth. When he was at the apex of his fame, a group of

Columbia University professors of science, anxious to examine the basis for the Ruth legend, submitted the Bambino to various tests. When it was shown that his eyesight was that of one man in ten, his sense of timing that of one man in ten, his wrist power that of one man in ten, and so on, it was easy to establish by use of the multiplication table the fact that George Herman was one in a million.

Ruth did not haunt the night clubs; he preferred to hold court in his suite, and lucky were the jesters who were in on the party. For that was what life was then to Ruth: mash notes, a gallon of ice cream, all the blessings of Bacchus, and hot dogs dripping with mustard.

Famed for his lack of memory, Ruth merely towered so above his opposition that he never bothered to learn their unimportant names. "Where wuz you sittin'?" he asked Horace Lisenbee, a young Washington pitcher off whom he had just hit a home run when Lisenbee later sought his autograph. The Babe remembered the important things, though, and never forgot to show up for a crowd.

The ability to rise to the occasion was his most poignant source of greatness. The biggest crowds saw his most dramatic achievements. A titan in world series play, he even hit a home run in the first All-Star game in 1933, when he was 38 and on his last legs. And on the opening day of his last and saddest season, with the Boston Braves in 1935, he hit a homer off Carl Hubbell, who was then at his left-handed peak.

Cobb may have had more baseball genius and more fire, Wagner or Chase may have had more grace, but for dramatic interest no player in the game ever approached the Babe. And although he was bitter in his last days because he had never been given a managerial job in the game that he had saved, he was on the scene when he was needed, and it was a simple matter for him to leave his Riverside Drive apartment and hit a final homer off Walter Johnson or take part in the festivities for Lou Gehrig.

Perhaps it is just as well that Ruth never did manage a team. The job is not one that requires the abundant talents that were his; he could never have become a successful martinet. But why some club, facing financial problems as all teams sometimes do, did not exploit the Ruth name as manager in order to lure reluctant customers through the turnstiles is incomprehensible.

An entirely different man was Judge Landis, the son of a country doctor who had been a Union Army surgeon and who had lost a leg at Kennesaw Mountain. It was in commemoration of the amputation that the name, in misspelled form, was passed on to baseball's future czar. Landis was born at Millville, Ohio, November 20, 1866, a hamlet not far north of Cincinnati. When he was very young, his family moved across the Indiana line and eventually settled near Logansport, where young Landis earned his first pennies hawking Chicago newspapers. His rise was in the Alger tradition, and his philosophy was the cracker barrel creeds picked up at the general store. Naturally alert, he learned to chew tobacco and punctuate his conversation with picturesque profanity.

It might have been that Ken Landis, like many a bright boy before him, would have succumbed to his environment and wasted his talents as a rustic raconteur had he not learned shorthand. But by mastering that specialized skill he became a court reporter, and then the trail led to the Y.M.C.A. Law School in Cincinnati, and as a young fan he watched baseball in that city before Ban Johnson and Charlie Comiskey met there.

Success in life comes not only through hard work, Alger to the contrary, but through good fortune, and in the case of Landis the liaison with pleasant fate was brought about by Judge Walter Q. Gresham, a Federal judge in Chicago named Secretary of State by Grover Cleveland. Gresham had known Landis' father in the Army, and when he went to Washington to assume his cabinet post, he took along the young attorney as his secretary. Landis spent two years in the capital, but despite the intimacy he enjoyed with the administration, he became a lifelong Republican.

Appointed a Federal judge by Theodore Roosevelt in 1905, Landis immediately attracted attention to his court by his colorful and unpredictable decisions. He liked to banter with the accused, and with attorneys and witnesses, and he was, in turn, cynical and tender. His attitude seemed to depend more on whim than any set pattern of belief.

Landis knew how to do dramatic things, and he got national publicity in 1907 when he fined the Standard Oil Company $29,240,000. The fine didn't stick because the Supreme Court later reversed the verdict, but by the judgment Landis endeared himself to the liberals and scared the pants off the Union League set. However, Landis was not to be a Chicago liberal in the tradition of John P. Altgeld, Gene Debs or Clarence Darrow; he hated Big Bill Haywood's "Wobblies" as much as he did the Rockefellers.

Like most American young men, the Judge was a baseball fan. Ten years old when the National League was born, he watched the progress of the game with avid interest, and he was a particular follower of Cap Anson's Chicago White Stockings. But he had no intimate contact with the game until he was called upon to hear the litigation brought by the Federal League. When he sat on that case, delaying any verdict until peace was made between the majors and the Feds, the magnates misinterpreted his purpose, and first began to think of him in terms of administering the pastime's affairs.

After he took office and began to delve into the affairs of baseball, Judge Landis apparently became fascinated by the game's structure. Unlike all previous czars of the game, who had been trained from within, Landis was an outsider and, in the eyes of some, an interloper.

The magnates were horrified to discover that they had bestowed unlimited powers on a despot who did not share their views. But to the ball player the Judge appeared to be a gift from heaven. It was as if John Montgomery Ward had been chosen to rule the game, and the ambitions of the Brotherhood, so illusionary in 1890, attained reality in the Landis administration.

Club owners wanted the Judge as a front of respectability, as they had wanted Morgan Bulkeley in 1876. But, unlike Bulkeley, Landis loved the game and devoted the remainder of his life to it. For more than twenty years he shook an ominous finger at the magnates. The Black Sox scandal did not in itself bring Landis into the game; he had been thought of before that. But the exposure of the Black Sox did force a decision in the matter, and, viewed in that light, the dereliction of the Chicago players in 1919 was a blessing in disguise.

It was Ruth who put the fans back into the parks, but it was Landis who made sure that what the spectators witnessed was as honest as the reflection from a mountain pool. Between them, working separately, they saved the game. The Sultan and the Czar worked different streets.

A Few
Final Scandals 22

THAT SUCH positive personalities as Ruth and Landis should eventually clash appeared to be inevitable, and when those titans finally did collide, the Judge was definitely the victor; this established the principle that no player, however lionized by the galleries, was bigger than the game itself.

The old National Commission had made a rule that players who appeared in the world series were not permitted to engage in barnstorming tours afterward, a rule designed to prohibit the players from exploiting themselves in the tank towns, risking injury on poorly equipped fields while under reserve to major league clubs.

During the world series of 1921 between the Yankees and Giants, the Bambino announced plans for a month of barnstorming arranged by a New York promoter, a series of games that was to net Ruth $1,000 a day. Outfielder Bob Meusel, Catcher Wally Schang and pitchers Carl Mays and Bill Piercy were to accompany him, and the team was to be filled out with players from the semipro ranks. Hearing of the venture, Judge Landis called Ruth's attention to the rule against such a trip and warned that his participation in it might bring drastic punishment.

But Ruth was a popular hero, and he misjudged public sentiment enough to defy the Commissioner and proceed with his plans. Schang and Mays were wise enough to cancel their part in the undertaking, but Meusel and Piercy strung along with the Bambino.

Today the jurisdiction of the Commissioner's authority is so well established that no player would be rash enough to defy such an order, but it must be remembered that Ruth's action took place when Landis had been on the job for only a year. Besides, the temper of the times was such that Americans who were normally law-abiding had such contempt for the eighteenth amendment that they welcomed any defiance of discipline and order.

The barnstorming tour itself was a complete fizzle, and was abandoned at Scranton after only six days. The daily gate was just about enough to meet Ruth's guarantee of $1,000, and any expense beyond that was a total loss. Landis meanwhile withheld the world series checks that would have gone to Ruth, Meusel and Piercy, checks for more than $3,000 each. Later, he announced that the players were suspended until May 20, 1922, which would deprive them of playing the first full month of the following season.

Ruth probably expected that such a popular clamor would be made on his behalf that Landis would be forced to back down. But, strangely, it was Landis who emerged the hero of the clash, for the Black Sox scandal had taught fandom that stern leadership was necessary to the game.

The Reach Guide, although an American League organ, lyrically observed:

> "If Ruth, next May,
> Returns to play,
> And knocks 'em far and high,
> The birds will sing
> Their song of spring
> Beneath a smiling sky.

"If Ruth, next May,
Declines to play
As in the days of yore,
The birds will sing
Their song of spring
As they have sung before."

Ruth's dereliction cost him dearly, as he participated in only 110 games in 1922 and his home run total fell to 35, four fewer than the number smashed by Ken Williams of the Browns. However, he did finally recover his world series check, as did his fellow vagabonds, Meusel and Piercy.

The popularity of home runs mounted steadily year by year, and the magnates were continually making plans to penalize the pitcher and aid the batter. When Ruth clouted 29 homers in 1919, the rule-makers observed how many runs he batted in, and provided that a compilation of tallies driven across the plate be incorporated into the averages, in accordance with the interest in hitting feats. It was also ruled that any home run made in the last half of the ninth with the winning run on base would count as a home run in the records provided the ball was hit out of the park and the batter made the tour of the sacks.

Pitchers were ordered to stop using freak deliveries, and the shine ball, the emery ball and other such exotic offerings were banned. The pitcher was forbidden to discolor the ball, treat it with any liquid, roughen it, or apply licorice, soapstone or anything else to it. An exception was made on behalf of those flingers who regularly applied saliva to the pellet. No new spitballers were to be admitted to the majors, but practitioners of the damp delivery were allowed to continue their craft.

These changes in rules had the desired effect, and the emphasis on batting became more noticeable with each year. The following table, showing the games played, hits and home runs made in each of the major leagues demonstrates the trend:

YEAR	NATIONAL LEAGUE			AMERICAN LEAGUE			BOTH LEAGUES		
	G.	H.	H.R..	G.	H.	H.R.	G.	H.	H.R.
1918	508	8,583	138	508	8,505	97	1016	17,088	235
1919	558	9,603	206	560	10,071	240	1118	19,674	446
1920	616	11,376	261	617	11,899	370	1233	23,275	631
1921	613	12,266	460	616	12,505	477	1229	24,771	937
1922	620	12,579	530	618	12,041	525	1238	24,620	1055

The ball was also changed, although the leagues denied it except to admit that the addition of Australian wool in 1921 might have made the sphere more lively. But the fans did not care. Base hit and home run totals soared like the bullish stock market, and the game reflected the inflationary aspects of life in general. Greater attendance, greater salaries and greater public interest all helped drive out the memory of the sordid Black Sox business.

But just as the departure of disease from a human body leaves the patient suffering from minor aches and pains, the Black Sox purge left baseball's structure the victim of a host of minor scandals, and a few more years were to pass before the suspicion of crooked work was entirely gone.

One of the first of these incidents was the case of "Shufflin' Phil" Douglas, a pitcher with John McGraw's New York Giants. Douglas, a Georgian who had bounced about from one club to another because of his bibulous proclivities, was a tremendous pitcher when he felt he was treated right, but a surly workman when despondent. During the season of 1922 he won 11 and lost 4 for the Giants, but he was frequently in trouble with McGraw because of carousing. Finally, after a particularly savage lecturing by his manager, he brooded over his mistreatment and determined to obtain revenge. Befuddled by drink, he wrote a very stupid letter to a player named Leslie Mann, who was an outfielder with the Cardinals, offering to "go fishing" and miss a few pitching turns if Mann would make it worth his while. This piscatorial proposal might well cost the Giants the pennant, Douglas figured, and he would have his revenge against McGraw.

Douglas might just as well have sent the letter to Judge Landis, for Mann was a player who made a fetish of physical condition and who spent his leisure hours in Y.M.C.A. work. Sorry for Douglas because he could understand that his troubled mind was alone responsible for the silly letter, Mann was nevertheless aware that he had better turn Phil in. So many players had been expelled under the new code for having guilty knowledge of crooked proposals, Mann felt that he had to keep himself in the clear. So he gave the note to his manager, Branch Rickey, who in turn gave it to Landis. When the Judge confronted Douglas with it and asked if he were the author, Phil confessed and was banned from the game for life.

It is doubtful if Douglas, in his right mind, ever would have made such a suggestion, and some followers of the game have felt that permanent exile was too severe a price for him to pay. Chances are if Phil had written to Mann in 1918, nothing would have happened. But the Black Sox series taught everyone connected with the game the importance of avoiding the slightest suspicion of crookedness. It is that policy, which in a few instances seems extremely harsh, that has kept baseball more highly regarded by the public than such other sports as racing and boxing.

The decisions of Judge Landis were not always consistent, and some were extremely difficult to figure out. Two contradictory edicts were made in the cases of Bennie Kauff and John (Rube) Benton. Kauff, the swaggering Federal League batting king who became something of a Broadway sport when he was sold to the Giants following the collapse of the Feds, was declared permanently ineligible by the Judge following his acquittal on charges of receiving stolen automobiles. Kauff was tried in the Bronx in May, 1921, and while on trial was not permitted to play for the Giants; after his acquittal he applied for reinstatement, but Landis made the ban permanent, explaining only that Bennie was undesirable and that his presence would have a bad effect on other players. Kauff secured a temporary injunction restraining Judge Landis and John Heydler from preventing him from making a living, but when he tried to obtain a permanent injunction, he was turned down.

Benton, a North Carolinian and by nature much like Phil Douglas, had been unofficially blacklisted by the National League because it was believed he had guilty knowledge of the 1919 series fix. Heydler considered him undesirable in the same fashion that Landis considered Kauff persona non grata. But Heydler's domain extended only to the eight National League cities, and the Rube was able to make a living by pitching for St. Paul of the American Association. When Garry Herrmann, still president of the Reds, purchased Benton from St. Paul and announced that he would pitch for Cincinnati in 1923, Heydler almost blew a fuse. But Herrmann appealed to Landis, who ruled that Benton was eligible to perform on National League slabs.

The saddest case was that involving Jimmy O'Connell, a sensational young outfielder the Giants had purchased for $75,000 from San Francisco following the 1922 campaign. O'Connell broke slowly with the Giants in 1923, but in the following year began to attain real stardom. In the final series of the year the Giants, gunning for their fourth consecutive flag, were one and one-half games ahead of their nearest rivals, the Dodgers, with only the Phillies between them and the pennant. All that McGraw's club had to do was split the last two games with the seventh place Phils.

On the field that final Saturday of 1924, September 27, O'Connell approached Heinie Sand, the Philly shortstop and a man he had known in the Pacific Coast League, and said out of the side of his mouth, "If you don't bear down too hard today it will be worth $500 to you."

Sand walked away without comment, but became more startled after thinking O'Connell's suggestion over, and, perhaps thinking of what Les Mann did in a similar position with Phil Douglas, he reported the remark to his manager, Art Fletcher. That started a double play over the telephone, Fletcher to Heydler to Landis.

Following the exact procedure he had used in the Douglas case, the Judge rushed to the scene as soon as possible and conferred first with Heydler and Sand, then with O'Connell.

Again, as in the Douglas case, O'Connell readily admitted his guilt. But this was no idea born of a hangover; there was no resentment involved. O'Connell's story was that a Giant coach, Alvin (Cozy) Dolan, had asked him to carry the fateful message to Sand. O'Connell also claimed that three Giant stars, Frankie Frisch, George Kelly and Ross Youngs, knew all about the matter.

In view of O'Connell's tacit admission that he had propositioned Sand, even though he had no idea in whose brain the scheme originated, Landis had no alternative except to blacklist him. But getting to the bottom of the business was a different matter.

Landis summoned Dolan in an attempt to clear things up, but the Giant coach proved to be a very poor witness indeed. Acting as if he had been rehearsing his answers, he claimed that he couldn't remember anything at all. Frisch, Kelly and Youngs all denied knowledge of the affair and were exonerated, but Dolan, because of his "poor memory," joined O'Connell on the ineligible list. Neither has ever been reinstated.

William J. Fallon, whose legal gymnastics have been perpetuated in literature by Gene Fowler's "The Great Mouthpiece," bobbed up as Dolan's attorney, and the talk was that Dolan was to sue the Commissioner for a million dollars. It was discovered that Dolan, the impecunious coach, had received the money for such costly counsel from John McGraw. But Dolan never went through with the suit, and although the real story has never been unearthed, there is reason to believe that Judge Landis got Charlie Stoneham, the Giant president, to call the whole thing off or face the publication of a mess that would have ruined the game, or at least the New York club, once and for all.

Jimmy O'Connell, only 23 at the time of his exile and quite possibly the participant in what he interpreted as a joke, drifted to Oklahoma and played outlaw ball around the oilfields for many years. More than a decade after the affair, tears would come to his eyes whenever he discussed the strangeness of his ruin. "I didn't know what it was all about," Jimmy insisted, and quite probably he didn't.

But the O'Connell case proved that such a subject as the throwing of ball games was not even to be joked about, and ever since ball players have shied away from conversation about such matters. You could spend thousands of hours in major league dugouts and clubhouses without hearing a reference to thrown games, and many modern players don't even know who Jimmy O'Connell was. All players, however, know better than to kid each other about "bearing down."

O'Connell was the last major league player to be found guilty of any incident of suspected crookedness, although there have been a few instances of such accusations being made. One of the expelled Black Sox, Swede Risberg, made the headlines briefly in 1927 when he charged that the Detroit Tigers had thrown a series of games to the White Sox in 1917. But Landis conducted an open hearing and exonerated all the Detroit players involved.

At the same time two of the greatest players in the game's history, Ty Cobb and Tris Speaker, were eased out of the American League when the aging Ban Johnson thought he had evidence that they had bet on a game between Cleveland and Detroit in 1919. Johnson permitted each to resign, Cobb as manager of the Tigers, Speaker as pilot of the Indians, then sent his file on the matter to the Commissioner. But Landis startled Johnson by making the matter public and calling another hearing at which Cobb and Speaker were completely cleared.

Because so many of the problems that plagued baseball had originated in the years before his reign, Landis properly put a statute of limitations on such charges. And with the exoneration of Cobb and Speaker passed the final aches and pains that infested the most diseased era the game had known. That strange pair of dissimilar physicians, Landis and Ruth, had restored the pastime's vigor.

Rickey
and His Redbirds 23

W HEN KENESAW Mountain Landis donned his toga as the game's Commissioner, the first case to come before him was a routine dispute between the two St. Louis clubs, the Cardinals and Browns, over title to the contract of a former highschool first baseman named Phil Todt. Though Landis had been a lifelong fan, his first intimate contact with the backstage aspects of the game came when he heard the Federal League suit. Now, as Commissioner, he was to discover that the legal life of baseball was a strange law unto itself, and that various magnates of the pastime were complex individuals who employed methods that covered a wide range, varying in ethics.

Landis blinked his eyes when he discovered that Todt had been signed by Branch Rickey, vice president and manager of the Cardinals, only to be subsequently signed and released by two teams in Texas, Sherman and Houston, clubs for which he had never even contracted to play. Meanwhile, the Browns had signed Todt, and now both St. Louis clubs claimed him. Landis ruled that Todt should remain with the Browns because it seemed evident that Rickey was introducing something new to baseball, or at least new to Landis, secret agreements with both the Sherman and Houston clubs.

Actually the option, that device by which a major league club retained title to a player while he was performing in the minor leagues, was nothing new.

It was first suggested by the Emporia, Kansas club in January, 1887, when an Emporia magnate proposed to the Cincinnati Reds that if they would send a pitcher and catcher to Emporia, the Kansas team would pay them the same salaries they would normally receive at Cincinnati and then return them to the Reds at the end of the season.

But baseball was slow to adopt businesslike methods, and for years major league club owners controlled players in the minors without any written agreements whatever. Most of the decisions forced on the old National Commission were the result of stupid business methods and dubious ethics. Club owners found themselves able to cover up numerous minor leaguers by giving financial aid to small teams without bothering to detail the transactions on paper. There are still men in baseball who are owed back salary from the era that antedated Landis. But just as the good Judge had to impose a statute of limitations on crooked playing, he had to apply the same rule to thievery on the part of the owners.

Wesley Branch Rickey or Branch Wesley Rickey (his correct name is as mysterious as some of his printed statements) was born at Stockdale, Ohio in barren farm country drained by the Scioto River north of Portsmouth, December 20, 1881. His father, Jacob, was a humble farmer celebrated throughout the backwoods for the unrelated accomplishments of piety and skill at wrestling. His mother, a deeply religious woman, early extracted a promise from young Branch that whatever he did in life he wouldn't do it on Sunday.

Today Branch Rickey is apt to drop out of the skies in his Beechcraft at any ballpark in the nation, but his early excursions in life were made first on foot and then by bicycle. His early training had all the conventional virtues that preface a career in American politics:

the one-room township school, the job of country schoolmaster at $35 a month, the pay from baseball and football that enabled him to work his way through Ohio Wesleyan.

Rickey at first considered baseball as a means to an end. He played professionally at Lamar, Wyoming in 1903 and the following year performed as a catcher for Dallas. When the Cincinnati Reds acquired his contract, Rickey astounded the Redleg manager, Joe Kelley of the old Orioles, by stating that he would not play on Sunday. Cincinnati promptly released him, but he went on to catch in the American League with the Highlanders and Browns and with indifferent success. His name appears in the record books just once: while catching for the Highlanders on June 28, 1907, the opposing Washington team stole 13 bases, an American League record. Rickey's critics have pointed to that reverse achievement with glee, but since bases are almost invariably stolen on the pitcher, Branch would seem to be technically in the clear, as he is in so many more important disputes.

Rickey has long resented the accusation of hypocrisy created by his attitude towards the Sabbath. He insists that he has nothing against Sunday baseball in principle, that his personal observance of the day is merely the fulfillment of that promise to his mother. That is logical enough, but the test of hypocrisy would come if one of Rickey's players should decide that his own religious scruples prevented him from taking the field on Sunday. It seems doubtful that Rickey would respect the conscience of such a contract violator. Also, there are in St. Louis today sports writers who will point to the Y.M.C.A. across the center field fence from Sportsman's Park and tell you that that is where Rickey watched Sunday ball games, with binoculars, during the years he ran the Cardinal show. Rickey's

Sunday manager in those years was his alter ego, Burt Shotton, who is still around but who now works seven days a week.

Had it not been for Robert Lee Hedges, president of the St. Louis Browns from 1903 to 1915, baseball might never have known Rickey as an executive. Branch's health failed in 1912, and he drifted west to Idaho, where he tried to survive as a frontier lawyer at Boise. Despite his fertile brain he almost starved, and had he not returned to baseball, it is likely that he would have turned to politics. Certainly he has all the necessary talents for political intrigue, and when baseball gained him, Idaho perhaps lost another William E. Borah.

But Hedges was aware how much Rickey knew about baseball, and a meeting of the pair at Salt Lake City resulted in Branch going to the Browns, first as assistant to Hedges, then as field manager. When Phil Ball acquired the American League franchise in St. Louis following the collapse of the Feds, Rickey transferred his allegiance to the Cardinals.

It was with the Cardinals that Rickey demonstrated how his baseball wisdom was to change the structure of the game. He was to have as much influence on front office affairs as Ruth had on the field. For years the Cards had been a weak sister in the National League sorority. They had never won a pennant in the National, and had not triumphed in any circuit since the days of Christ Von Der Ahe and his four-time American Association champs.

Rickey took over the field management of the Cardinals in 1919, but so little money was available that the team had to train at home, in the gymnasium of Washington University. Stock in the club was available at $3.50 a share or even less; and the National League wondered if its St. Louis representative, which finished eighth in 1918, might not be forced to abandon the franchise. Then Rickey put his brain to work and the results, though gradual, were as far-reaching as the roots of the oak trees that drew amazing vigor from the soil of his native Sciotoland.

Sam Breadon, a frosty, hard-bitten product of New York's storied sidewalks who fought his way to affluence in the automobile business at St. Louis, became president of the Cards in 1920. Sam was as hard as nails in business, but after hours he enjoyed singing and lifting a few highballs, a type of activity in which the ascetic Rickey quite naturally never joined; but he marveled at the baseball brain of his manager, and felt that they made a good team. Their principal problem was in recruiting players, for the wealthy clubs of the east, notably the Giants, were able to pay outlandish prices for athletes, and there was little chance for the Cards to compete. It was this economic situation that threatened to make the second division the St. Louis club's permanent address, a state of affairs that called for revolutionary action.

Rickey told Breadon of a radical scheme he had worked out for beating the Giants to the punch by acquiring players at an earlier age. Rather than pay for polished performers in the high class minors, Rickey would sign rookies to contracts in the lower minor leagues, hundreds of them, in the hope that a few would attain stardom in the majors. Breadon agreed that the plan was a sound one, and the experiment was launched. In those days rookies without professional experience were not ordinarily given bonuses; that development did not come to the game until Rickey's agricultural idea was copied by virtually every major league team. Highschool boys and sandlot players were delighted at the chance of signing with a big league team or one of its affiliates on any terms.

The first expansion in the aggression that accomplished the Cardinal empire occurred in 1919 when Rickey acquired about one-fifth of the stock of the Houston club of the Texas League. Fort Smith, Arkansas of the Western Association was next, then came Syracuse, in which Breadon, not Rickey, bought a half-interest. The Cards found it was to their best advantage to own clubs outright rather than work with them, and that was the policy generally pursued. From that axis of Houston, Syracuse and Fort Smith the Cardinal imperialism began to radiate through baseball's entire minor league structure. Rickey's chief scout, the peripatetic Charlie Barrett, seemed to have his finger on the pulse of every player in the country.

New athletes began to arrive in St. Louis and add luster to the Cardinal box scores. Before long it became apparent that the downtrodden days were done and that a formidable new club was being forged. The Cards climbed from eighth to seventh in 1919, moved into a tie for fifth in 1920, advanced to third in 1921 and tied for third in 1922. A temporary slump derailed the Redbirds as they sagged to fifth in 1923 and sixth in 1924, but they climbed back to fourth in 1925 and then won their first pennant in 1926.

This surge was accomplished with a host of homegrown stars, such creamy products of the lush Rickey crops as Jim Bottomley, Clarence (Heinie) Mueller, Charles (Chick) Hafey, Eddie Dyer, Howard Freigau, Ray Blades, Lester Bell, Tommy Thevenow, Taylor Douthit, Flint Rhem, Bill Hallahan and Roscoe (Wattie) Holm.

Even those young farmhands who never did quite sparkle on the main line at least enriched the game's nomenclature. Rickey's colorful rosters were dotted with athletes bearing picturesque names. It would be difficult to imagine players more engagingly designated than Bill Pertica, Arthur (Tink) Riviere, Lester Sell (as distinguished from Lester Bell), Clyde Barfoot, D'Arcy Flowers, Guilford Paulsen, Firmin Warwick and Carlisle Littlejohn.

In those early years Rickey divided his time between office and field. He was a theoretician but also a practical baseball man, and if he drew charts and diagrams for his players on blackboards, it was because that was the best way to demonstrate a point. He has been sneered at as a starry-eyed strategist, but even the gruff, extremely practical and unusually skilled Rogers Hornsby cheerfully admitted that he learned plenty about baseball from him. If the players could not follow Rickey's ideas, that was the fault of the players. Rickey's way was not to drive men as if they were oxen, as did John McGraw. Although the Giants retained enough class to win four consecutive pennants starting in 1921, McGravian methods were on the way out, and Muggsy himself had not much longer to go. Rickey could think faster than his players, but he wanted them to think for themselves, and his faith paid dividends in the end. Baseball today is completely permeated with Rickey's ideas, and a whole covey of lesser Rickeys occupy executive chairs and parrot his theories.

But in spite of the progress that was made, Breadon had occasion to feel that Rickey's talents were better suited to the front office than the dugout. After the team skidded to sixth in 1924 he became sure of it, and when the Redbirds got off slowly the following year, he decided to take action. On Decoration Day the Cardinals found themselves decorated with a new manager, forthright Rogers Hornsby. Breadon had finally induced Rickey to step inside the office door for good. The team responded to the lash of the fiery Rajah by bracing immediately and then climbing pennantward.

When the Cardinals won their first pennant in 1926 and followed it up with a conquest of the mighty Yankees in a seven-game world series, Hornsby was the recipient of most of the bows, although the legendary hero of that fabled set of games was Grover Cleveland Alexander, the veteran pitcher who plodded his way from the bullpen in the seventh inning of the final game to strike out Tony Lazzeri and quell a Yank uprising and pinch off the victory. But that Cardinal victory was also a triumph for Rickey, who had built the team; and who knows what his thoughts were as he watched Hornsby so brilliandy succeed with the club he had provided.

But it was Rickey who won in the end, for two months after the series the populace was electrified to read that Hornsby had been traded to the hated Giants for another sizzling second baseman, Frankie Frisch, and a once capable though by now inconsequential pitcher named Jimmy Ring. It was Hornsby's stubbornness over the cancellation of an exhibition game that taught Breadon that the Rajah must move on. Sam could not tolerate a manager who did not yield to his suggestions. It was a great triumph for the front office over the manager, and it set an important precedent: big league managers today follow instructions as often as they give them. Hornsby, who had batted .424 in 1924, the most stratospheric mark of modern times, and who was to lead the league in hitting seven different years, had made the first move of what was to be a most nomadic baseball existence. The era of the general manager had arrived.

Rickey's early brush with Judge Landis over Phil Todt, who, incidentally, finally became a big league first baseman with the Red Sox, was only the first of many visits he was to pay to the Commissioner. Landis felt that baseball, at every level, should belong to the people. He believed that local teams in the lower regions of the minors should be owned by local capital; he felt that because Rickey controlled so many players he could retard their progress if the fancy struck him. It seemed to Landis that the suave and subtle manipulations of Rickey constituted as serious a threat to the game as the syndicate proposed by Andrew Freedman at the turn of the century. But Landis hesitated to anger the Cardinal mogul enough to drive him into court. The Commissioner loved baseball but took a dim view of the legality of the professional game's form; he was well aware that even if he were upheld in court against Rickey, the entire structure might topple and wreck the game. Some of the most important decisions made by Landis came when he decided to do nothing. His knowledge of the law was tremendous, but many of his verdicts came from the heart.

So instead of fighting openly at his agricultural adversary, Landis instead sniped at him, curtailed his operations where he could, made new rulings that he must observe, and generally fenced him in. Occasionally the Commissioner erupted, as he did finally in March, 1938, when the bubbling lava washed away in free agency more than 80 intended Cardinals of the future, including a fine young outfielder named Pete Reiser, who was to become the league batting champion for Brooklyn only two summers later.

Rickey, however, could build a pretty good case against Landis. Statistics, in the hands of the proper people, can be used to prove almost anything, and Branch always contended that his farm operation benefited the player rather than otherwise. Rickey believes that he saved minor league baseball, that the game's competition from the automobile, the movies and from other sports made independent operation in the minors almost impossible. It is likely that Rickey views himself as the savior rather than the destroyer of players, and it would be simple for him to prove that he has speeded up the process by which a rookie reaches major league stature.

Perhaps the average fan is not particularly interested in the ideological battle between the forces of Landis and Rickey that occupied attention in the game for more than two decades, but it was that battle that determined the type of baseball that would survive. And apparently it was Rickey who won.

Changing
of the Guard   24

IT IS not a careless generalization to say that the 1927
New York Yankees constituted the most memorable
ball team of all time because a poll of the game's
savants conducted by *The Sporting News* established
that fact beyond all doubt. The Chicago Cubs of 1906
won more games (116 to 110), the 1930 Giants hit for a
higher composite average (.319 to .307), and the 1947
Giants smashed more home runs (221 to 158), but
none of those clubs was able to arouse and excite the
populace like the Yanks of '27.

That was the year that Ruth reached his epic total
of 60 home runs. He was spurred on to that figure
when his young mate, the piano-legged Lou Gehrig,
demonstrated a propensity for grabbing headlines
by hitting homers himself. Brisding at the challenge,
the Babe excelled himself, but Gehrig ended up with
47 and even surpassed Ruth in runs batted in, 175 to
164, and in batting average, .373 to .356. Those figures
aptly show what the heart of the Yankee batting order
held for enemy pitchers, but Ruth and Gehrig, great as
they were, represented only two of the eight regulars,
aside from pitchers, that enabled the team to zoom to
greatness.

For instance, Earl Combs, the fleet center-fielder
and leadoff man in the order, hit .356, making 231
hits and splashing 23 triples between the fielders. Bob
Meusel, the left-fielder, hit .337 and batted in 103 runs.
Tony Lazzeri hit .309 while playing second base, and

added 18 homers to the strategic Yank stockpile that reached 158. No wonder pitchers shuddered when they contemplated an afternoon of facing the horrendous hirelings of Miller Huggins.

Mark Koenig at short, Joe Dugan at third and Pat Collins, who bore the brunt of the catching chores, were the other regulars, and they too, at times, entered into the picnic aspects of the attack.

The following table shows the regularity with which Ruth bombarded the parks in achieving the home run total that has withstood the assaults of 22 seasons since:

NO. DATE	ENEMY PITCHER	OPPONENT	PLACE
1 April 15	Howard Ehmke	A's	N.Y.
2 April 23	Rube Walberg	A's	Pha.
3 April 24	Hollis Thurston	Senators	Wash.
4 April 29	Slim Harriss	Red Sox	Bos.
5 May 1	Jack Quinn	A's	N.Y.
6 May 1	Rube Walberg	A's	N.Y.
7 May 10	Milt Gaston	Browns	StL.
8 May 11	Ernie Nevers	Browns	StL.
9 May 17	Warren Collins	Tigers	Det.
10 May 22	Ben Karr	Indians	Cie.
11 May 23	Hollis Thurston	Senators	Wash.
12 May 28	Hollis Thurston	Senators	N.Y.
13 May 29	Danny MacFayden	Red Sox	N.Y.
14 May 30	Rube Walberg	A's	Pha.
15 May 31	Howard Ehmke	A's	Pha.
16 May 31	Jack Quinn	A's	Pha.
17 June 5	Earl Whitehill	Tigers	N.Y.
18 June 7	Al Thomas	White Sox	N.Y.
19 June 11	Garland Buckeye	Indians	N.Y.

20 June 11	Garland Buckeye	Indians	N.Y.
21 June 12	George Uhle	Indians	N.Y.
22 June 16	Tom Zachary	Browns	N.Y.
23 June 22	Hal Wiltse	Red Sox	Bos.
24 June 22	Hal Wiltse	Red Sox	Bos.
25 June 30	Slim Harriss	Red Sox	Bos.
26 July 3	Hod Lisenbee	Senators	Wash.
27 July 8	Earl Whitehill	Tigers	Det.
28 July 9	Ken Holloway	Tigers	Det.
29 July 9	Ken Holloway	Tigers	Det.
30 July 12	Joe Shaute	Indians	Cie.
31 July 24	Al Thomas	White Sox	Chi.
32 July 26	Milt Gaston	Browns	N.Y.
33 July 26	Milt Gaston	Browns	N.Y.
34 July 28	Walter Stewart	Browns	N.Y.
35 Aug. 5	George F. Smith	Tigers	N.Y.
36 Aug. 10	Tom Zachary	Senators	Wash.
37 Aug. 16	Al Thomas	White Sox	Chi.
38 Aug. 17	George Connally	White Sox	Chi.
39 Aug. 20	Walter Miller	Indians	Cie.
40 Aug. 22	Joe Shaute	Indians	Cie.
41 Aug. 27	Ernie Nevers	Browns	StL.
42 Aug. 28	Ernie Wingard	Browns	StL.
43 Aug. 31	Tony Welzer	Red Sox	N.Y.
44 Sept. 2	Rube Walberg	Athletics	Pha.
45 Sept. 6	Tony Welzer	Red Sox	Bos.
46 Sept. 6	Tony Welzer	Red Sox	Bos.
47 Sept. 6	Jack Russell	Red Sox	Bos.
48 Sept. 7	Danny MacFayden	Red Sox	Bos.
49 Sept. 7	Slim Harriss	Red Sox	Bos.
50 Sept. 11	Milt Gaston	Browns	N.Y.

51 Sept. 13	Willis Hudlin	Indians	N.Y.
52 Sept. 13	Joe Shaute	Indians	N.Y.
53 Sept. 16	Ted Blankenship	White Sox	N.Y.
54 Sept. 18	Ted Lyons	White Sox	N.Y.
55 Sept. 21	Sam Gibson	Tigers	N.Y.
56 Sept. 22	Ken Holloway	Tigers	N.Y.
57 Sept. 27	Lefty Grove	A's	N.Y.
58 Sept. 29	Hod Lisenbee	Senators	N.Y.
59 Sept. 29	Paul Hopkins	Senators	N.Y.
60 Sept. 30	Tom Zachary	Senators	N.Y.

But although Ruth's home runs and the clouting of Gehrig and the others played such a vital part in the success of the Yankees, the work of that team's pitchers has been largely overlooked by the historians. Although the Bronx Bombers won about as they chose that year, and crushed the memory of their 44 defeats with 110 triumphs, there were days when Murderers' Row was not functioning. But Huggins' hurling corps was so classy, it made little difference and the team generally won anyway. This can best be shown by considering the runs scored by the Yanks against each opponent and the runs that they yielded:

OPPONENT	YANKEE RUNS	OPPONENTS' RUNS	GAMES WON	GAMES LOST
Philadelphia	157	106	14	8
Boston	171	80	18	4
Washington	135	79	14	8
Detroit	136	113	14	8
Chicago	111	59	17	5
Cleveland	115	97	12	10
St. Louis	150	65	21	1
Totals	975	599	110	44

Although it is seen that New York outscored each of its opponents, it will be noted that the Yankees scored fewer times against the White Sox than any other club. But the New York pitchers were equal to the task, and held the Sox to a paltry 59 runs in the 22 games.

Waite Hoyt had the best record of the pitchers, winning 22 while losing 7; Herb Pennock won 19 and dropped 8; Urban Shocker spitballed his way to a mark of 18 and 6; Dutch Ruether won 13 and lost 6; and young George Pipgras got into the spirit of things with 10 and 3. But the surprise of the mound corps was Wilcy Moore, a veteran Oklahoma dirt farmer who had toiled long and often in the lower minors. Rewarded with a chance to join such a fabulous club, grateful Wilcy worked in 50 games, starting and relieving, and won 19 while being smeared with defeat in only 7.

Starting in 1921, the Yankees were to win 16 pennants and 12 world championships in 29 years, but most witnesses agree that the club reached its zenith during 1927. The team was not out of first place for a single day all season long, then climaxed the year by blasting the Pirates in four straight world series engagements. Pittsburgh had shot to prominence in the National League with a team built around the Waner brothers, Paul and Lloyd, a pair of capable Oklahomans who hit mostly singles. The Yanks went for the long one, and it proved to be a better system.

But their interest in the home run did not prevent Huggins' club from showing fascination with hits of assorted sizes: Gehrig led the league in doubles, Combs in singles and triples. The team averaged more than six runs a game, and its favorite number was eight, scoring exactly that many runs in 19 different struggles. New York won the first 21 games against the Browns before dropping the final one, and was not shut out by any club until Lefty Grove accomplished the miracle on

September 3, holding the murderous brigade to four hits and winning, 1 to 0.

Although it was humiliating for the Pirates to endure the nightmare of a world series against the Yankees, at least the National League had the satisfaction of not contending against such a club all season long. It was slugging that fans wanted in the twenties, and, led by the incredible Ruth, the Yankees showed to what a fine degree the art could be developed. If Branch Rickey with his hungry, fighting farm chattels interpreted his 1926 victory to mean that the style of baseball played in the major leagues was again to change, the Yanks made clear his error. And as long as the nation remained prosperous the New York Americans, laced with dynamite, remained in power. Rickey did not win a world championship again until 1931, when a nation that knew breadlines applauded his scrawny heroes.

But the dethroning of the Yanks came from within their own league when Connie Mack, fifteen years after destroying his invincibles of 1914, reached the top again. A trio of brilliant pitchers, Lefty Grove, George Earnshaw and Rube Walberg, throttled opposition to the Athletics, enabling such swatsmiths as Al Simmons, Jimmy Foxx, Bing Miller and Mickey Cochrane to blast the ball often enough to enable the A's to win in 1929. That year was capped by the fantastic world series against the Cubs in which Connie by-passed his regular pitchers and watched Howard Ehmke, a fading veteran who had not been expected to work, even in relief, whiff 13 Bruins for a series record in the opening game. That was also the series in which the A's, trailing, 8 to 0, rallied for ten runs in the seventh inning of the fourth game, one of the most remarkable exhibitions of batting ever recorded.

But when the Yankees were in full flower, Ban Johnson, the great builder of the American League, entered into a period of personal senescence that ended in his retirement and ultimate death.

Ban never could get used to the idea that the commission form of baseball government made subordinate his activity. He had fathered the American League and had seen it grow from a leaky roof circuit to a position of national dominance. To yield his powers to a new god seemed ironical, and instead of mellowing with the passing years, he grew more bitter.

Ban's iron leadership had caused him to break with his oldest friends, and his hatred for Charlie Comiskey, which was returned, became the most intense feud in the history of the game, even exceeding in heat the enmity between Barney Dreyfuss and Garry Herrmann over the disposition of George Sisler. The fissure originally developed when Johnson ordered that Pitcher Jack Quinn be awarded to the Yankees in 1919. Comiskey had brought up Quinn to the White Sox when the Vernon club of the Pacific Coast League disbanded in July, 1918, because of the war. But the cause of their dispute was forgotten as the breach widened with the years, and the two men who devoted their lives to baseball after starting on their executive paths together at Cincinnati in the nineties both died without a hint of reconciliation.

Johnson's last years as president were a sad contrast to his buoyant days as a builder of the game. Shorn of his power, aged before his time and embittered by what he considered the perfidy of men he had helped create, he slowly and definitely declined. His stubborn refusal to attend the 1924 world series in the belief that the games should be cancelled because of the Jimmy O'Connell scandal gained him nothing, and his occasional printed outbursts against Judge Landis only embarrassed his colleagues. When Ban cried out that Landis had made a mess of the Cobb-Speaker case, the

Judge, deciding to rid himself of the hostility once and for all, asked the American League officials in effect, "Look here, are you fellows sincere about getting rid of Johnson or not?"

The league that Johnson built then decided that he should continue in office in name only, and finally, on July 8, 1927, Ban resigned, effective at the end of the baseball year. He spent his last days at St. Louis and died there, March 28, 1931. Oddly enough, his successor as league president, Ernest Sargent Barnard, who had previously been the president of the Cleveland team, expired the day before, dying in office at Cleveland, March 27. Barnard's successor, William Harridge, still occupies the presidential chair. He started his career as a clerk in a railroad office, served as Johnson's secretary and then as secretary of the league. The need for strong men of Ban's inclinations and abilities is no more.

In the year that Ruth was hitting his homer peak and Ban was handing in his resignation, Charlie Comiskey enlarged his ball park, adding $900,000 to the original investment of $750,000 to increase the seating capacity to 55,000. But the Old Roman was likewise saddened by the events of the years. Broken-hearted by the sellout of his 1919 club, he was never able to restore the White Sox to their previous position of mastery even though he could remodel his park. Comiskey, too, did not have long to go, and late in October, 1931, the same year that witnessed the passing of Johnson and Barnard, he died at his country place at Eagle River, Wisconsin.

Another who died that year was Garry Herrmann, who had retired as president of the Reds the same year that Johnson resigned his presidency. Increasing deafness made it impossible for Garry to determine what was going on, and he got out of the business rather than go through the motions.

Other great figures of the game were calling it quits on the playing field, and it seemed to be a time for the changing of the guard. Ty Cobb and Tris Speaker laid down their gloves after winding up their careers as teammates with the Athletics in 1928, a year after Walter Johnson had ceased his fireballing after two decades with Washington.

Baseball, reaching another plateau of maturity in its evolution, no longer needed its pioneers, either in executive chairs or in the dugouts. And the game, which roared through the postwar boom as an exciting example of American opulence, was ready to adjust itself to the requirements brought on by the nation's depression.

Depression Baseball

25

W HEN THE stock market crashed on Wall Street in late October, 1929, it received only an over-the-shoulder glance from baseball folk who were still preoccupied with their own affairs. There was no way of knowing that America had reached the end of an era and that a period of grim economy was in sight. During the week the market collapsed magnates, players and fans were more upset and saddened by the news that Walter Lerian, a fine young catcher with the Phillies, had been crushed to death by a motor truck in Baltimore. And less than a week after the Wall Street debacle the Chicago Cubs, by way of demonstrating their faith in the pastime's future, paid Boston $80,000 for the contract of Third Baseman Lester Bell.

The season of 1930 proved to be more prosperous than ever, especially in the National League. Home runs were the order of the day, and the Heydler circuit produced 892 of them, a record number. Lewis (Hack) Wilson, a rotund outfielder with the Cubs, even threatened Babe Ruth's individual total and wound up four shy with 56. The souped up ball enabled 71 National League batters in ten or more games to hike their averages above .300, and the entire league had a composite mark of .303. Baseball, slow to catch on, still reflected the boom market. There was not quite so robust a display of hitting in the American, but the difference was not too great.

The first pinch was felt in the lower regions of the minor leagues, and became noticeable when there was a strange dearth of attendance in Mississippi Valley cities in 1930. Still, 21 minor leagues operated that year, only four fewer than in 1929. And it was thought that the slump was temporar y, just as Congress felt that the depression itself was a momentary nuisance.

But by 1931 the game had changed enough to reflect the national concern. Hitting declined when the ball was deadened, in the belief that fans were surfeited with home runs, and when the sacrifice fly rule was abolished. This gave rise to a concentration on the more scientific aspects of play, and there was a revival of interest in base-stealing, the bunt, and the hit-and-run. The game did not go all the way back to the era of the dead ball, but it seemed headed that way.

John (Pepper) Martin, hero of the 1931 world series, in which the Cardinals defeated the Athletics in seven games, demonstrated the shift in style. An unkempt hero who had once ridden to his training camp in a box car, hungry and unshaven, Martin blazed across the baseball sky in that series not so much because he hit .500 in the seven games, but more because he stole five bases, completely upsetting Mickey Cochrane, the affluent and stylish Philadelphia catcher who had reputedly lost a fortune in the stock market. The underprivileged were about to come to power.

By 1932 the situation was much more serious, and the minor leagues were dying on the limb. A federal tax on admissions and a levy on sporting equipment imposed a twin burden on the game. Judge Landis and John Heydler voluntarily reduced their own salaries to set an egregious example, and the magnates, infinitely wiser than their forbears, pruned the stipends of players carefully and not cruelly.

Only fourteen minor leagues operated in 1933, but all survived their seasons under the solid leadership of the minors' czar, Judge William G. Bramham, who supervised the affairs of the lesser leagues from his headquarters at Durham, North Carolina.

"Our national game has weathered the most critical year in its history," said Heydler at the conclusion of the 1933 campaign, "Things should go better from now on."

One major league creation of the depression days was the annual all-star game, the mid-season exhibition between stellar clubs of the National and American Leagues which has come to be looked upon by fans as an event almost equal in importance to the world series. The idea for the "dream game" was hatched in the fertile mind of Arch Ward, sports editor of the Chicago Tribune as a promotion that would give baseball a part in the Century of Progress exposition at Chicago. Originally it was not planned as an annual event. But although fans had long dreamed of seeing all-star teams upon the same field, Ward had considerable difficulty in selling the game to the magnates, even though his paper agreed to underwrite all costs in the event of rain.

The players were selected by popular ballots in the Tribune and other papers, and the game was played at Comiskey Park, July 6, 1933. John McGraw, who had retired as manager of the Giants the previous year, and Connie Mack, the by now patriarchal pilot of the Athletics, managed the two squads, the first time they had clashed since the world series of 1913. The game was not intended for the glorification of any single player, but the redoubtable Ruth, rising to the occasion as always, hit a towering home run into the right field stand and paced the American League to a 4 to 2 victory.

The popular clamor became so great that the game was made an annual feature of the schedule, with the

American League usually winning. Magnates and players have never particularly cared for the contest, and there has been considerable bickering about the methods used to select players and criticism of various managers for keeping certain athletes out of the lineups once they were chosen. Yet, the game, always played before a jammed park, has held its high caste with the fans, and some of the greatest sources of nostalgia have been derived from all-star feats, such exciting exhibitions as the accomplishment of Carl Hubbell in striking out five consecutive batters at the Polo Grounds in 1934 and the climactic, game-winning home run of the mighty Ted Williams at Briggs Stadium in 1941.

John Heydler was right when he predicted that 1934 would see better days for baseball, but he did not stay around long to watch the improvement in baseball's fortunes. The league's good and faithful president, with tears in his eyes, summoned newspapermen in November, 1934 and announced that failing health forced his retirement. He left at its crest the league that he loved, a few months after the Cardinals had again given the National one of its rare world series victories, a triumph over the Tigers in seven games, the series that starred the Dean brothers, Jerome and Paul.

The National League chose as Heydler's successor Ford Christopher Frick, a product of Wawaka, Indiana, a village celebrated for the culture of onions and a shipping point for muck farmers. Graduating from DePauw College where he attained proficiency as a public speaker, Frick drifted to Colorado as a schoolteacher and worked on the Colorado Springs Gazette. There a printer who also happened to be a friend of Arthur Brisbane took a liking to Frick's stuff, and when Brisbane also read and enjoyed it, Ford was called to New York as a writer for William Randolph Hearst. He also did radio work, and at the time of his election as president he had run the National League's service bureau for a year.

Frick did not remain in the presidential chair for long before learning that there were times when it could be a hot seat. During the 1937 season he ran afoul of Jerome (Dizzy) Dean, the great pitcher of the Cardinals who was as colorful a performer as the National League has ever produced. Dean, like his team-mate, Pepper Martin, was an ideal hero for depression days, a gaunt, ageless Oklahoman who had spent his youth as an itinerant worker in the cotton fields of Arkansas and who had worn the drab khaki of an Army private. Though lacking in formal education, Dean was a shrewd personality, blessed with native wit and bolstered with tremendous self-confidence. He won thirty games for the 1934 Cardinals, and his fiery fastball and baffling curve were only slightly less interesting than his fantastic and boisterous claims of his own talent.

The trouble between Frick and Dean began on a Wednesday afternoon, May 19, 1937. Although St. Louis at that time was not known for its vast outpourings of fans at Sportsman's Park, 26,399 of them were lured to the grounds that day to witness a pitching duel between Dean and the great southpaw of the Giants, Carl Hubbell. Frick had instructed his umpires that year to enforce a provision of the balk rule that requires a pitcher to come to a definite pause in his windup after the preliminary stretch with runners on bases.

Umpire George Barr called such a balk on Dean for not obeying the letter of the law, and Dizzy then proceeded to blow up and lose the ball game, 4 to 1. The balk call was made in the sixth inning, and for the remainder of the contest it appeared that Dean was throwing at the batters. At least the Giants thought so, and when, in the ninth frame, Dizzy and Jimmy Ripple, a New York outfielder, tangled at first base after a close play, players from both sides began swinging at each other in a series of free-for-all fights. Dean was fined fifty dollars for his part in the proceedings.

When Dizzy made his next start, against the Phillies four days later, he made a burlesque of the balk rule, pausing in his windup so long it delayed play. When he repeated this three times, Umpire John (Beans) Reardon called a ball, and Dean immediately staged a sit down strike, squatting on the mound, his arms folded in front of his chest. St. Louis players, converging on the slab, induced him finally to resume pitching, and he finished the ball game, winning, 6 to 2.

Two nights later Dizzy made a speech at the Father and Son banquet of a Presbyterian church at Belleville, Illinois. The Belleville Daily Advocate quoted Jerome as having included in his postprandial remarks one to the effect that "Ford Frick and George Barr are two of the biggest crooks in baseball."

The new league executive, his feathers ruffled by this absurd but amusing allegation, then dispatched Ernie Quigley, his superannuated supervisor of umpires, to Brooklyn, where the Cardinals were playing, with a long apology for Dean to sign. Quigley did not put in an appearance with the document until June 2, eight days after the speech at Belleville.

When Dean, backed by his manager, Frankie Frisch, and the club president, Sam Breadon, refused to sign the statement, Quigley then handed him still another piece of paper, this one containing the following notice:

"For conduct detrimental to the best interests of baseball, Player J. H. Dean of the St. Louis club is this date indefinitely suspended.

"Ford Frick"

Frick's document had asked Dean to apologize not only for what he said at Belleville but for deliberately throwing at the Giant players and for violating the balk rule although he understood its provisions. Dizzy then snorted what has come to be one of baseball's greatest quotes: "I won't sign nothin'."

Frick perpetuated the nonsense by issuing a solemn statement in which he said, "It's down to the question of whether Dean is bigger than the National League."

Apparently he was, for the pitcher never did sign an apology and the suspension was lifted after only two days. Numerous conferences were held between Frick and Dean in the presence of baseball writers, and though Diz denied making the statements credited to him by the Belleville newspaper, he stubbornly refused to sign any disavowal of them.

Completely baffled, Frick finally backed down and agreed to reinstate Dean if he would take part in a little game of "question and answer" before newspapermen who were to act as witnesses. Overjoyed at the possibility of further conversation, Diz agreed, but all his answers were in the same vein, "I didn't say nothin'; I won't sign nothin'."

Diz resumed pitching, but not before telling the Associated Press, "All the guy (Frick) wants to do is make a heel outa me and a hero outa himself. If he stays in office very long, why, he'll have us all wearing tennis shoes. Why, we never had any trouble when Highlander (sic) was president."

Ford Frick did stay in office and has increased in stature with the years, but he has had no other Dizzy Deans to cope with.

Diz suffered a broken toe in the all-star game of that year, and when he resumed pitching too soon afterward, he had to use an unnatural motion that injured his arm. Branch Rickey sold him to the Cubs where, pitching with courage alone, he lasted a few more years. He then took his picturesque personality into a St. Louis broadcaster's booth, but his uninhibited remarks have led to no suits for slander. He was one of the greatest pitchers in baseball when he had it, and those who remember him at his peak recall a man who combined sheer baseball talent with a vivid personality that has been all too rare in National League affairs.

Baseball moved on through the depression, recovering slowly as did the country. Player limits were decreased slightly, but the reduction in rosters actually made for better baseball. The players were still major leaguers; the game attained a degree of proficiency that many consider the zenith of its evolution.

Six Thousand Full Moons

26

"MacPhail is making a circus of the game. Night baseball is synthetic; Washington fans will never see it"

Clark Griffith, 1935.

"Night baseball appeals to more people, more people are able to attend games, and interest is intensified. Seven games are not enough."

Clark Griffith, 1939.

ALTHOUGH THE major leagues survived the nation's worst depression without moving a single franchise to some other city, the going was difficult for many clubs, particularly Cincinnati, the smallest city in the majors with a population of about 450,000. The team had been purchased in September, 1929, at the height of the bull market, by Sidney Weil, a native who had pyramided a fortune built from profits in the automobile business. Victim of the worst possible timing, he held onto the reins as long as possible but finally turned the operation over to a bank, the Central Trust Co.

Larry MacPhail, who had exploded onto the baseball scene while running the Columbus franchise of the American Association with all the energy and excitement of a Barnum, was then brought to Cincinnati to revive the moribund Reds. MacPhail, soon to be known throughout baseball as Loud Larry, achieved a master stroke when he was able to induce the Cincinnati industrialist, Powel Crosley, Jr. to buy a controlling interest in the Reds. Crosley had previously turned down all such suggestions, but MacPhail painted such a rosy picture of the future of baseball's first professional club that he fell victim to the salesmanship.

In one of their preliminary conversations, MacPhail told Crosley how many paid admissions he had drawn at Columbus, but added, "Of course we played under the lights."

"Why can't we put in lights at Cincinnati?" Crosley asked.

"Oh, that's out of the question," Larry said.

"Is there any rule against it?" Powel persisted.

"No, but—"

"Why don't we try?"

At the National League meeting in December, 1934, MacPhail pleaded with his fellow magnates to allow the Reds to install the arcs on a limited basis, for seven games a year, pleading that Cincinnati represented a peculiar situation.

"Give me seven night games a year, one with each opposing club, and I will give you seven additional Sunday crowds," Larry promised.

The idea of playing baseball by artificial light was horrifying to the dignified National League executives, but when MacPhail mentioned the possibility of profit, they reluctantly yielded, telling themselves that they were doing it only to make it possible for the Reds to compete with larger cities in the purchase of playing talent. But the resolution was adopted unanimously, provided that no team play at night on Saturday, Sunday or on a holiday, that visiting teams be given the right to refuse to play nocturnally, and that any team which played more than seven night games would suffer a drastic penalty at the hands of the league office.

Oddly enough, it was MacPhail who insisted that night games be limited to seven, saying, "Too many games would defeat the purpose of stimulating attendance."

However, Larry did hope to schedule a few night exhibitions with American League clubs, in an effort to pay for the initial installation of lighting equipment. But the National League tagged on an amendment to the rule prohibiting such a scheme, and as a consequence when the Cincinnati board of directors voted to install lights and play seven night games in 1935, MacPhail voted against it, feeling that his inability to schedule the exhibition games would prevent him from making a profit. But the club's directors went ahead with plans and told MacPhail to get busy.

All National League clubs save the haughty New York Giants agreed to participate in the Cincinnati venture, but the Giants scoffed at the innovation, calling it "bush league stuff," and refused to take the field against the Reds in any after dinner antics. MacPhail was looked upon as a literal lunatic who was ruining the game.

The American League was even more hostile, and the distinguished Connie Mack, who was not to install lights of his own for four years, considered after-dark baseball a form of hippodroming.

It is interesting to observe that George Wright, shortstop on baseball's first professional club, the Red Stockings of 1869, was still alive when the first night game in major league history took place, May 24, 1935. Wright was invited to the game, but could not make the trip from Massachusetts because of illness. Judge Landis was also absent because of ill health, but a crowd of 20,422, including Ford Frick, who threw out the first ball, and William Harridge, watched the history-making festivities.

MacPhail put on a good show at the overture, including a thunderous display of blazing fireworks and deafening bombs, and the lighting system was turned on when Franklin D. Roosevelt, seated in the White House, pressed a button that launched the new chapter in baseball's story. Umpire Bill Klem, the veteran arbiter selected to work behind the plate that night, took a suspicious view of the whole proceedings until the light streaming from the 616 1,500-watt mazdas satisfied him that the game could be played without difficulty.Here is the box score of the game:

Philadelphia	AB	R	H	PO	A	Cincinnati	AB	R	H	PO	A
Chiozza, 2b	4	0	0	1	3	Myers, ss	3	1	1	2	3
Allen, cf	4	0	1	0	0	Riggs, 3b	4	0	0	0	2
Moore, rf	4	0	1	0	0	Goodman, rf	3	0	0	3	0
Camilli, 1b	4	0	1	15	0	Sullivan, 1b	3	1	2	8	2
Vergez, 3 b	4	0	1	0	4	Pool, if	3	0	1	0	0
Todd, c	3	1	1	3	0	Campbell, c	3	0	0	5	0
Watkins, if	3	0	0	5	0	Byrd, cf	3	0	0	4	0
Haslin, ss	3	0	1	0	5	Kampouris, 2b 3	3	0	0	4	3
Bowman, p	2	0	0	0	2	Derringer, p	3	0	0	1	2
[3]Wilson	1	0	0	0	0						
Bivin, p	0	0	0	0	0						
	32	1	6	24	14		28	2	4	27	12

PHILADELPHIA	0	0	0	0	1	0	0	0	0-1
CINCINNATI	1	0	0	1	0	0	0	0	x-2

[3]Wilson

3 Wilson batted for Bowman in eighth. Errors: None. Runs batted in: Bowman, Goodman, Campbell. Two-base hits: Myers. Stolen bases: Vergez, Bowman, Myers. Double play: Riggs to Kampouris to Sullivan. Bases on balls: off

The Cincinnati experiment was greeted with a mixed reaction. Opponents of the night game said that it was artificial, that fans would not take to it, that it was dangerous to spectators and players alike, and that a permanent gain in attendance was unlikely. Some players complained that outfielders could not follow high flies, that the batters could not see well enough, that the damp air affected their throwing arms, that the ball became wet and difficult to handle, that it led to irregular hours, and that an unfair advantage was given the pitcher.

In rebuttal, supporters of the project maintained that most of the objections were based upon watching night games in the lower minor leagues, where cheap lighting systems caused the difficulties mentioned. But these people said that if night baseball was desirable in the minors, it was infinitely more desirable in the majors, which can afford better lights. It was also observed that most of the opposition came from the timid and/or recalcitrant owners who dismissed nocturnal play with the careless generalization, "baseball is a day game."

Like it or not, night baseball was definitely here to stay; in fact it had been around for quite a time. Though it was long believed that the first night game ever played took place at Fort Wayne, Indiana on the evening of June 2, 1883, with professional players from Quincy beating a club known as the M.E. Church Nine, 19 to 11, it has now been determined that a game had been played by artificial light seventeen days before that one. A team with the charming name of George Pensinger's Paint Shop defeated Clay Henninger's

Bowman, 1. Struck out: by Bowman, 1; Bivin, 1; Derringer, 3. Hits off Bowman, four in seven innings. Losing pitcher, Bowman. Umpires: Klem, Sears and Pinelli. Attendance: 20,422.

Nine at Chambersburg, Pa., May 16, 1883. The score of that contest is not known, but the light was supplied by a portable dynamo which rested on a flat car.

The real pioneer of night baseball, however, was George F. Cahill, an inventor from Holyoke, Massachusetts, who devised a practical lighting plant as early as 1909. Cahill journeyed about the country trying to interest ball clubs in his invention, and though he was permitted to stage numerous games, his idea was never taken seriously. Fortunately he lived long enough to attend the game at Cincinnati in 1935, the realization of his dream.

The General Electric Company in 1927 demonstrated that night baseball was practical and induced the Boston Braves to meet a picked team at Lynn, Massachusetts under the sponsorship of their arcs. But it was not until depression struck the country that teams actually considered playing championship games by night.

Independence, Kansas, a club representing the Western Association, played a night exhibition with the House of David, April 18, 1930, a contest that was quite widely publicized, and a few weeks later, Des Moines and Wichita of the Western League engaged in a championship struggle at Des Moines on the evening of May 2. Other minor league clubs, noting the success of the experiment, began to install plants, and before long the lights were blazing at such points as Omaha, Decatur, Sacramento, Portland, Asheville, Jeannette, Wheeling and Muskogee.

Within a very few years minor league teams discovered that the application of night ball actually tripled their attendance, and magnates began to ask themselves why it had never before occurred to them to play at a time when most working people were at leisure. By 1934, 15 of baseball's 19 minor leagues had one or more parks equipped with lights, and a total of 65 teams depended upon plants that ranged in cost everywhere from $3,000 up to $50,000.

After the Cincinnati venture succeeded, other major league teams began to show more interest. MacPhail himself moved on to Brooklyn, where he blazed another trail for night ball at Ebbets Field, having the extraordinary good fortune to see Johnny Vander Meer, Cincinnati's ephemeral sensation, pitch the second of two successive no-hit games in the game that marked night baseball's debut at Flat-bush.

The first American League convert was Connie Mack, who conveniently forgot his hippodroming charge of four years before. Though 76 years old at the time, Connie gurgled like a schoolboy when he contemplated the lights he had erected at Shibe Park in 1939.

"Why, it's even brighter out there on the diamond than it is on a sunshiny afternoon," Connie cooed into the field microphone, not knowing it was turned on. "It's wonderful; why, it's perfect for a ball game."

By this time one of the few die-hards was Ed Barrow, the beetle-browed tycoon of the New York Yankees, who said as late as October, 1939, "Night baseball is a passing attraction which will not live long enough to make it wise for the New York club to spend $250,000 on a lighting system at the Stadium." But when the Yankees became the thirteenth major league club to install lights in 1946, Ed Barrow was on hand and watched the reversal of his prophecy take place.

Here is how night baseball came to the major leagues:

CLUB	DATE	ATTENDANCE
Cincinnati, NL	May 24, 1935	20,422
Brooklyn, NL	June 15, 1938	38,748

Philadelphia, AL	May 16, 1939	15,109
Philadelphia, NL	June 1, 1939	8,000
Cleveland, AL	June 27, 1939	55,305
Chicago, AL	August 14, 1939	30,000
New York, NL	May 24, 1940	22,460
St. Louis, AL	May 24, 1940	24,827
Pittsburgh, NL	June 4, 1940	20,319
St. Louis, NL	June 4, 1940	23,500
Washington, AL	May 28, 1941	25,000
Boston, NL	May 11, 1946	35,945
New York, AL	May 28, 1946	48,895
Boston, AL	June 13, 1947	34,510
Detroit, AL	June 15, 1948	54,480

Today the Chicago Cubs are the only major league club not yet called upon to play by night at home, although the management has exhibited a friendliness towards the arcs that demonstrates the day is not far removed when Wrigley's hirelings will strut their stuff after the sun goes down.

Each succeeding major league plant has poured down more benign though more powerful rays than its predecessor, and when the Detroit installation enabled the Tigers to play beneath 2,750,000 watts, engineers gleefully explained that this was the equivalent of six thousand full moons.

At first the clubs held themselves to the schedule of seven games a season, the number insisted on by MacPhail. But the lure of the lamps and the clicking of the turnstiles were too compelling to ignore, and when President Roosevelt asked for increased night ball to provide decent leisure for warworkers, the magnates blissfully assented. Today night baseball in the majors is almost entirely unrestricted.

MacPhail was right; attendance was stimulated beyond all belief. Teams in the National and American leagues attained a composite attendance of ten million, thanks to the lights, for the first time in 1945. This figure was upped unbelievably to eighteen million in 1946, nineteen million in 1947, and the peak of twenty million in 1948. The men who scoffed at Larry MacPhail in 1935 and considered him a carnival barker can now thank him for making it possible for them to enjoy a comfortable old age. But will they? Such genuflections do not seem to be standard equipment in their code of etiquette.

"Break Up
the Yankees!" 27

"Organize, regulate, promote, but battle the Yankees by building up to them, not by any un-American methods of putting a premium on mediocrity "
Dr. Erle V. Painter, trainer,
New York Yankees, in 1939.

NOT EVEN the bright lights of night baseball could dim the glory of Babe Ruth, whose passing from the baseball stage coincided with the shift of the spotlight to play under the stars. On May 25, 1935, the afternoon that followed the first night game in major league history, the Bambino, by now a hobbling, forty-year-old outfielder, pinch hitter and vice president of the Boston Braves, burst into explosive grandeur for the last time when he unloaded three tremendous home runs against the Pirates in a single game at Forbes Field. Three summers later the Babe was a spectator at Ebbets Field when the lights were turned on there, and so tumultuous an ovation did he receive that four days later the Dodgers hired him as a coach.

After that, they let Ruth alone, left him with his scrap-books and his memories to sit out his days in his Riverside Drive apartment, embittered because he had never been given a chance to manage a big league team. And when he died, hideously, of cancer of the throat in 1948, they all said he was the greatest of them all.

A fate that was perhaps even sadder pursued Ruth's great team-mate of the twenties, Lou Gehrig. Possessed of an unparalleled stubbornness and a burning zeal to play and win that is seldom seen, Gehrig was a fixture at first base for the New York club for fourteen years, and his record of playing 2,130 consecutive games is one that probably will never be broken.

There are some curious circumstances surrounding that mark. Prior to Gehrig, the most successive games ever participated in by a major league player was 1,307, the figure achieved by Everett Scott, an extremely talented American League shortstop. Scott was benched at the conclusion of his skein while with the Yankees early in 1925, and his place was taken by Paul (Peewee) Wanninger, an obscure rookie. Only a few days later, on June 1, 1925, Gehrig went up to the plate as a pinch-hitter for this same Wanninger, and it was in that box score that Lou began his record-shattering total of games. On the following day he replaced the veteran Wally Pipp, who had a headache, at first base, and from that time on he plodded to fame as baseball's Iron Horse, remaining in the lineup despite all sorts of minor injuries, serious beanings, and lumbago. Finally, not knowing that he was suffering from amyotrophic lateral sclerosis, a form of paralysis, he benched himself in a game at Detroit, May 2, 1939. Gehrig had been approaching his twenty-second birthday when the string began; he was graying as he neared thirty-six when it ended.

When Gehrig died in 1941, there were many who considered him the greatest first baseman of all time. He left a lifetime batting average of .340, and his feats of slugging still dot the record books. Certainly he and Ruth were the most fearsome duo a pitcher was ever called upon to face in one inning.

But Colonel Jacob Ruppert, the owner of the Yankees, was well aware that baseball had changed. The Yankees had been able to purchase Ruth from the Red Sox when he was an established star; they had found Gehrig on their own doorstep, endangering the windows that surround South Field of Columbia University. The Colonel knew that he could not build a great baseball machine by counting on the purchasing of talent from other organizations, or the mere accident of finding a Gehrig in the streets.

Ruppert knew that Branch Rickey had the right answer in his farm system, that an organization must be developed. Well, if the Yankees had to go into the farm business, they would. The Colonel considered baseball fifty years behind the times, and he knew that with his business acumen and vast resources he could construct an empire that would make Rickey's look feeble by comparison.

Ed Barrow, whose career dated back to the previous century, supplied Ruppert with the ideal executive to head the formidable front office. George Weiss, a suave and urbane executive of magnificent talents, nevertheless had the knowledge of baseball's bucolic aspects to head the farm chain. Paul Krichell, a former mediocrity as a player but a very shrewd judge of baseball flesh, made his contribution as chief scout.

Ruppert and Barrow found the field manager they wanted in Joe McCarthy, who had never reached the majors as a player but who had led the Cubs to a pennant in 1929. McCarthy moved to the Stadium in 1932 and for more than 15 years he was to sit in the Yankee dugout, manipulating the most skilled players in the game with an occult insight. McCarthy had great judgment in handling pitchers, in picking and coordinating players. Like Huggins before him, he paid great attention to small details, knowing that they added up to victory.

Replacing Ruth was something else again, but the Yankees were fortunate enough to find a great star in Joe DiMaggio, a young outfielder from the Pacific Coast League. Because he had hurt his knee getting off a bus and there was some question as to whether the injury would have a permanent effect, Barrow was able to obtain DiMag for only $25,000 and five players, the most fortunate baseball bargain of all time. Although he never excited public attention the way Ruth did, DiMaggio was a super player in his prime, an inspirational athlete who seemed to do everything without effort. If the script called for a home run, Joe hit a home run. If it required him to dash several hundred feet to snare a fly ball, he did that. He would tip his cap to the crowd perfunctorily, for that was part of his job too, but he never had the love for humanity that was in Ruth.

The Yankees finished second to Detroit in 1934, the last season that Ruth was in their employ, and remained there the following year. But by 1936, the season that DiMaggio joined the ranks, the Bombers were ready for an assault on every previous approach to perfection. No team in history had ever won more than two consecutive world championships. The Yanks, the scourge of baseball, won four in a row, defeating their National League opponents in each world series as handily as they breezed through each championship season in their own circuit.

Here is the statistical story of that cyclone:

YEAR	YANKEES		MARGIN	DATE		WORLD SERIES	
	WON	LOST	OVER 2ND PLACE CLUB	PENNANT WAS CINCHED		WON	LOST
1936	102	51	19 1/2 games	September	9	4	2
1937	102	52	13 games	September	23	4	1
1938	99	53	9 1/2 games	September	18	4	0
1939	106	45	17 games	September	16	4	0

During this four year period the Bombers won sixteen world series games while losing three, two of them to the great Carl Hubbell and one to Hal Schumacher. The last nine of the world series victories were in succession, and actually the team increased it to ten by copping the first series game from the Dodgers in 1941. In the history of the inter-league competition there is nothing to approach it, and some critics believe that this modern Ruppert machine even surpassed the 1927 club.

It is idle to try to compare those wonderful machines, because there are too many intangibles. The earlier team had Ruth and Gehrig and better pitching. The later nine had better defense, especially in the infield. On a pure position by position comparison between the squads of 1927 and 1939, Gehrig was better than Babe Dahlgren by a wide margin, Joe Gordon perhaps was a shade better than Tony Lazzeri, Frankie Crosetti was far more impressive than Mark Koenig, and Red Rolfe was a better performer than Joe Dugan. In the outfield Ruth surpassed any of the others, but DiMaggio excelled Combs and Bob Meusel and George Selkirk were about equal. Bill Dickey, behind the bat, was far superior to either Pat Collins or Bennie Bengough of the 1927 club.

Judge Landis watched the growth of the farm idea with mounting exasperation, but he could find no violation of the game's rules by the Yankee brain trust, which played the game according to the code. It did seem, though, that the New Yorkers had succeeded in stifling competition by their superiority, and fans actually thought it best that the club be broken up. Colonel Ruppert died when his club was still at the crest, in January, 1939, and he always insisted, "Let the other teams build up to our level."

But if Landis could not catch the Yankee imitators of the Rickey idea, he could trap several more careless operators. Within two years after making free agents of more than 80 Cardinal farm hands, the Judge, in January, 1940, emancipated a total of 91 athletes who thought they belonged to the Detroit Tigers, a decision which cost the Bengals an estimated half million dollars at the time. Only two of the players, Infielder Benny McCoy and Outfielder Roy Cullenbine, were of proven major league stature, but among those who were just starting out and were derailed en route to Detroit was Johnny Sain, later a three-time twenty-game winner for the Braves.

The executive bungling done by Detroit was old stuff, and included the manipulation of players, contract irregularities, secret agreements and the deliberate violation of known rules.

By this time the other fifteen teams, shocked by what the Commissioner had done, wondered if they too were suspect. By now, two decades after Rickey had conceived the idea, all had their farm chains. All, presumably, were mystified by what they could and could not do under the rules.

Instead of pledging to obey the rules, the magnates snorted, "What has Landis ever done for the game? If he doesn't like the farm system idea, let him suggest some alternative."

The Judge was willing to oblige. Within two weeks he came forth with a radical proposal that, had it been effected, would have changed the entire fabric of the game. Landis proposed that his office be given jurisdiction over all minor league players, a clearing house or pool, and that he be charged with the instruction, development and placing of recruits. He further suggested that the major leagues finance the minors, and that subsidies be paid to minor leagues of low classification to help them operate. Cash accrued from the sale of players was to make up for the subsidies, and all players not sold at the end of each playing season were to be subject to unrestricted draft.

Judge Landis was a man of many contradictions, and for a lifelong Republican he seemed strange in the role of father for such a hodgepodge of pure socialism. And yet the magnates reacted to his suggestion with great restraint, pointing out that there were some virtues to his scheme. But it was never seriously believed that any such plan would be adopted.

Landis had courage, and yet he muffed his greatest chances to exhibit it. Consider the case of Bob Feller. An Iowa farm boy, Feller had been signed by the Cleveland Indians in 1935, when he was but sixteen years old, or rather he had been signed to a contract with the Fargo-Moorhead club of the Northern League. Fargo-Moorhead assigned him to New Orleans in January, 1936, and two months later Feller was granted voluntary retirement. During the 1936 season he pitched batting practice for Cleveland, and when he struck out eight Cardinals in a three-inning exhibition stint, his name careened dizzily into the headlines. Cleveland then had him reinstated and purchased him from New Orleans, and he was used in championship games.

The Des Moines club of the Western League then claimed that it had attempted to sign Feller but had been thwarted because Cleveland snared him despite the clause of the Major-Minor agreement which prevented major league teams from signing sandlotters. Had Cleveland taken the ordinary precaution of becoming the owner of the Fargo-Moorhead team, and designating Cyril C. Slapnicka, the man who signed Feller, as a vice president of that club, all would have been legal, for that is the device major league teams habitually use to violate their agreement with the minors. But Cleveland slipped up.

The Landis decision in the Feller case is a maze of double talk, but since he awarded the aggrieved party, Des Moines, $7,500 damages, he obviously believed that the Indians were in the wrong. Feller might easily have been given his free agency, as were the various Cardinals and Tigers.

But perhaps this was a decision of the heart and not the head. Had Feller been made a free agent, the bidding for his services would have reached fantastic proportions, and he would probably have ended up as a member of that wealthiest of clubs, the Yankees. It is likely that Landis, foreseeing that contingency, felt that the correct legal decision in this instance would only serve to unbalance the game even further.

Bobby remained with the Indians and became one of the most brilliant pitchers of all time. It is probable that if he had become a Yankee the Bombers would not have lost for at least five more years. As it was the Yanks were nosed out by Detroit in 1940 when the old sparkplugs, Bill Dickey and Red Rolfe, could not quite equal their previous heroics.

It is likely that baseball reached its pinnacle of playing skill in those years just before World War II.

And atop that pinnacle, if such a thing can be, were the Bronx Bombers of Colonel Jacob Ruppert, who demonstrated that business sagacity combined with capital might rout all opposition and provide the public with a juggernaut.

Under
the Green Light 28

T HE BASEBALL fan is by his very nature isolationist in spirit. The real follower of the game pursues his interest in the sport at the exclusion of everything else. To him there is nothing worse than winter, which means no baseball at all, and even in season he carps at anything that delays play, whether it be rain or darkness or the more animate and unnecessary spectacle of a governor or mayor prolonging a pre-game ceremony with rhetoric. This type of fan even considers global war as a personal affront designed to ruin his enjoyment of baseball.

By the autumn of 1939 even the die-hards of baseball must have known that the invasion of Poland by Herr Hitler would necessarily change life in the western hemisphere. And yet the Spalding-Reach guide, issued in April, 1940, made no editorial reference to the war which had engulfed the world.

However, on St. Patrick's Day, 1940, baseball made its first gesture to the war-torn world. All-star teams from the National and American leagues clashed at Tampa for the benefit of the Finnish Relief Fund, and the game, won by the National, 2 to 1, netted almost $20,000 for the valiant Finns who were fighting the Soviets in the snows. Bill McKechnie piloted the National League forces, and it heralded the start of a banner year for the veteran. In July a McKechnie managed all-star club shut out the American, 4 to 0, in the regular "dream game," and in October his Reds won the world championship in a seven-game set with the Detroit Tigers. The season constituted a refreshing oasis in the sands of National League fortune.

Baseball first felt the impact of war when all American men between the ages of 21 and 36 registered for militaryservice, October 16, 1940. When Bill Embrich, an obscure outfielder with Harrisburg of the Inter-State League, was called for duty less than six weeks later, the game had its first reminder that its personnel owed their first duty to the nation. Hugh Mulcahy, a pitcher for the Phillies, soon became the first major leaguer to change the color of his uniform to khaki, and clubs had to set up a "National Defense List," which provided automatic retirement for athletes called to the colors. By April, 1941 the Spalding-Reach guide, no longer able to disregard the military aspects of life, ran a rather negative editorial under the head, "Baseball Never A Slacker," which was true enough.

But the game as played in the major leagues in 1941 was still close to perfection. Fans that year were excited by two remarkable hitting performances. Joe DiMaggio, attaining more laurels with the passing of each campaign, hit safely in 56 consecutive games, a record. Starting on May 15, DiMag was not stopped until the night of July 17, when an outpouring of 67,468 at Cleveland's cavernous Municipal Stadium watched two pitchers, Al Smith and Jim Bagby, shut him out. The best previous streak of this kind, 44 games, had been established by diminutive Willie Keeler for the Baltimore Orioles in 1897.

The other event in the slugging world that captivated the populace was Ted Williams' season batting record of .406. The Red Sox outfielder became the first player in eleven years to bat better than .400, Bill Terry of the Giants having swatted .401 in 1930. But Williams' mark was the highest since Rogers Hornsby had hit .424 in 1924, the modern record.

Those two magnificent batting accomplishments highlighted the last year in which baseball was to continue unmolested by the war. When the Japanese bombed Pearl Harbor December 7, the question became not merely whether baseball would be worse but whether it would continue at all.

It was really the Selective Service system that saved the game, because fans knew that a player's draft status was a personal matter between him and his local board. That made for a much better situation than had existed in 1918, when the "work-or-fight" order made any player in uniform, baseball uniform that is, feel something like a slacker. Throughout 1942 enough players were deferred by their boards for various reasons to assure the continuance of the game.

But by 1943 the situation, to use a word popular in the communiques of the era, worsened. Draft boards, politicians and various others involved seemed uncertain whether the national game was important enough to continue. That it was not essential seemed obvious.

Joseph B. Eastman, the director of defense transportation, warned all clubs that in 1943 they must conserve transportation. The two majors then adopted playing schedules that saved more than 46,000 miles, and also scheduled benefit games in each major league city, with the proceeds turned over to war charity. Eastman's office also demanded that teams train closer to home, north of the Ohio and Potomac rivers and east of the Mississippi, an exception being made in the case of the two St. Louis clubs, which were permitted to condition in Missouri.

In complying with this order, major league clubs pitched their camps in this exotic pattern:

NATIONAL LEAGUE	AMERICAN LEAGUE
Braves — Wallingford, Conn.	Red Sox — Medford, Mass.
Dodgers — Bear Mountain, N.Y.	White Sox — French Lick, Ind.
	Indians — West Lafayette, Ind.
Cubs — French Lick, Ind.	Tigers — Evansville, Ind.
Reds — Bloomington, Ind.	Yankees — Asbury Park, N.J.
Giants — Lakewood, N.J.	Athletics — Wilmington, Del.
Phils — Swarthmore, Pa.	Browns — Cape Girardeau, Mo.
Pirates — Muncie, Ind.	Senators — College Park, Mary
Cardinals — Cairo, 111.	land.

It took some time for the athletes to accustom themselves to their chilly locales, and they were wont to recall that in 1942 eleven teams had trained in Florida, four in California and one in Cuba.

Another victim of the war in 1943 was the baseball used by major league teams. Made without the use of critical materials, it contained a strange core made of balata, a reclaimed compound, instead of rubber. Dead as the hopes of a cellar team it plunked off the bats and rolled weakly to the infield or sagged in mid-air. When 11 of the first 29 games played in the majors resulted in shutouts, the magnates screamed to the manufacturers, and a new ball was soon produced. The Cooper Union Institute of Technology submitted the wartime sphere to a series of tests which showed it was 25.9% less resilient than the old ball, and hitters looked for a similar reduction in their batting efficiency.

For the first time a shortage of skilled players became apparent, but teams took the attitude that they would play as long as they could field nine men, which seemed to be in accordance with governmental thought in Washington. But baseball had no lobby in Congress. Judge Landis was extremely squeamish about even having officials of the game visit men in office. The game sought no favors.

In January, 1942 Landis had written to President Roosevelt, inquiring as to the status of baseball in wartime so that clubs would know whether to bother to start training. The President replied that he thought it best to keep baseball going, that it provided legitimate occupation for the leisure hours of war workers, and that he wished more night games could be played. This famous document came to be known as the "green light letter," and it served to clear up the game's traffic snarl that resulted when some of the magnates thought they were seeing amber. Baseball did not continue in the brilliance of its pre-war days, but at least it continued to glow, however dimly, under the green light.

The suggestion that clubs play more at night was hailed with glee, and the restriction of seven night games was waived. The nocturnal game has since succeeded so well as a siren of customers that it is virtually certain no limit on them will ever again be imposed.

Wartime baseball produced other strange tinkerings with the clock. In order to please and entertain workers from the night shift, morning games were introduced, a custom in which teams never had indulged save on the mornings of holidays in some cities. Other tilts were started at twilight, sometimes as the first games of what came to be known, horribly, as twi-night double headers. The players got more inept with the passing of each month, but the grandstands were jammed, not only with war workers of both sexes but with soldiers, sailors and marines who were admitted free of charge. Passes were also given to those who donated their blood to banks, and playing the national anthem became standard procedure in all parks, whether it was canned music or the warbling of some bosomy canary.

By 1944 the shortage of players was really acute, as all men between the ages of 18 and 38 were either in the armed forces or in essential work, as ordered by War Manpower Commissioner Paul V. McNutt. Players long forgotten re-appeared on the major league scene. Others who never would be ready for the major leagues went through the motions of playing big league ball. Scouts no longer asked if a player could throw, run and hit. They sought men with punctured ear-drums, epileptics, and mutes. The Cardinals introduced a pitcher considered highly desirable because as a baby he had swallowed a lump of coal and the subsequent operation to remove it left him unfit for military duty. Cincinnati used a pitcher named Joe Nuxhall more than a month before his sixteenth birthday, the youngest player of all time.

By 1945 the game had reached its alltime low. Only 12 minor leagues operated beneath the two majors. The play became so incompetent that when one Chicago writer was asked whether he thought the Cubs or Tigers would win the world series, he replied, with considerable justice, "I don't believe either club is capable of winning."

But by that time it was obvious the worst was over, and the surrender of Japan made certain that baseball would survive. War veterans began to get back into civvies, and into the flannel of their respective clubs. Baseball, which had survived everything in its history, had staggered through World War II.

Judge Landis, who had guided the game for almost a quarter-century, did not live to see the completion of the war. Falling ill in 1944, he died of coronary thrombosis at St. Luke's Hospital, Chicago, November 25. His death left baseball in the hands of the advisory council, a group consisting of the two league presidents, Ford Frick and William Harridge, and Landis' assistant, Leslie M. O'Connor. Landis hoped that O'Connor, who had written so many of his decisions, would be elected as his successor. But the magnates felt that O'Connor had fathered the Landis proposal of a pool for players as an antidote to the farm system, and they feared to entrust their properties to one with such revolutionary views.

But the election of a one-man commission was viewed as inevitable, and there was no shortage of candidates both in and out of baseball. The first move was to appoint a committee of four to sift the candidates, a group which included Alva Bradley of the Indians, Don Barnes of the Browns, Sam Breadon of the Cardinals and Philip K. Wrigley of the Cubs. The committee moved slowly, and though numerous meetings were held little progress was made.

It was at Cleveland in April, 1945 that the new commissioner was finally selected. The explosive Larry MacPhail, by now president of the Yankees after blazing previous trails with the Reds and Dodgers, accosted Barnes in Cleveland just before the meeting and said, "I understand your committee is going to recommend a stopgap commissioner or else move for further delay."

"That's right," Barnes said.

"Well, that's all nonsense," MacPhail thundered. "You'll be the laughing stock of baseball."

This led to a heated exchange of words, and the ebullient MacPhail was so angered that he returned to his hotel and tried to get plane reservations for New York, but without success.

On the following day, April 24, the club owners met in the Rose Room of Hotel Cleveland, and MacPhail was in attendance. Barnes read the report of his committee and revealed that a list of more than one hundred aspirants for baseball's biggest job had been reduced to six, as follows: Ford Frick, president of the National League; James A. Farley, former Postmaster General and an executive of the Coca-Cola Company; War Mobilizer Fred Vinson; Robert P. Patterson, Undersecretary of War; Robert Hannegan, head of the National Democratic Committee; and Frank Lausche, Governor of Ohio.

"Why isn't Senator Chandler of Kentucky on that list?" MacPhail shouted.

"I have nothing against Chandler," Barnes said. "Let's put him on and make him the seventh."

The magnates then voted and were surprised to note that Senator Chandler's name appeared either one, two or three on every ballot, and either first or second on 13 of the 16.

The next move was to discuss all seven of the men and eliminate those who appeared doubtful. Vinson was the first to be eliminated, then Patterson, and finally all but Chandler and Hannegan. A vote was then called for, and on the first poll Chandler had 11 votes and Hannegan five. Horace Stoneham of the Giants then switched to the Chandler camp, and on the third ballot Chandler was elected unanimously.

Who baseball's commissioner would have been had MacPhail succeeded in obtaining plane reservations the day before is uncertain, but on such whims of fate rest even more important decisions.

Albert Benjamin (Happy) Chandler was born in the dusty hamlet of Corydon, Kentucky, July 14, 1898, son of a tenant farmer who eked out an existence by doing such odd jobs as lugging the mail from the depot to the post office. The boy grew up in extremely humble circumstances but early in life helped better his lot by finding chores of his own to do. He worked his way through Transylvania College and first demonstrated his talent for politics as a joiner in almost every campus activity imaginable. It was at this stage of life that his perpetual grin secured for him the nickname of "Happy."

A wealthy Louisville distiller and Transylvania alumnus helped him through Harvard's Law School, and Chandler returned to Kentucky to practice. His first political post of any consequence was a seat in the state Senate. "Happy" had an affable manner, and his youth became a political asset as the road led to the lieutenant-governorship, the governorship and the United States Senate.

Chandler brought to his job, the realization of a long ambition, a love for baseball and devotion to its welfare. But he was amazed to discover that the commissionership carried with it as much criticism as any political post. He was almost immediately attacked by the press, which expected him to be a carbon copy of Judge Landis. The public had grown so used to the pictured image of Landis, chin thrust out and white hair cropping out from under his battered hat, that his successor was expected to be a virtual replica. Baffled and hurt by this reception, Chandler systematically set his course.

"If anywhere in the world social barriers are broken down it is on the ball field. There are many men of low birth and poor breeding who are the idols of the rich and cultured; the best man is he who plays best. Even men of churlish disposition and coarse hues are tolerated on the field. In view of these facts the objection to colored men is ridiculous. If social distinctions are to be made, half the players in the country will be shut out. Better make character and personal habits the test. Weed out the toughs and intemperate men first, and then it may be in order to draw the color line

Newark *Call*, October, 1887.

THE BASEBALL field is hardly a good laboratory for the study of race relations. This was discovered early in the game's history by Moses Fleetwood Walker, a Negro catcher for Toledo of the American Association in 1884, and his brother, Welday Wilberforce Walker, an outfielder with the same club. The Walker boys, unquestionably the first Negroes to appear in major league box scores, were the sons of a fugitive slave who made his escape to Mt. Pleasant, Ohio, an important stop on the Underground Railroad. "Fleet" Walker, as the catcher and more prominent of the brothers was called, grew up around Steubenville, attended Oberlin College and later the law school of the University of Michigan.

But though the Walkers were the first actual Negroes in the majors, they were not the first to feel the sting of taunts about their pigmentation. That distinction went to Vincent (Sandy) Nava, a Cuban catcher who appeared in 1882 with Providence of the National League. Nava, the target of players, fans and the press because of his sallow complexion, turned into a lush and ended his days as a bouncer in a dive on Harrison Street in Baltimore.

"Fleet" Walker almost went the same route. Deprived of his occupation by the unwritten law against Negroes that came about in 1887, he lived for a while at Syracuse and attained notoriety when, on April 9, 1891, while in a drunken stupor, he stabbed and killed a convicted burglar named Patrick Murray. After his acquittal he went back to Ohio and pursued a literary life, writing numerous pamphlets on the social problems of the Negro in America and a book on the same subject, "Our Home Colony." He lived out his days quietly and died at Steubenville in 1924, aged 66. Brother Welday, three years his junior, lived until 1937.

Newspapers of the 1880s took a curiously cynical and brutal view of non-Caucasians. On June 29, 1884 one major league paper's baseball writer printed this gem of ignorant prejudice against the Chinese: "Sam Gee, the Chinaman that Grady of the Reading team tried to kill recently with a beer bottle, did not die. He is still able to say 'No checkee, no washee' to absent-minded customers. Grady's fun, however, cost his club $112 in the way of court expenses and doctor bills."

The Walkers were not accepted by their mates on the Toledo team, nor, of course, by opposing players. When the club visited Louisville, urchins followed them in the streets, hooting at them and pelting them with sticks and stones.

Late in the 1884 campaign Richmond, Virginia acquired a franchise in the American Association, which caused four of the local xenophobes to dispatch the following communication to the Toledo manager, Charles H. Morton:

Richmond, Virginia
September 5, 1884.

Manager, Toledo Baseball Club.
Dear Sir:

We, the undersigned, do hereby warn you not to put up Walker, the Negro catcher, the days you play in Richmond, as we could mention the names of seventy-five determined men who have sworn to mob Walker if he comes on the ground in a suit. We hope you will listen to our words of warning so there will be no trouble, and if you do not, there certainly will be. We only write this to prevent much bloodshed, as you alone can prevent.

Bill Frick
James Kendrick
Dynx Dunn
Bob Roseman

Morton released the letter to the press, and when Toledo accepted the hospitality of Richmond on the thirteenth of the month, Walker did not catch, his place going to the unmistakenly fair John Thomas (Tug) Arundel of Auburn, New York. The major league had ended its first experiment with Negroes.

But despite the shoddy treatment given the Walkers, numerous Negroes continued to find employment in the minors. "Fleet" Walker went to Newark where he became the battery mate of a famed Negro pitcher, George Stovey. And by 1887 there were about twenty Negroes scattered through the minor leagues. Stovey was such a good pitcher that John Montgomery Ward tried to buy him for the Giants, but Cap Anson, manager of the White Stockings, found out about the deal and blocked it.

When Anson took his celebrated White Stockings to Newark for an exhibition in 1887, he refused to play unless Stovey and Walker were removed from the field, and when the home club reluctantly acceded to his demand, a precedent was established. Thereafter, even minor league teams barred the Negro. One of the last holdouts, the Harrisburg club, dismissed all its Negroes in order to gain admission to the Atlantic Association in 1890. By 1891 there was not a single Negro playing professionally.

More than half a century passed before there was more than occasional agitation for the removal of the unwritten law. And not until World War II, when Americans of all creeds began to examine their consciences, did the question of why Negroes were not represented in the major leagues prove embarrassing to the magnates.

When the Brooklyn Dodgers were in training at Bear Mountain, New York in 1945, Nat Low, sports editor of the Communist Daily Worker, and two other newspapermen put in a surprise appearance with two Negro players, First Baseman Dave (Showboat) Thomas and Pitcher Terris McDuffie, and demanded that they be given a trial. Obviously, this was a stunt to test the Quinn-Ives bill, legislation adopted by New York State which made it unlawful for industry to practice discrimination and provided for suitable prosecution. But the promoters unfortunately selected two players who were poor prospects. Thomas was 34, McDuffie 32.

They were given a complete workout and thoroughly examined by the Dodger board of strategy. Branch Rickey, furious at the methods which had been used to gain the tryout, shook his head and advised, "I'm more for your cause than anybody else you know," a statement which proved to be remarkably true, "but you are making a mistake using force. You are defeating your own aims."

Seven months later, on October 23, 1945, Hector Racine, president of the Montreal club of the International League, a farm team of the Dodgers, called a press conference, immediately causing speculation among the writers that the Royals might have been granted major league status. When they gathered expectantly in Racine's office, the forthcoming announcement was almost an anticlimax: Montreal had signed a Negro shortstop named Jack Roosevelt Robinson, former star football player at UCLA and Army lieutenant who had played with the Kansas City Monarchs, a Negro team, the previous year.

The baseball world was startled at this first break in the color line, and Rickey, in Brooklyn, was bombarded with questions from all sides. No, he did not sign Robinson because of fear of the Quinn-Ives bill. Yes, Robinson was a major league prospect, but he had been assigned to Montreal because he was not ready for the National League. No, he didn't anticipate trouble.

Jackie himself, introduced by Racine to the Montreal writers, shook hands all around and said, "If I can make good here, then it will be a new deal in baseball for people of my race. It could be that I'll be subjected to abuse, but I'll take the chance."

When Robinson reported for spring training at Daytona Beach prior to the 1946 season, he found that another Negro, Pitcher John Wright, had been signed to keep him company. Rickey visited the camp and made a plea to the players for fair play, pointing out that the team's manager, Clay Hopper, though a Mississippian, felt that Jackie could make the grade. But at first there was some doubt. Working out first at short and then at second, he was tense and unimpressive. But as the training grind wore on, he became more at ease and settled down to enter the battle with four experienced candidates for the second base job.

If there was any doubt that Jackie could meet with the requirements of International League play, it vanished in the opening game of the championship season when he made his debut at Roosevelt Stadium in Jersey City and thrilled a mob of 25,500 by smashing a home run and three singles, stealing two bases, batting in four runs and scoring four himself as the Royals romped over their hosts, 14 to 1. In the following days he performed so consistently that he became the most popular player on the club, not because of his novelty but only because of his skill.

Only in Baltimore was his appearance greeted with hostility, and though the reception given him there made his young wife go back to their hotel room to sob, Jackie merely bit his lip and maintained a discreet silence. He was still under wraps. Coached thoroughly by Rickey, who had foreseen every situation that developed, he kept his distance from umpires and handled close plays at second with decorum. Pitchers threw at him regularly, but soon learned that he could take it.

By September it was apparent that he could probably make the grade with Brooklyn. Bruno Betzel, the Jersey City manager, called him a better bunter than Ty Cobb. He was a line drive hitter who occasionally pulled the ball a long way to left field, but it was on the bases that he was at his best; constantly upsetting the pitchers with his daring. When the season closed, he was the league's leading batter with a mark of .349

and also the finest fielding second base guardian with a figure of .985.

But where could he play if he did make the Brooklyn club? The Dodgers had Harold (Peewee) Reese at short and Eddie Stanky at second, both major league stars. Robinson had worked out at third for a few games at Montreal, but he was not particularly brilliant at that post.

During the winter Rickey let Robinson remain on Montreal's list, delaying the formality of his purchase as long as possible. It was his hope that when the Dodger players saw Jackie in training, they would ask that he be brought up. Because of the segregation laws in Florida, both the Dodger team and the Montreal club trained at Havana, and had to fly 2,600 miles to Venezuela to find major league competition with the Yankees. Jackie was moved to first base, a position entirely foreign to him.

Some of the Brooklyn players were antagonistic towards him, and there were mutterings, but a few of the athletes were in his corner. Most outspoken was the Brooklyn coach, Jake Pitler, who said, "It would be a crime not to let this boy come up because of his color. Wait until you see him in action." As for Robinson, he said that if the players resented him he didn't want to play in the majors, that his only interest was an economic one.

Finally, on April 10, Rickey announced that Jackie's contract had been purchased from Montreal, and Jackie was in the lineup when his team opened the season against the Boston Braves, going hitless in three trips. But soon afterward he began to click. The Dodgers accepted him, and half the battle was won.

The other half of the battle, winning over his opponents, was something else again. Early in the season the Robinson experiment entered its most dangerous phase. Ben Chapman, the fiery Alabaman who managed the Phils, was charged with heaping abuse on Robby from the bench.

"So what?" Chapman told a sports writer for a Negro paper in Pittsburgh. "If Robinson has the stuff, he will be accepted in baseball the same as the Sullivans, the Lombardis, the Schultzes and the Grodzickis. All that I expect him to do is prove it."

Shortly afterward there was a more sinister development. Stan Woodward, writing an exclusive story in the New York Herald-Tribune, charged that certain St. Louis players planned to strike rather than take the field against Robinson, and that the plot aborted only when President Sam Breadon, after talking to Ford Frick, pointed out the folly of such a stupid move. Breadon, who had rushed to New York from St. Louis to meet with his team, denied that any such plot was in existence. But Frick gave proof of the authenticity of Woodward's story when he admitted what had taken place.

In a magnificent statement, showing how greatly he had gained in stature since his unfortunate bungling of the affair with Dizzy Dean, Frick, through Breadon, told the sulking Cardinals, "If you do this, you will be suspended from the league. You will find that the friends you think you have in the press box will not support you, that you will be outcasts. I do not care if half the league strikes. Those who do it will encounter quick retribution. All will be suspended, and I don't care if it wrecks the National League for five years. This is the United States of America, and one citizen has as much right to play as another."

From then on Jackie's lot was easier. Improving in his first base play as the year grew older, he became an accepted part of the National League scene. Closing the year with a batting average of .296, stealing 29 bases and demonstrating defensive skill and team value, he was chosen as "rookie of the year" by the game's bible, The Sporting News. When the Dodgers then lost a seven-game world series to the Yankees, Robinson, the first of his race to appear in the fall festival, held up his end for the losing cause.

Since that day, Jackie's career has been a succession of mounting triumphs, climaxed when he won the league batting championship in his third year, 1949, with a mark of .342. It was a long, hard road, but he took the turns in stride.

It should not be thought that all who opposed his entrance into major league baseball were motivated by bigotry. Many sincere players and fans took the position that baseball had such a unique code of ethics that it did not furnish the proper laboratory for a sociological experiment. Players representing other minorities had had to bear up under the most outrageous slurs. But their followers never attended games in a bloc; Jackie's did. The dynamite inherent in the situation was not on the playing field but in the stands. The Negro press urged its readers to welcome Robinson calmly, to avoid cheering when he made a routine play, to beware of demonstrations that would only embarrass him. And for a year Negroes kept their enthusiasm for the trail-blazer within bounds. But after he attained stardom, they found it difficult to restrain their exuberance, which led to a situation unique in baseball, the spectacle of home fans cheering the opposition in seven National League cities.

The obvious answer was for other magnates to sign Negro players. So it came about that Bill Veeck, the publicity-conscious generalissimo of the Cleveland Indians, bought a Negro infielder named Larry Doby from the Newark Eagles in July, 1947. Moved to the outfield the following year, Doby also succeeded as a big league player and starred when his club defeated the Boston Braves in the 1948 world series.

By 1949 the Dodgers had three Negroes in their starting lineup, as Catcher Roy Campanella and Pitcher Don New-combe achieved stardom with the Flatbush club. Though a freshman, Newcombe appeared to many observers as the best pitcher in the National League, and Campanella's work behind the bat in the world series of 1949 forced numerous observers to the conclusion that he was the game's best catcher.

Branch Rickey, his farm system idea now the property of every major league club, had tapped another source of playing talent, and the question of why Jackie had been signed answered itself.

The Land
of Tequila 30

THE ANNUAL minor league meetings held at Columbus, Ohio in December, 1945 and attended by major league officials in addition to numerous job-seekers and writers were utterly unlike the usual hot stove league gathering. Optimism reigned supreme as baseball, weary after the war years but excited by the future, heralded the reconversion to peace. Players were streaming back from the armed forces, and all of them seemed to have hit more than .400 while in service. The New York Giants boasted of their fabulous recruit, Clint Hartung, reputed to be, simultaneously, the greatest hitter and pitcher in the annals of the game; and every club, all the way down the ladder of baseball's minor league structure, had its particular reason to welcome the postwar world. Many lesser minor leagues were being organized without thought to territorial intelligence, and all the minors, led by the strident Pacific Coast League, which considered itself a major, clamored for an advance in classification. Lavish bonuses were handed to free agents, salary raises were granted indiscriminately, and baseball headed for what was to be the greatest era of prosperity it had ever known.

After the meetings the magnates prepared to train in Florida or California again, following the three springs of exile north of the Eastman line. Contracts were sent out, schedules for exhibitions were drawn up, and the great game was ready to move.

Branch Rickey, examining daily his formidable stack of mail, sniffed when he noted that two of his Montreal chattels, Pitcher Jean Pierre Roy and Outfielder Roland Gladu, thought so little of the terms he proffered that they were jumping to an outlaw circuit in Mexico. But a few days later, when Outfielder Luis Olmo, who was counted upon as a gardener at Ebbets Field, announced that he had accepted $40,000 for three years of play in Mexico, Rickey phoned Commissioner Chandler and asked what this Mexican business was all about.

It developed that the Mexican League was run by five fabulous brothers named Pasquel: Don Jorge, Alfonso, Gerardo, Bernardo and Mario. Jorge seemed to be the spokesman for the family and the boss, and his wealth was reputed to total thirty million dollars.

When it was published that Rickey had prevailed upon Chandler to act, Jorge landed in the public prints with a statement of his own, saying, "I'm very much surprised at Branch Rickey complaining of our raids. For many years, while our Mexican League was struggling to get along, major league scouts in general and Joe Cambria of the Washington Senators in particular stole our players when they were signed to Mexican League contracts."

Other players from other clubs then leaped south of the border, such athletes as Alex Carrasquel, a Venezuelan pitcher sold by the Senators to the White Sox, and Infielder Nap Reyes and Outfielder Danny Gardella of the Giants. But no "name" players headed for the land of tequila until Catcher Mickey Owen of the Dodgers and Shortstop Vern Stephens of the Browns jumped their reserve clause.

But all of these men were holdouts; no players signed to 1946 contracts leaped across the Rio Grande until Sal Maglie, George Hausmann and Roy Zimmerman of the Giants vaulted into the Mexican camp. Of these only Hausmann was counted upon as a regular, and the threat from the Pasquels was still in the nature of a nuisance rather than a problem.

Commissioner Chandler issued an ukase warning all the jumpers that if they did not rejoin their clubs by the opening game of the season, they would be suspended from organized baseball for a period of five years. The only one to heed the warning was Stephens, who reported back to the Browns after playing two games in the Tamale Circuit.

Stephens, a fun-loving player of real class, reported that he was tired of frijoles and enchiladas and that life in Old Mexico was not half so glamorous as painted. He moaned about the skinned diamonds in vogue, the poor clubhouse facilities, the custom of players smoking and drinking beer on the bench, and the long bus rides in decrepit vehicles that frequently paused to take on peon passengers accompanied by goats and chickens. Vern had to hide his identity to get back to the United States, a mission replete with cloak-and-dagger aspects, but accomplished in the nick of time.

Despite the warning of Stephens, more players flirted with Pasquel, who visited New York after the major league seasons got under way and continued to offer fantastic sums for top players. Ace Adams and Harry Feldman of the Giants, both pre-war major leaguers, made the leap; and then Pasquel pulled his neatest coup when Max Lanier and Freddy Martin, Cardinal pitchers, and Infielder Lou Klein of the same club deserted. Lanier had won his first six games of the year, and his southpaw slants were considered likely to spark the Redbirds to a flag.

Even the great Babe Ruth, still bitter in retirement, visited Mexico, and the rumor mill worked overtime reporting that the Bambino was to become Commissioner of the outlaws. Ruth had no such intentions, but he did spend several weeks being idolized by Mexican fans, and put on an exhibition of hitting that included his specialty, the home run. Returning to New York, he announced that he was willing to manage a team of AAA classification, but no offer ever reached him. His offer to pilot the Yankee farm at Newark was never replied to by Larry MacPhail.

Shortly after Lanier, Martin and Klein crossed into the cactus, Pasquel and Owen bobbed up in St. Louis and consulted the National League's greatest player and drawing card, Stan Musial. The offer they made him was certainly something to think about: $130,000 for five years, with $65,000 in cold cash supplied in advance. Musial was on the fence, but finally decided to remain with the Cardinals.

But by this time Sam Breadon, the president of the Red-birds still, made up his mind the time had come for action. Without consulting either Ford Frick or Commissioner Chandler, he boarded a plane and headed for Mexico City. His hope for secrecy was blasted when he encountered Gordon Cobbledick, a vacationing Cleveland sports writer, but at least he met Don Jorge and came to some sort of an agreement. Pasquel and Breadon understood each other as only two businessmen can, and when their session was finished, Pasquel announced that he would steal no more players from "my friend, Sam Breadon."

Although Breadon made it clear that he went to Mexico simply as a private citizen and not as an ambassador of the game, Chandler quite naturally felt that his trip put organized baseball in a compromising position, making it appear that the magnates were willing to bargain. Chandler summoned Breadon to a conference at Cincinnati, and when Sam failed to agree to come, he was fined $5,000 for disobeying the summons. Later, the fine was rescinded when Breadon explained his position. He had told Pasquel that he did not represent the game and was only protecting his own interests, and he was afraid that Jorge would interpret his visit to Chandler as the work of a stool pigeon.

No more players made the trek to Mexico after that, and Pasquel stopped making his mad offers. Baseball in Mexico was apparently not on a paying basis, and the competition was nothing like that the National and American leagues had suffered in their fight with the Brotherhood or Federals.

Mickey Owen, a dejected figure with a plea for sympathy and reinstatement, returned to the United States during the summer, a sadly disillusioned man who repeated all that Vern Stephens had said about conditions among the outlaws.

Owen had originally been hired to manage the Torreon club, but when he reached Mexico he was made boss of the Vera Cruz team instead. All went well at Vera Cruz until Jorge Pasquel, visualizing himself as a manager, suddenly made an appearance on the bench. Pasquel switched Owen to first base, and then dropped him as manager. It was Mickey's contention that this act made void his contract and enabled him to return to the United States without misgivings.

For more than three years the ineligible players made a living as best they could. Owen, his reinstatement denied, played outlaw ball and worked as an auctioneer in rural Missouri. Lanier, who later became disgusted and departed from Mexico, found that his pitching talents could best be employed in Quebec. Gardella, only an ordinary player, found that even the semipro ranks were closed to him, and he assumed the occupation of a hospital orderly.

Amnesty was finally granted when the Commissioner allowed the jumpers to return during the season of

1949. Owen, not wanted by the Dodgers, was sold to the Cubs and filled out the season as a Bruin, finding it difficult to start all over at 32. Lanier, Martin and Klein rejoined the Cardinals, and played an important part in that team's bid for the pennant. Since Lanier and Martin had filed tremendous lawsuits against the St. Louis club, fandom for a while watched the strange spectacle of players trying their best on the ballfield for clubs they were suing. Olmo also rejoined the Dodgers and appeared for that team in the 1949 world series, and several lesser lights took advantage of their eligibility, but soon slipped back to the minors.

When Fred Saigh, the Cardinal president, induced Lanier and Martin to drop their suits, organized baseball assured itself of victory. The only remaining holdout was Danny Gardella, the Giant outfielder whose lawyers threatened to blow the game wide open. But finally, during the 1949 world series, it was announced that Gardella too had settled and would sign a contract with the Cardinals in 1950. The cancellation of his date in court spared baseball the embarrassment of holding the reserve clause up to the light again for all to see. The Mexican hayride was over!

Another serious threat to the status quo in baseball was the organization of the American Baseball Guild, an independent labor union announced by Robert Murphy, a Boston lawyer, during the midst of all the excitement about Mexico. A graduate of Harvard Law School and examiner for the Labor Relations Board, Murphy hoped to junk the reserve clause, or at least see to it that players got a share of the purchase price if sold, submit financial disputes between a player and his club to a board of arbitration and establish a minimum wage for big league players. He claimed that in April, 1946 half of the sixteen major league clubs had on their rosters members of his guild.

The movement apparently had started when Murphy, a fan, listened to the gripes of various members of the Boston Braves. "Why don't you organize a union?" he asked. When they expressed interest and outlined their suggested improvements in a letter, Murphy set up the organization. Because Pittsburgh was a highly industrialized city, he concentrated on the Pirates and claimed that ninety per cent of that team's players were members.

Fans who attended a scheduled night game at Forbes Field on the evening of Friday, June 7, noticed a peculiar reversal of baseball custom. The home team always takes batting practice first and drills for a longer period than the visitors, but on this occasion the Giants hit first, and the Pirates did not put in an appearance until almost game time.

They had been detained at the clubhouse by a vote on whether or not to strike. Two days before Murphy had visited William Benswanger, president of the team, and had asked for recognition of his guild, which was denied. He then threatened a strike, but Benswanger averted it by making his first clubhouse appearance in twelve years and winning over his players. It was finally agreed that the players should vote in a closed meeting whether to strike for recognition of the union. It was decided that a three-fourths vote would be necessary to call the walkout, and the poll showed 20 players in favor of striking, 16 against.

That ended baseball's closest brush with unionization. Thoroughly frightened by this time, the magnates put an end to Murphy's hopes with what amounted to the formation of a company union. In a surprise meeting at Chicago in July they agreed to the formation of a committee of players (shades of John Montgomery Ward!) that would draw up a new player contract form.

Ford Frick then stepped forth and revealed that he had thought the player's contract to be inequitable for some time, that, in fact, he had drawn up a revised contract in 1936. What had become of it? Frick replied that he could only plead inertia. Frick also admitted that 19 players in the National League received less than $5,000 a season, and that there were 31 such athletes in the American.

When the players made known their demands, the public found little to become excited about. Not a single mention of the reserve clause was made. The players wanted a pension plan, a minimum salary of $5,000, no withdrawal of waivers after they were once asked and a player was claimed, the elimination of the ten-day clause in favor of 60-day notice with severance pay.

Baseball officialdom yielded to most of these demands, and the players eventually got their pension plan, the privilege to barnstorm 30 days instead of ten at the expiration of each season, 30-day notice instead of ten, $25 a week expense money during spring training, and a provision that their salaries could not be cut more than 25 per cent at one sitting.

By way of asking the athletes to pay for these demands, the magnates then announced the adoption of a schedule that called for 168 games annually instead of 154. Immediately there was a howl from players and fans. All baseball records are based on a schedule of 154 games; to adopt one of any other length would be to throw the record book out of the window. The magnates, never having given thought to the game's records, which seldom interest them, then realized what a blunder in public relations they had fallen for. Almost immediately the 168-game idea was abandoned, and when it was, Larry MacPhail, the perpetrator of the scheme, angrily quit his job on the game's steering committee.

And so, frightened by the twin perils of the Mexican League and the unionization scheme of Robert Murphy, the game of baseball, late in 1946, adopted some of the reforms that John Montgomery Ward had sought in 1887.

L'Affaire
Durocher   31

THE BASEBALL scene that followed World War II failed to follow the script. Instead of developing into an era of good feeling, as anticipated, it evolved into an age featured by short tempers, unnecessary harangues, and front office sensitivity unmatched in the game's past. Grandstands became full of the most intolerant fans yet, many of them former soldiers and sailors bearing resentment against their officers that they sublimated by screaming at umpires, managers and players. Magnates accused each other of stealing players, players went to court to collect back salary, and everyone connected with the game seemed anxious to shout his grievances in public. The Mexican League mess and the Murphy union attempt were only two aspects of the noisy prosperity that greeted A. B. Chandler when he took over as Commissioner.

Three men—two magnates and a manager—seemed involved in more than their share of the bickerings. They were: Leo Ernest Durocher, field leader of the Brooklyn Dodgers who was generally known as The Lip; his boss, pious Branch Rickey, the shrewd president of the same club; and Leland Stanford (Larry) MacPhail, formerly Leo's boss at Brooklyn but now president of the New York Yankees and a man whose public eruptions were just as well publicized and every bit as regular as those of Old Faithful.

Durocher was born on the wrong side of the tracks of West Springfield, Massachusetts, July 27, 1905.

He survived an atmosphere of poolrooms and gang fights because his skill at baseball enabled him to flee the environment. When he was only 20, he played shortstop so brilliantly for the Hartford team of the Eastern League that little Miller Huggins, manager of the wondrous Yankees, personally scouted him and bought him despite the low blood count of his .220 batting average. Perhaps Huggins saw in Durocher a replica of himself, for Miller had also been an infielder slight of stature who did little hitting.

The Yankees immediately decided the Leo was the freshest recruit who ever entered their clubhouse. Instead of being awed at finding himself a member of the club, Durocher palled around with Babe Ruth and brashly adopted the Ruthian mannerisms of speech and dress. A potential boulevardier, he tried to spend money as the Bambino did, which was something of a feat inasmuch as he earned one-tenth as much.

Durocher was adept at any activity that involved the use of the hands: playing shortstop, playing cards or manicuring a pool cue. There seemed to be an interlocking of his finger tips and intuitive brain, and his hands responded to his nimble wit feelingly and spontaneously. This made him as graceful an infielder as had ever been observed.

But despite his many talents, no other American League club wanted him when he was shipped to Cincinnati during the winter following the season of 1929, exchanged on waivers for an obscure infielder named Clarke Pittenger. He joined the Reds accompanied by a flood of debts which the Cincinnati president, Sidney Weil, tried to square by means of salary withholdings. Weil, his first spiritual father, set the pattern for Rickey's handling of him, and tried to keep his buoyancy within bounds. Durocher was traded to Rickey's Cardinals in May, 1933, in a deal involving Pitcher Paul Derringer, a transaction which helped both clubs. But the Cardinals were aided first, as Durocher fitted right into the Gas House Gang tradition, and his flamboyant play at short helped make possible the world championship of 1934.

MacPhail and Durocher first joined ranks at Brooklyn in 1938, and after that season Larry made him manager of the Dodgers. Leo then entered the most successful stage of his career, and set the stage for the Durocher who will be remembered: the nervous, intuitive firebrand who stormed out of the dugout to snarl at umpires, changed pitchers frantically and usually was right, and hurled epithets over his shoulder at those who taunted him from the box seats.

He was an anachronism in those days, an atavistic throwback to John McGraw, and fans who saw him kick dirt on an umpire's shoe or throw a towel in an arbiter's face wondered how he got away with it. Often he didn't, and his career was punctuated with fines and suspensions. But baseball people used to say that "the game has been pretty good to Leo Durocher," an observation which implied that retribution of some kind was inevitable.

Fortune caught up with Leo in the year that followed World War II. Still manager of the Dodgers under Rickey, who succeeded MacPhail at Brooklyn in 1943, he started the 1946 season by being cleared in a Brooklyn court of charges that he and Joe Moore, a park policeman, had broken the jaw of one John Christian under the stands at Ebbets Field. Leo said that Christian fell down while talking to him, but a civil suit for $6,750 was settled.

Larry MacPhail experienced a bad year with his Yankee managers in 1946, firing both Joe McCarthy and Bill Dickey, and ending the year with Johnny Neun at the helm. It was thought logical that MacPhail would reach over from the Bronx to Flatbush and snare Durocher to pilot the Bombers. Larry did induce Chuck Dressen, a coach at Brooklyn, to come to the Yanks, a move which caused ill feelings between the two clubs. Dressen had agreed to terms with the Dodgers for 1947 but had signed no contract. Rickey viewed Dressen's dereliction as unethical.

Even when MacPhail signed Bucky Harris to pilot his club for 1947 the furor over Durocher did not cease. Leo claimed that MacPhail had offered him the managerial job; Larry retorted that The Lip had sought the position but had been turned down.

Durocher, off the field, was as picturesque as he was in uniform. His office at Ebbets Field became general headquarters for a set of Hollywood characters, such people as George Raft, the movie gangster, and Danny Kaye, a comedian. Where John McGraw before him had found conviviality at the Lambs Club, Leo found his spiritual affinity in going Hollywood. He was no drinker, but he liked the ladies. All during 1946 he posed for cheesecake pictures with Edna Ryan, a Powers model from Brooklyn, and there were rumors that they were married.

Late in November, 1946, when Durocher was in Hollywood, he was called to Oakland by Commissioner Chandler for a little chat. This mysterious conference was held in the rough of the eighteenth fairway of the Claremont Country Club. After two hours of conversation, they split up, and Leo dismissed the confab as a "discussion about a business deal."

It developed later that the subject touched upon was a charge by Columnist Westbrook Pegler that in 1944, when the Dodgers were on the road, Durocher gave the key to his apartment to a friend so that his place might be used as a setting for dice games. Chandler tried to find out the circumstances of Leo's relations with various unsavory people.

"Do you know a man named Buggsy Siegel?" the Commissioner asked.

"I have a nodding acquaintance with him," Leo said.

"Don't nod to him any more," Chandler warned.

A few days after meeting with Chandler, Durocher was named co-respondent in a divorce action by Ray Hendricks, an airline executive who was filing an answer to his wife's plea for a divorce. Hendricks' wife was Laraine Day, a movie star, and it was charged that Durocher "clandestinely pursued" her affections "while posing as a family friend." They both denied the charges.

Leo and Laraine flew to Mexico where she obtained a divorce, crossed back over the border to El Paso and were married by a Texas Justice of the Peace before her California decree became final. Hailed into court by Judge George A. Dockweiler to show cause why the California judgment should not be set aside, Durocher then was quoted as calling the judge an "unethical and publicity conscious servant of the people," a speech which almost caused him to be cited for contempt.

By this time Branch Rickey began to wonder whether he had been wise in signing Durocher to manage the club again, a wonder which grew when the Catholic Youth Organization withdrew its support from the Brooklyn Knothole Club, saying that Durocher had "undermined the moral training of Brooklyn's Roman Catholic youths" by his conduct on and off the field.

But it was a chastened manager who reported to lead the Flatbush flock in training at Miami Beach. There were to be no more card games for stakes of any kind, and, above all, the new Durocher was to avoid gamblers.

That winter Durocher had been conducting under his name a column in the Brooklyn Eagle which was amazingly outspoken about baseball affairs and which appeared to be whipped up mainly to stimulate the rivalry between the Dodgers and Yankees. It was generally believed that the column was written by Harold Parrott, a former newspaperman who served the Dodgers as traveling secretary. When Larry MacPhail read what he interpreted as libels on his character, he unveiled the curtain on the next stage of the Durocher drama, filing oral charges with Commissioner Chandler against Durocher, Parrott and Rickey. Though Rickey was not writing any column, MacPhail had heard that the Mahatma had accused him of playing host to two gamblers in a box at the ball park at Havana. "Apparently there are two sets of rules in baseball," Rickey is supposed to have said. "One for Durocher and another for the rest of baseball." MacPhail considered this as slander.

Chandler closeted himself with Rickey, MacPhail, Durocher and the others involved in two secret sessions, the first at Sarasota and the second at St. Petersburg. MacPhail carried a brief of 50,000 words to substantiate his charges against Rickey, and these two adults engaged in an opéra bouffe of unparalleled childishness. The Commissioner enjoined all the participants to brush off questions from the press with "no comment," the only sensible means of shutting the three famous mouths.

When the evidence was sifted, Chandler's decision was firm enough to put an end to the nonsense. Durocher, found guilty of conduct detrimental to the game, was suspended for the entire playing season of 1947. MacPhail was fined $2,000 for permitting Durocher to use the threat of jumping to the Yankees as a squeeze against Rickey for better terms, Brooklyn's management was fined $2,000 for indulging in the silly squabble, and Harold Parrott was fined $500 for writing the pieces that brought matters to a head.

The decision made clear that Durocher's banishment was not brought about by the MacPhail charges but by "an accumulation of unpleasant incidents." Dressen was also suspended for thirty days because of the manner in which he left the Dodgers for the Yankees.

It is probable that MacPhail never dreamed when the charges were filed that they would result in such drastic penalties, and he immediately disregarded the order to maintain silence about the matter, telling a press conference that he felt the public was entitled to some facts about the hearing. He also wrote to William Harridge, his league president, asking that he intervene with Chandler, getting him to reconsider his decision. What Loud Larry forgot was that when he originally filed the charges, Chandler suggested that he wait a while and see if he still wanted to press them.

Laraine said it was all "terribly unfair."

Ford Frick implied that he too had been silenced, but then he lapsed into biblical rhetoric, saying, "If there is one among you without sin, let him cast the first stone." This was at the Brooklyn Knothole Club's annual dinner, and the audience inferred that Frick had found a way to evade the silence order. Interpreting it as a blast, however subtle, at the Chandler decision, the audience roared its ovation. If this was Frick's method of criticizing the man who held the job he had been so prominently mentioned for, it served as a demonstration of how timid had executives become since the days that another league president, Ban Johnson, openly opposed another Commissioner, Judge Landis.

MacPhail's continual talking about the case landed him in the Commissioner's lap again, and he talked to

Chandler for six hours and a half when summoned to Cincinnati to explain why he had ignored the order to preserve silence. That was the last of Larry. His Yankees won the 1947 pennant and defeated the Dodgers in the world series, then MacPhail departed from the scene. It was Burt Shotton, Rickey's old Sunday manager, who came out of retirement to fill in as Flatbush pilot.

After a maze of double talk over a period of months, Rickey finally appointed Durocher as his manager again in 1948. But in a surprising mid-season transfer, Leo crossed the East River to become the leader of the Giants, and Shotton again took over in the Dodger dugout.

As a Giant, Durocher was no longer debonair, no longer jaunty. He remained discreetly in the dugout, victim of the game's new code. It was a strange psychological study; he could no longer act like the Durocher of old, and the new Durocher became just another manager.

There was only one more unpleasant episode to mar his baseball life. Charged with assaulting a fan after a game at the Polo Grounds, he again appeared in Cincinnati before Chandler and was cleared of blame.

The departure of MacPhail from the game and the reconversion of Leo into a blushing violet left only Rickey unscathed. Baseball seemed vastly quieter to the fans.

Peace, It's Wonderful! 32

THE CRITICS of Albert B. Chandler as Commissioner of Baseball, many of whom thought the job should have gone to Ford Frick, complained of various things during the first few years of his administration. They resented the fact that he did not bear a physical resemblance to his predecessor, Judge Landis, felt that it was not dignified for him to sing "My Old Kentucky Home" at banquets, were annoyed because he set up his headquarters at Cincinnati instead of New York, and criticized his handling of the Durocher case.

As far as Landis wa

s concerned, Chandler could no more have been expected to be like him than Ford Frick could be expected to be like the man he succeeded, John Heydler. Chandler, however, was exactly like Landis when it came to protecting the welfare of the game. Landis lived in fear that baseball would be invaded by gamblers, and kept an ever-watchful eye on that contingency. Chandler adopted equally stern measures of dealing with the betting gentry, with the result that there has not been a breath of scandal in that direction during his administration.

Landis endeared himself to the press by his contempt for the game's magnates, although he was not always consistent in his decisions. Chandler had contempt for certain magnates too, but the general level of decency among men who owned ball clubs was considerably higher in 1945 than it had been in 1920. Landis was required by his times, so was Chandler. As a matter of fact, when Chandler did make a ruling of the Landis type, as he did in the dictatorial suspension of Leo Durocher, those who objected the most strenuously were those who had compared him to Landis and found him wanting.

Knowing little of baseball history, Chandler's critics failed to understand why he had set up shop in the smallest major league community. Actually, the historical precedent for such a move was strong. Cincinnati contributed the very idea of professional baseball to the nation, a fact which may eventually dawn upon those charged with selecting candidates for the Hall of Fame, and when that time comes, Harry Wright will perhaps be recognized for his contribution, even though Cooperstown is not the proper place to honor him. The idea for the National League was a western idea solely the property of William A. Hulbert, and the circuit succeeded despite the defection of clubs in New York and Philadelphia which opposed honesty in baseball in the first place. The American League was first visualized in Cincinnati by Ban Johnson and Charlie Comiskey, and was made a reality because of other westerners such as Al Spink. Finally, when baseball was run by a three-man commission, the chairman, Garry Herrmann, presided at Cincinnati. No more logical choice for the seat of the game's government could have been made than the one Chandler selected.

When Chandler took office, the game was plagued by numerous problems of the most thorny variety, including the Mexican League ruckus, the unionization threat, and the hullabaloo raised by Rickey, Durocher and MacPhail. The Commissioner solved all of these intricate puzzles with the greatest possible neatness, including the Danny Gardella lawsuit, an aftermath of the Mexico episode that threatened to topple the game's entire structure.

Babe Ruth Day was celebrated at Yankee Stadium on Sunday, April 27, 1947, and when Chandler stood there by the microphone at home plate, he was lustily booed by many of the 58,339 throats in attendance. Knowing full well that the fans had been poisoned by what they read of his handling of the Durocher case, he jutted his jaw, held up his head and went on with his speech. The boos changed to cheers during the progress of his talk, just as the boos have changed to cheers during the progress of his administration.

Why baseball had never held a Day for Babe Ruth before Chandler came into the game might seem inconceivable at first glance, but the important thing is there was one held for him at last, even though he was dying of cancer at the time.

In order to understand fully how well Chandler is adjusted to his times, it is necessary to compare baseball of modern days with the game of three decades ago. In that dim age clubs cared nothing about the welfare of young players, cheated them in salary, manipulated their contracts and left them to shift for themselves. Branch Rickey's farm system idea revolutionized the business because scouts had to deal with teen-aged boys and their parents and were not simply buying baseball flesh on the open market. As an outgrowth of the highly competitive farm systems set up by the clubs, bonuses were awarded boys without previous experience. With so much invested in their recruits, clubs learned to see that the boys married properly, visited the dentist and knew something about sex hygiene. Sissified? Perhaps, but it saved numerous careers, and besides it only reflected the paternalism that was going on in America's national life starting in March, 1933.

If John McGraw were alive today, it is extremely likely that he would conform to the times. McGraw would be much too shrewd to operate in any other way.

The point is, when Chandler talks of setting an example for youth and making baseball a profession any man would be proud to have his son engage in, he isn't dealing in corny cliches but is talking facts. The evils that were paramount in baseball when Landis took over in 1920 are no longer present.

Some fans, who remember what was good in the old days, yearn nostalgically for the long ago. But there is no turning back. Possibly baseball was more competitive before there were trainers and rubbing tables and sanitary clubhouses, but when an oldtimer such as Grover Alexander boasts that he never had a sore arm he forgets that many pitchers of his time did and had to leave baseball because there was no known treatment for such an affliction.

Players today are criticized because they are business men, just as in the eighties they were criticized because they were not. But there are still men who slide hard, throw hard, run hard and hit hard, and they do all these things before huge crowds, much larger than the gatherings that used to delight in throwing pop bottles from the wooden stands of blessed memory.

Chandler's view of the function of the commissionership is not necessarily that of a man with a club, and he has succeeded admirably in promoting baseball among youngsters. But the club is there and can be used if necessary.

Meanwhile, the game goes on, looking ahead to further development, although the form it will take is not yet clear. Branch Rickey, having seen his farm system copied by all his competitors, is searching for something new to give his organization an advantage.

Quite possibly he has found it in the assembly line system of player production he has installed at Vero Beach, Florida.

Rickey apparently has cut the time it is necessary for a young player to spend in the minors by two years. Annually the Dodgers look over more than a thousand prospective players. The best of these report for observation and specialized instruction at the Rickey factory, and those who are not prospects are weeded out instantly. The others receive the benefit of advice from the masters of all departments, learning hitting from George Sisler and base-running from Pepper Martin, for example. What they learn in this course of cramming is reflected in their summer's work, and in the following spring their progress is charted and they are advanced up the ladder that leads to Ebbets Field.

Life at Vero Beach is regimented, run by bells and the clock, and mimeographed instructions on the bulletin boards. But it provides an infinitely more satisfactory means of learning big league baseball than the haphazard life of early training camps that included snipe hunts.

This is not to say that major league baseball has yet achieved the degree of skill that was prevalent just before World War II. There are still problems that carry over from the days of the war. The bonus rule has deprived many boys of gaining much needed experience in the minor leagues. There is still a shortage of playing talent caused by the war, but that will be alleviated because more boys are playing baseball today on the lots than ever before, despite a general impression that the game has lost some of its charm for youngsters.

There are too many minor leagues. Boys who have no business doing so are playing professionally because the rosters of all the clubs in all the circuits must be filled. Major league teams are thus required not only to find prospects but "service players" for the numerous teams in the chains.

The style of play employed in recent years is to the disadvantage of the pitcher, and if Henry Chadwick were around today he would be horrified by the interest in the home run. Even the little fellows, infielders weighing 150 pounds or so, are swinging for the fences, knowing that the money goes to the man who hits the ball out of the park. This fact, combined with the elimination of the sacrifice fly rule, has caused a decline in batting averages. But baseball styles are ephemeral. If one club would move back its fences, raise its pitching mound, slow down the infield by letting the grass grow, and WIN — then the entire structure of the game's strategy might enter another phase. There is no particular reason to become alarmed because of the accent on hitting. A similar howl was raised about the lively ball in 1894, and the game soon entered a phase that gave every advantage to the pitcher.

The temporary decline in efficiency caused by the war is slowly being forgotten as each succeeding year produces more and more fine young recruits. Baseball has not lost its hold on the people and is steadily moving on to maturity with the nation. What course it will take and just how it will evolve remain to be seen, but since the days that Boss Tweed ran the Mutuals the game has found ways of copirt with whatever problems developed. That something exciting is in store for fandom is assured; the axiom about taking nothing for granted in baseball is as true today as it was when it was first mouthed.

The New York Evening Sun seems to have said it happily, in an editorial in 1915:

"Wars are declared, fought and ended. Elections are called, held and decided. Floods rise, ravage and subside. And each has its transient hold upon the populace. But to the American in whose veins the wine of April is bubbling there is nothing which has the perennial fascination which baseball holds for its votaries. The fan is back in his element, as happy as a landed fish returned to its native waters. He breathes again the diamond dust, he hears once more the cry of 'Batter UP!'"

DISCOUNTS. OFFERS. EXCLUSIVE CONTENT.

The Bibliopoesy book publishing company is an independent publisher promoting beautiful books on a wide range of topics and genres.

To keep up with all the latest, Sign up to our newsletter where you will receive exclusive content, early-bird discounts and special offers not found anywhere else.

http://bibliopoesy.com/newsletter/

See you soon!!

One Last Thing

Word-of-mouth is crucial for any author to succeed. If you enjoyed the book, please consider leaving a review at your point of purchase, or on Facebook, Twitter, or perhaps on your personal blog (if you have one). Even if it's only a line or two; it would make all the difference and would be very much appreciated. Make it as short or as long as you prefer. Thank you again for your support!

Made in the USA
Middletown, DE
29 September 2021